Biographical Sketches
on
Burke County Georgia Persons

(Volumes 1 & 2)

Compiled by:
Albert M. Hillhouse

Southern Historical Press, Inc.
Greenville, South Carolina

This volume was reproduced
from a personal copy located in
the Publishers private library

Please direct all correspondence and book orders to:
SOUTHERN HISTORICAL PRESS, Inc.
PO Box 1267
Greenville, SC   29602-1267

New Material Copyright 2024 by:
   Southern Historical Press, Inc.
ISBN #978-1-63914-204-0
Printed in the United States of America

FOREWARD

Biographical Sketches of Burke County, Georgia includes short biographies of 250 persons within the period, 1777-1981. This volume is for those interested in the History of Burke County, Georgia, which is still at the printer's.

Many persons have aided the author with information for the sketches. The author had two excellent typists in Mrs. Susan Reynolds and Mrs. Cecily Armstrong of Danville, Kentucky. Further the author owes much to two real friends, Joyce and Alex Gray of Waynesboro, Georgia, for their help in rescuing the manuscript.

Biographical Sketches will also be found in the Georgia Historical Society in Savannah and the Archives in Atlanta.

November 1, 1982

Albert M. Hillhouse

The <u>Biographical Sketches of Burke County, Ga.</u> include 250 persons within the period 1777-1980. This small volume will aid the reader, interested in the <u>History of Burke County, Ga.</u>, which has not been completed. A second small volume will also follow soon and will serve the same purpose.

Many persons have aided the author with their sketches and the first small volume will be found soon in the Burke County Library, and also placed in the library of the Georgia Historical Society (Savannah) and the <u>Archives</u> in Atlanta.

The author has two excellent typists in Danville, Kentucky. Mrs. Susan Reynolds and Mrs. Cecily Armstrong, who have produced two excellent manuscripts for the printing press. Further, the author owes also two real friends, Joyce and Alex Gray of Waynesboro, Ga., who recouped the material which the author was not able to do over a period of several months.

April 1, 1981   *Albert M. Hillhouse*

VOLUME I. BIOGRAPHICAL SKETCHES
OF BURKE COUNTY

1. Zillah Lee Bostick (Redd) (Agerton)
2. Elisha Anderson Allen
3. Joseph P. Applewhite
4. Douglas Attaway
5. Nell Hillhouse (Baldwin)
6. Goodwin Malcolm Barnes
7. Simeon Bell
8. Lloyd Jones Belt
9. Henry Berol
10. Major John Berrien
11. Laura Maria Berrien
12. Thomas Moore Berrien
13. Edward Hosea Blount
14. Hugh M. Blount
15. Stephen W. Blount
16. Marcus P. Borom
17. Rev. Edmund Botsford
18. Braswell Family
19. Judge Edward L. Brinson
20. William Leslie Brinson
21. William H. Bryan, Sr.
22. William H. Bryan, Jr.
23. Thomas Burton
24. Adele Johnston Bussey
25. Needham A. Buxton
26. Samuel Buxton
27. Rev. Edmund Byne
28. James Miller Byne, Sr.
29. James Miller Byne, Jr.
30. Enoch Howard Callaway
31. John Wright Carswell, Sr.
32. Arabella Walker Carswell
33. John Devine Carswell
34. John Wright Carswell
35. Porter Wilkins Carswell
36. Patrick Carr
37. Brig.-Gen. John Carpenter Carter
38. Francis Marion Cates, Sr.
39. Francis Marion Cates, Jr.
40. Cates Families
41. Hodges Family

42. Alexander Carter
43. Isaiah Carter, I
44. William Chandler
45. G. Frank Cherry
46. Kennedy Canty Childers, Sr.
47. Paul Coalson
48. Joseph E. Cooley
49. Frank G. Corker
50. Palmer L. Corker
51. Stephen A. Corker
52. George F. Cox, Jr.
53. Jackson Elliott Cox
54. P. Duncan Cox
55. Sidney C. Cox, III
56. William D'Antignac
57. Henry Carlton Daniel, Sr.
58. Henry Carlton Daniel, Jr.
59. J. H. Daniel
60. Myrick Davies
61. Marion Tracy Davis
62. William Hudson Davis
63. John Marshall Dent
64. Capt. Wm. Henry Dickinson
65. Eve Walker Armstrong Dixon
66. Arnold Joseph Dolinsky
67. Troy Drew
68. David Emanuel
69. Arthur Forte Evans, Sr.
70. Thomas B. Felder, Jr.
71. Lewis R. Ford
72. Alonzo Lee Franklin
73. George W. Fryhofer
74. Edwin Fulcher, Sr.
75. Edwin Fulcher, Jr.
76. Edwin Dent Fulcher
77. Capt. William Marcus Fulcher,
78. William Marcus Fulcher, Jr.
79. George Galphin
80. Carroll Blount Garlick
81. Cicero Garner

82. Evelyn Ward (Gay)
83. Howard Washington Givens
84. A. Holland Gnann
85. Francis Robert Goulding
86. Simeon Alexander Gray
87. John Green
88. William Green
89. Henry D. Greenwood
90. Ross Ullman Harden
91. Roy Belmont Hargrove, Jr.
92. Capt. John A. Harlow
93. Southworth Harlow
94. Herbert Clifford Hatcher
95. Linwood Clinton Hayne
96. Lovick Pierce Herrington, Sr.
97. Lovic Pierce Herrington, Jr.
98. Albert Miller Hillhouse
99. William Chambers Hillhouse, II
100. Josiah Holland
101. Wm. Wycliffe Hillis
102. Mary Louise Olliver Herrington

103. W. J. Herrington
104. James Killock Hines
105. William R. Holmes
106. Allison T. ("Pooley") Hubert, Sr.
107. C. W. Hurst
108. Jared Irwin
109. Alfred Iverson, Sr.
110. Abraham Jackson
111. Rev. George L. Jackson
112. C. Preston Johnson
113. Herchel Vespasian Johnson
114. L. D. Johnson
115. Philip Pelatiah Johnston
116. Allen W. Jones
117. Batt Jones
118. John James Jones ("Jenks")
119. John J. Jones
120. Margaret A. Jones
121. Philip Jones
122. Inez Florida Wilkins (Jones)
123. Henry A. Jones

125. Seaborn H. Jones
125. Warren W. Jones
126. William Everett Jones
126. Capt. William Wilkins Jones
127. Andrew Zadock Kelsey
128. Rev. James Hall Tanner Kilpatrick
129. Rev. James Hines Kilpatrick
130. Rev. Washington Lafayette Kilpatrick
130. Thomas Jackson Lance
131. Joseph Law
132. Alexander J. Lawson
133. Edward F. Lawson
134. Hugh Lawson
135. Isam Samuel Lee
136. Rufus Ezekiel Lester
137. Clifford Lewis
138. Jonathan Lewis
139. Rev. Josiah Lewis
140. Thomas Lewis, Sr.
141. George Lisle
141. Alexander Lively
142. William Lord
143. Judson W. Lyons
144. Hugh Angus Macaulay
144. Annie Reid Mackenzie
145. Sidney J. McCathern
145. Walker McCathern
145. William Walker McCathern, Jr.
146. The McCloud Family
147. Evans Howell McElmurray
148. John F. McElmurray
148. Judson Sapp McElmurray
149. Mary Louise McElmurray
150. Second and Third Generations

151. Thomas J. McElmurray

151. William Leslie McElmurray

152. Hugh Buchanan McMaster

153. Baldwin Buckner Miller

154. Julia Carter (Miller)
154A Joseph Baldwin Miller
155. Robert Lee Miller

155. Ellis W. Mills

156. Charles T. Milner

156. John Milton

157. William St. Clair Morris

158. Robert Madison Murphree

158. Robert A. Murphy

160. Alvin Wilkins Neely, Sr.

161. Lillian Wilkins Neely

162. Horace P. Odom

163. Joyce Pittman Odom

164. James Oglethorpe

165. James H. Oliver, Jr.

166. C. L. Pagenhart

167. Howard E. W. Palmer

168. James P. Palmer

169. Jesse Campbell Palmer, Sr.

170. Jesse Campbell Palmer, Jr.

171. John Turner Palmer, Sr.

172. John Turner Palmer, Jr.

173. Atton Pemberton

174. Edward Alonzo Perkins

175. John Harrell Perkins

176. Heman Humphreys Perry

177. Roderic Pettigrew

178. Louis Pintchuck

179. Thomas Polhill

180. Rev. Joseph Polhill

180-A John Powell

181. William Henry Powell

182. John Carter Poythress

183. James Lawrence Pugh

184. Ella Mary Rainwater

185. Kate Thomas (Wilkins) (Dowell) (Rauers)

186. Joseph Jones Reynolds, Jr.

187. Margaret Story (Riordan)
189. Grattan Whitehead Rowland
190. John Wesley Sanderford
191. George W. Sapp
192. The William Sapp Family
193. The William Sapp Family
194. Floyd Lawson Scales
195. Henry Jackson Schley
196. Robert Lee Scott, Jr.
197. Adiel Sherwood
198. Burke Shewmake
199. John Troup Shewmake
200. Charles W. Skinner, Sr.
201. Franklin Monroe Skinner, Jr.
202. Henry Hansel Stembridge, Jr.
203. Major John R. Sturges
204. Samuel Sturges
205. Thomas F. Tanham
206. Ben James Tarbutton
207. Andrew E. Tarver
208. Charles F. Tarver
208. Charles F. Tarver
209. Ethelred Thomas

209. George C. Thomas
210. Jethro Thomas
211. J. Pinkney Thomas
212. Peyton Wade Thompson
213. Wall Tatnall Thompson
213. Memory King Tucker
214. John Twiggs
215. Kate C. Wakelee
216. The George Walker Family
217. The George Walker Family
218. John Woolfolk Walker
219. Thomas W. Wall, Jr.
220. W. T. Walton
220. George O. Warnock
221. Eli Warren
222. Lott Warren
223. Amos Grattan Whitehead
224. Amos Grattan Whitehead
225. Florence Byne (Routzahn) (Whitehead
226. James Harper Whitehead
227. John Philpot Curren Whitehead, II
228. William Dowse Whitehead
229. Ezekiel Williams

VOLUME II - BIOGRAPHICAL SKETCHES

1. Roy F. Chalker, Jr.
2. William H. Craven, Jr.
3. Henry J. Fullbright
4. Charles Gray Green, Sr., M.D.
5. Charles Gray Green, Jr., M.D.
6. Job Gresham, Jr.
7. Edmund Byne Gresham
8. John Jones Gresham, C.S.A.
9. Captain Richard Milledge
10. Emmett Burdell Gresham
11. Oscar Milledge Gresham
12. Lena Shewmake Gresham (Stevenson)
13. Evans Virgil Heath, Jr.
14. Preston Brooks Lewis, Jr.
15. Robert Caldwell Neely, Sr.
16. Robert Caldwell Neely, Jr.
17. Marion Neely (Walker)
18. Samuel Gaines Story, II
19. Elizabeth Jones (Wade)
20. Young John Allen

ZILLAH LEE BOSTICK (REDD) (AGERTON), Waynesboro genealogist, historian, and poet, was born in New Orleans on July 16, 1871, the d/o Alma Marshall and John E. Bostick. In 1881 the Bostick family moved to Augusta and later, Miss Bostick graduated with first honors from Tubman High School.

Georgia State College for Women, first called the Georgia Normal School, was a new college in 1891, and Miss Bostick, having won a scholarship, entered the sophomore class after successfully completing the freshman examinations. After three years she completed the requirements of the college and was awarded a diploma and certificate to teach in the public schools in Georgia.

The first teaching position held by Miss Bostick was in Anniston, Ala., where she taught for two years before coming to Waynesboro.

In the early spring of 1895, Miss Bostick came to Waynesboro as secretary to the law firm of Lawson and Scales. One afternoon shortly after her arrival, she was typing out legal briefs in the office with her back to the entrance door. Upon hearing sounds in that direction, she turned to see a group of six or eight men staring at her. When she inquired as to the nature of their business, one man spoke up and said "we have never seen a female secretary before and were curious to see if the rumor that one was working for Lawson and Scales was true."

After her marriage to John Allen Redd in 1896, she resigned her position in the law office and devoted her attentions to domestic and civic affairs. In 1927, five years after Mr. Redd's death, she married Edward Thompson Agerton.

When the Edmund Burke Chapter of the Daughters of the American Revolution was organized in 1924, Mrs. Agerton became interested in genealogy--this interest which was a hobby at first became part of her livelihood. As she began tracing her ancestry for membership in the patriotic organization, Mrs. Agerton became so involved that she volunteered to do research for 14 other prospective members in order that they might qualify for membership. Since that time countless genealogical records and family trees have passed through her hands.

"I am working on several lines now and expect to have them finished within the next few weeks," Mrs. Agerton said. "If I had to depend on this for my entire income, I would have starved to death long ago, but the money I earn from this does come in handy," she said.

At the present time, Mrs. Agerton holds fifteen offices in state and national historical and patriotic organizations. As late as 1960, she belonged to 42 organizations, but in recent months, she has resigned from several because, "I could not take long trips to attend the conventions which are held all over the country." Among the many tributes which have come to Mrs. Agerton the one she cherishes the most was an invitation from the Duke of Argyle to be his guest at Inverness Castle and attend the coronation of Queen Elizabeth II. Next in line was an invitation to be part of the greeting party which welcomed Princess Elizabeth to the United States in the late 1940's.

From early childhood she began writing verse. In time her poetry received recognition. The Eugene Fields National Poetry Society made her an honorary member and at least two anthologies included some of her poems. In 1938 The Second Poetry House Anthology contained seven, and in 1939, Poems of Trees, A Sidney Lanier Memoria included four. Her own volume of forty-four poems, If Your Heart Attends, was published in 1951 by the New Anthenaeum Press. Two of her poems, Emily Plays the Fifth Nocture and Resurrection, have been read over national and state broadcasting stations on several occasions.

Mrs. Agerton served for a number of years as historian of the Waynesboro Presbyterian Church. The church published at the time of its bicentennial her History of the Presbyterian Church of Waynesboro, Georgia, 1760-1960. Mrs. Agerton also worked on the history of the Women's Auxiliary of the Presbyterian Church. She organized the group in 1924 and has read the history to the Women's Auxiliary.

Mrs. Agerton was the poet laureate of the Washington Family Descendants, Colonial Dames of the Seventh Century, Dames of the Court of Honor, Clan Campbell Association of America, and the Huguenot Society and Founders of Manakinantown, Va.

On Sunday, July 16, 1961, The True Citizen celebrated her 90th birthday with a fine article in T.C., Jul 19, 1961. She went to her Maker in 1967 and is interred in the Waynesboro Magnolia Cemetery.

ELISHA ANDERSON ALLEN, one of Burke's three signers of the Ordinance of Secession, was the son of Robert Allen, who invented the Allen plow, and Elizabeth Anderson, the only child of Elisha Anderson.

They had five daughters and two sons. Allen was a prosperous planter and a slave owner. In 1861 when he voted for Secession he was 46 years old and owned 65 slaves. He died in 1863 just about two years after the Secession Convention.

His estate was appraised at $90,000; of this more than $64,000 was invested in slaves. The inventory also listed among his personal belongings a large library. His name place in McBean Creek included 1892 acres.

EQUITY 1ST BOOK, BURKE COUNTY
Appraisal and Distribution (pp. 268-276) of the Estate of the late Elisha A. Allen, January 1871.
Lot # 1   462 acres   Janette J. Allen $2081.75
    # 8   296 acres   Janette J. Allen   1086.75
    # 2   260 acres   Jennie T. Allen   1431.25
    # 3   243 acres   Annie E. Allen   607.58
    # 4   363 acres   Maggie C. Allen   1372.25
    # 5   362 acres   Robert H. Allen   1462.75
    # 6   362 acres   Pauline C. Allen   1119.72
    # 7   793½ acres   Daniel R. Allen   1597.74
The above is the Appraisal and Distribution only of the acreage.

E. A. Allen had a brother, Judge Robert Anderson Allen of Augusta. Judge Allen had two sons: Francis Marion and William Wirt.[1] Francis M. Allen moved to Burke, married Anna Evans, daughter of Daniel Richard Evans. Francis was about 39 years of age at the time of the Civil War. He had five children but enlisted as a private; was promoted to First Lieutenant, and was killed the second day of the Battle of Gettysburg.[2] William Wirt Allen, the second son,

---

1 A Lost Arcadia, pp. 20-21

2 Francis Marion. 1st Lieut. Co D 48th Ga. Inf. The Burke Volunteers, Co D. was with Wright's Brigade. His wife lived until Feb 9, 1858 and is interred in the Allen Cemetery.

had run away as a young man to Pennsylvania. He apprenticed himself for three years as a machinist, and during the Civil War period repaired Yankee weapons. Ultimately he returned to Burke, operated a plantation known as "Below", and later a merchantile business man near Green's Cut.

JOSEPH P. APPLEWHITE, president of the Bank of Millen, Jenkins county, and secretary and treasurer of the C. Parker Company, the leading mercantile concern of this thriving little city, was born on a farm in Burke county, this state, Nov. 1, 1864, and is a son of John N. and Sarah (Owens) Applewhite, both natives of Burke County, where the former was born on Sept. 13, 1837, and the latter on Nov. 13, 1836.

The father, who was a successful planter, passed his entire life in Burke county, where he died on July 13, 1893, having been one of the loyal sons of the Confederacy who did valiant service as a soldier in the Civil war. Sarah (Owens) Applewhite died Nov. 20, 1868. The paternal grandparents of the subject of this sketch were John and Caroline (Fullford) Applewhite, the former of whom was born in Wayne county, N.C., and the latter in Jefferson county, Ga. The maternal grandparents, John and Sarah Owens, both passed their entire lives in Burke county.

Joseph P. Applewhite secured his earlier educational training in Waynesboro academy and Hephzibah high school, after which he was matriculated in Mercer University, where he was graduated as a member of the class of 1884, with the degree of Bachelor of Arts. For two years thereafter he was clerk and bookkeeper in the mercantile house of Maj. W. A. Wilkins, of Waynesboro.

In 1886 he took up his residence, now the judicial center of the recently organized county of Jenkins, and here he was employed six years as cashier and bookkeeper in the mercantile house of Daniel Sons & Palmer. On Jan. 1, 1892, he became an interested principal in the mercantile firm of Daniel & Co., this association continuing until 1898, when he purchased an interest in the large mercantile firm of C. Parker & Co., in Millen. Crawford Parker, the head of the firm, died in 1899, and in the following year the business was incorporated by Messrs. Sidney C. Parker and Joseph P. Applewhite, the former being the eldest son of the the late Crawford Parker. At that time the present corporate title of the C. Parker Company was adopted, Mr. Parker being president and Mr. Applewhite secretary and treasurer of the company, whose business is extensive and whose establishment is metropolitan in equipment and appointments.

In 1892 Mr. Applewhite was one of the organizers of the Bank of Millen, of which he has been a director from the start. He was vice-president of the institution six years, and since December, 1905, has held the office of president. He is a director of the operating companies of the Millen mills and the Morton oil mills, and is the owner of extensive plantation property in Jenkins and Burke counties. Mr. Applewhite is aligned as a staunch supporter of the cause of the Democratic party, and he served four years as commissioner of Burke county, before the new county of Jenkins was organized, and he also held the office of mayor of Millen one year.

He and his wife are members of the local Baptist church, in which he is a trustee, and he is affiliated with the Knights of Pythias, of which he is a past chancellor. Mr. Applewhite is recognized as one of the progressive and public-spirited business men of Jenkins county and is one of the representative citizens of Millen. On April 3, 1892, he was united in marriage to Miss Lou Parker, daughter of the late Crawford Parker, of Millen, and of Jeannette (Burke) Parker, who still resides in this city. Mr. & Mrs. Applewhite have four children, namely: Joseph P., Jr., born Feb. 7, 1893; John C., born Feb. 4, 1896; Sidney, born Nov. 10, 1899, and Emerson, born Nov. 1, 1904.

DOUGLAS ATTAWAY, newspaper publisher, was born in Waynesboro, Ga., Jan. 24, 1878, son of James and Frances (Cates) Attaway. His father was a farmer. Douglas Attaway received his preliminary education at public schools in Georgia and later attended business school in Jacksonville, Fla. After working as a bookkeeper in Richmond, Va., New York City, and Houston, Tex., he joined the Shreveport (La.) Journal in 1901 in that capacity. He became the paper's business and advertising manager in 1907, a stockholder and secretary of the newspaper's parent firm, the Journal Publishing Co., Inc., in 1911, and owner of a controlling interest in the paper in 1918. In 1923 he became president of the Journal Publishing Co., Inc., and publisher of the paper, maintaining both positions until the close of his life. The Shreveport Journal was founded in 1895 by J. E. Goodwin and was published under the name The Judge until 1897. When Attaway became publisher in 1923, its circulation was approximately 16,000, and by 1957 this figure had risen to about 53,000.

Aside from the above, he was a director and vice-president of the First Federal Savings and Loan Association and a director of the First National Bank. He also took an active role in Shreveport community affairs, serving as a director of the Norwela Council of the Boy Scouts of America and as a director of the YMCA, the local chapters of the American National Red Cross and the Salvation Army, and the Community Chest. He was a director of the Louisiana State Fair for several years. He was a member of BPOE and the Lions and Shreveport clubs. His religious affiliation was with the First Presbyterian Church, Shreveport. In politics he was a Democrat. Fishing and playing bridge were his principal recreational interests. He was married in Shreveport, Feb. 10, 1909, to Bessie, daughter of Levi Hill Fisher of that place, a physician, and had two children: Douglas Fisher, and Betty Cates, who married Robert Frederick Wiemer. Attaway died in Shreveport, La., July 1, 1957. [1]

---

[1] By permission this sketch was reproduced verbatim from the National Cyclopedia of American Biography, Vol. 47, p. 404. A short obituary notice appeared in The New York Times, July 2, 1957.

NELL HILLHOUSE (BALDWIN), the d/o Cornelia ("Nell") Miller Thomas and William Chambers Hillhouse II, was born June 23, 1906 at Waynesboro, Ga. Education: Waynesboro H. Sch; AB (1928) Agnes Scott Col.; post-graduate study at East Carolina Teachers Col. (now Univ.), Georgia State Teachers Col. (now Georgia Col.), Cornell Univ. and Georgia Southern Col. From the last mentioned earned a Master's degree (majoring in Guidance and Counseling Services.)

On Sept. 5, 1936 md. John Charles Baldwin, s/o Nell James and Nathaniel H. Baldwin of Fort Valley, Ga. His education: Grad. Fort Valley H.S.; student at Mercer University, member Sigma Nu fraternity. His occupation: U. S. Dept. of Agric. (Fort Valley). Later farmer in Burke County (Ga.).

Nell's occupation: Teacher of social science and history. During some 15 years she taught in Cordele, Moultrie and Fort Valley. During part of WW II was Exec. Sec. of Amer. Red Cross (Cordele). In 1944, upon the serious illness of her father, she and Charles moved to Waynesboro in order to help take care of his business. From 1944-66 she was a teacher in the Waynesboro H.S. At some point she became interested in local history and with a co-author, published An Intelligent Student's Guide to Burke County (Ga.) History (1956), 203 pp. This book was used in the Burke Co. H. Schools.

In 1957 the Senior Class at the Waynesboro H.S. dedicated their yearbook to her with the following inscription:
"Because of her achievements in her profession;
Because of her rich, warm personality, her humor,
Her qualities of sympathy and understanding;
Because of the ideas which she inspires;
We dedicate the 1957 Hurricane to . . .".

Nell was also selected in 1957 as Burke Co's "Teacher of the Year", having previously been elected to a similar honor of the Waynesboro H.S. by her fellow faculty members. After her Master's degree, she became the Guidance Counselor of Waynesboro H.S. In this capacity she also prepared a Handbook for Guidance and Counseling, 32 pp. for the Burke Co. Sch. system. She also served for a time in the Ga. State Textbook Selection Committee.

Nell also for many years was the SS teacher of the women's adult class, the First Pres. Church. She died after a three week's illness on April 20, 1966 and is buried in Magnolia Cemetery, Waynesboro. No children.

GOODWIN MALCOLM BARNES was born Dec. 31, 1882, at Warm Spring, Ga.,[1] son of Sarah Clements and John Monroe Barnes. He entered North Georgia Agricultural College, Sept. 1902, the first semester after his older brother, John C. Barnes, had graduated. He was initiated into Pi Kappa Alpha, Sept. 27, 1902. In the Student Cadet Corps he attained the rank of 2nd Lieutenant. He served as SMC (president) of the fraternity his senior year. Graduated, 1906 with the B.S. degree.

During World War I, he served as part of the training complement, First Officers Training Camp, Ft. McPherson, Ga., Company 10 of the 7th Provisional Regiment.

---
[1] Warm Springs was formerly Bullochville.

On Mar. 12, 1919 he married Elizabeth Smith of Midville, Ga., daughter of Patrick Barton and Mary (Murphree) Smith. He had already adopted Midville as home and was to become one of her leading citizens. From 1909-14, he was Superintendent of the Midville High School; for years, a farmer and merchant in a rich part of big Burke County, and for nearly ten years, Midville's postmaster (1934-1943). Death came, May 31, 1943; interment at Midville.

Active in the Methodist Church, he was made a Steward; also for sixteen years he taught a Sunday School class. Generous with his time in devotion to Midville and her future, he was elected several times to the City Council; also served as secretary and president of the Kiwanis Club, and later, the Lions Club.

Mrs. Barnes became well known for her local history research, and for the valuable insights into the county's and Midville's past which her articles provided.

SIMEON BELL, ex-mayor of Waynesboro and recognized as a representative merchant and planter of Burke county, is a progressive business man and public-spirited and loyal citizen, well meriting consideration in this publication. He was born on the homestead plantation of his parents, in Burke county, May 29, 1853, and is a son of Simeon and Elizabeth (Herrington) Bell, both of whom were likewise born and reared in this county, where they passed their entire lives, the father having been a successful planter. He died in 1869, at the age of seventy-two years, and his wife survived him by only thirty days, being sixty-nine years of age at the time of her demise. Simeon Bell, the subject of this sketch, secured his fundamental educational training in the schools of his native county, after which he took a course in Moore's business college in Atlanta. He continued to attend school until he had attained the age of eighteen years, and for the two ensuing years remained on the homestead farm. At the age of twenty-one years he became bookkeeper in the mercantile house of W. McCathern, of Waynesboro, and two years later was promoted to the position of general manager of the store. After the lapse of two more years his employer admitted him to partnership in the business, and the firm name of W. McCathern & Co. was then adopted. In 1890 this partnership was dissolved, and Mr. Bell then engaged in the same line of enterprise in an individual way, in the quarters at present occupied. He has a well equipped general or department store and has built up a large and representative trade, placing him in the front rank of the successful and popular merchants of Waynesboro. His financial advancement through his careful management of his mercantile business has been such that he has been enabled to acquire large landed interests in the county, and he now controls a large business as a planter and general agriculturalist. In politics Mr. Bell is found stanchly arrayed as a supporter of the principles and policies of the Democratic party; served seven years as a member of the board of aldermen of Waynesboro; held the office of mayor for eight years, giving a most thorough, businesslike administration and doing much to advance the interests of the city; and for fifteen years he was secretary of the board of education. He and his wife are members of the Methodist Episcopal church South. Mr. Bell was for several years a non commissioned officer in the Wilkins cavalry, and later was for a number of years first lieutenant in the Burke Troop of cavalry, having been identified with the state militia for a period of twenty years. He is affiliated with the blue lodge, chapter and commandry of the Masonic fraternity and also with its adjunct, the Ancient Arabic Order of the Nobles of the Mystic Shrine. He is past master of his lodge and past high priest of the chapter. In the Knights of Pythias he has served for many years as master of the exchequer, and for the past twenty years he has been treasurer of the local council of the Royal Arcanium. On Feb. 28, 1881, he was united in marriage to Miss Emma L., daughter of William Chandler, of Burke county. They have three children: Annie W., Simeon, Jr., and Winnie Davis. The elder daughter is a graduate of Brenau college and its conservatory of music, at Gainesville, and the younger daughter graduated in June, 1906, at the Lucy Cobb institute, at Athens. The son attended school at Waynesboro and spent some time at the University of Georgia, at Athens, becoming while there a member of the Phi Delta Theta fraternity. Upon leaving the university he took charge of his father's books and remained in that position for two years. In January, 1906, he was elected assistant cashier of the First National bank of Waynesboro. He is one of the representative young men of the city, having the respect and good will of all who know him.

Vol I, Cyc of Georgia, 161-162

LLOYD JONES BELT, M.D. was born on Woodstock plantation, Jefferson County, Ga., Mar. 15, 1856, s/o _____ and Dr. Lloyd Carelton Belt.

The literary education of Doctor Belt was secured in Georgetown University, in the District of Columbia, and his professional education was secured in the medical department of the University of the City of New York, in which he was graduated as a member of the class of 1885, duly receiving his degree of Doctor of Medicine and coming forth well fortified for the active work of his chosen profession. On July 4th of the same year he opened an office in Herndon, Burke county, and he there built up an excellent practice, continuing his residence there until 1897, when he removed to Millen, where he has farther added to his professional precedence and prestige, being one of the leading physicians and surgeons of Jenkins county. He is a member of the American Medical Association, the Medical Association of Georgia, and is a local surgeon for the Central of Georgia railway. On August 31, 1904, he was appointed, by Governor Terrell, a member of the Georgia branch of the American Anti-Tuberculosis League, of which position he is still incumbent. He is identified with the Masonic fraternity, is past chancellor of the local lodge of the Knights of Phthias and is treasurer of the Millen lodge of the Independent Order of Odd Fellows. In political affairs he is found arrayed as a stanch supporter of the principles and policies for which the Democratic party stands exponent, and he served as mayor of Millen in 1904, giving an able and progressive administration. He was for several years a member of the BurkeTroop of cavalry, in which he held the office of surgeon. On Oct. 18, 1900, Dr. Belt was united in marriage to Miss Susan Whitehead, (b. Sept. 21, 1862), daughter of Margaret Harper and the late John P. C. Whitehead of Waynesboro, Burke County.[1]

---

[1] Mrs. Lloyd Jones Belt d. Mar. 30, 1947 and is interred in the Waynesboro Magnolia Cemetery.

HENRY BEROL. The late Henry Berol, president of the Georgia Field Trial Association for 20 years, was elected to the Field Trial Hall of Fame during the Bicentennial year.

The squire of Di-Lane Plantation at Waynesboro, home of the Georgia Field Trial Association, will be remembered in this community for his vital role in the preservation of the field trials here and his help in retaining Waynesboro as the "Bird Dog Capital of the World."

His election was by unanimous vote.

Less than six months after his death (Feb. 14, 1976), he received this high tribute.

Berol was born in New York on August 8, 1896, and after graduation from Yale in 1917, he served as a Major in World War I. After completion of his military service, he joined his brother, Edwin Berol, in the family owned Eagle Pencil Company.

Berol was associated with Berol Corporation, formerly the Eagle Pencil Company, for over 50 years. He was honorary chairman of the firm at the time of his death.

Berol purchased 10,000 acres in Burke County which he named after his daughters, Diane and Elaine.

The vicinity had once been a proud place for the annual Georgia Field Trial Association trials, but the grounds utilized had passed their zenith.

Berol with his aggressiveness, took over as president of the Georgia Field Trial Association in the early 1950's.

He converted nearly 6,000 acres of the plantation into one tract with barns, kennels and a comfortable clubhouse.

Even in his years of declining health, Mr. Berol remained active in the Field Trials. He was preserved and gave an inspiring talk at the Handler's Banquet two weeks before his death.

Breeder, owner, dog handler, marshal, competitor, organizer, dedicated club official, business man, civic leader and gentleman he left hundreds of friends throughout the country, as well as a tremendous gap in the leadership of the organization he promoted for so long.

Among his many contributions was the founding of the Henry Berol Fellowship in Ophthalmology at Johns Hopkins University.

Sketch by Bonnie Taylor (T.C. Jan. 26, 1977).

MAJOR JOHN BERRIEN, the father of Hon. John MacPherson Berrien, came to Georgia at a very early age. At the dawn of the Revolution, when entering on the threshhold of life with a heart glowing with patriotic ardour, he visited Georgia, expecting to find a fold in which he might devote himself of the defense of his country. At fifteen years of age he was appointed a Lieutenant in the First Georgia Regiment. He was subsequently promoted to a Captaincy.

When General McIntosh was appointed to a command in the Northern Army, young Berrien was elected a Brigade Major and in that capacity he joined the grand army at Valley Forge. He was very conspicuous in the Battle of Monmouth and in several engagements and continued until the close of the Revolutionary War.

On the return of peace, being qualified by an active well-cultivated mind, and correct judgment for public usefulness a great part of his life in offices of. Never hurt, the duties of which he performed with integrity and diligence.

Toward the close of the Revolutionary War he married in Philadelphia, Margaret MacPherson, the sister of John MacPherson (aid-de-camp) of General Montgomery, General John MacPherson resigned from the British Army, and he finally got back to the Long Island shore where he was safe on the American side.

LAURA MARIA BERRIEN, was born Nov. 1, 1877 at Rome, Ga., the d/o Elizabeth Palmer and Thomas M. Berrien. She was the second child of four, and her mother died when "Maria" was about six years old. Her father remarried and Waynesboro became their home.

Educated at Waynesboro, and graduated from the Georgia State College for Women (Milledgeville) in 1896, at age 19. She taught in schools for 13 years, mostly at Waynesboro. She left teaching, however, when the Waynesboro School Board wanted her to succeed Mr. Graham, as principal of the Waynesboro High School, at half of his salary. She was a strong believer in women's rights and they angered her.

She moved to Washington, D.C., and found a government job, earned an M.A. at American University, and also a B.L. Law degree at Washington College of Law (1916). At age 39 years she began working in the Bureau of Internal Revenue. In 1931 she became the first woman in the legal branch to be named "Attorney" in the Bureau's Office of the General Counsel.

She became a leader in the drive for women's suffrage, which included opening doors to women in new fields and professions, and in the struggle to eliminate discriminations practiced against women. She was a charter member of the Women's Bar Association of the District of Columbia, and one of the first women members in the American Bar Association. In 1938 she was president of the National Association of Women Lawyers. She also was a member of the Georgia Bar and licensed to practice before the the United States Supreme Court. She was also associated, from the first, with the Inter-American Commission of Women and the Women's Club in Washington, D.C. She was a Taft Republican, but was not reconciled with Eisenhower's policies.

At a later date she formed in Washington, D.C. (in the Southern Building) a law firm, Matthews & Berrien, which was successful. They attracted many women clients and also men. She never lost, however, her ties in Waynesboro. She was especially close with Mrs. Clarence Rowland and Barbara Reynolds Rackley. Her roots went back to New Jersey and to the first Berriens in Georgia, including the famous John McPherson Berrien.

Death came in August 14, 1962 and was interred in the Old Cemetery (now the Waynesboro Confederate Memorial Cemetery).

THOMAS MOORE BERRIEN was born Jan. 7, 1844 near Rome, Ga. in Floyd County. He was the son of Weems Berrien and a nephew of Hon. John McPherson Berrien. He received a preliminary education at private schools. He then entered the United States Naval Academy at Annapolis and was there engaged in studying for the naval profession when the Civil War began. Leaving the Academy without delay he returned to his native state and soon embraced the establishment of the Confederacy and the Confederate Navy. He was in that terrible bombardment and storming of Fort Fisher and was favorably mentioned in the report of the Confederate Commander. At the capture of the "Waterwick", a Federal gunboat, he was in that expedition which captured by a hand-and-hand conflict on the vessel's deck. At the end of the War he held the rank of Passed Midshipman.

He moved to Burke County, married Miss Elizabeth Palmer, d/o Judge Edward Palmer. He began as a farmer and after was admitted to the Bar and practiced in Waynesboro. His first wife died and left four (4) young children: Noble, Laura Maria, Margaret and John. He remarried Eliza Godbee, the widow of Homer V. Godbee.

Mr. Berrien took an active part in politics and he was nominated and elected a Representative in the State Legislature. He also was much interested in education and was elected Superintendent of County Schools. He served two terms (1880-1888).

He died on Dec. 20, 1901 and is interred in the Waynesboro Confederate Memorial Cemetery. He sleeps in this old cemetery where his first wife and two children also are interred.

EDWARD HOSEA BLOUNT - Long active in Georgia affairs, Edward Hosea Blount, of Waynesboro, was a leader in both agricultural and commercial enterprises, and his labors brought him the esteem and high regard for all who knew him. He did much for the advancement of his church and in a variety of ways exerted an influence for the good of Waynesboro, which he left a better place than he found it. He was respected for his attainments, and at the same time was honored for his splendid qualities of character and personality. He was kind, generous, sympathetic and fair-minded, and will long be affectionately remembered as such by his host of friends.

Mr. Blount was born in Burke County, Georgia, on November 1, 1874, son of William Augustus and Georgia (Cates) Blount. His father, also a native of Burke County, born Oct. 25, 1841, was long a planter there, continuing in that work until his death on April 29, 1904. During the War Between the States he fought valiantly for the Confederate cause. The Blount family, of which he was a member, have for generations lived in the South. They came originally to the New World from England. Stephen Blount was a lieutenant in the Colonial forces in the War of the American Revolution, and for a number of years served as collector of customs in Savannah, Ga. William Augustus and Georgia (Cates) Blount were the parents of several children, three of whom, two brothers and a sister, survived Edward Hosea Blount. These three who survived were Mrs. Ada Bell, F. H. Blount, and H. M. Blount.

A man of Mr. Blount's diversified nature could not be content to contribute to only one branch of activity in his community and in the region where he lived. So it was that he extended his interests after a few years into the business sphere, establishing a general merchandising enterprise in Waynesboro and becoming increasingly successful in the conduct of this new firm. Operating under the name of E. H. Blount, he built up a strong and substantial enterprise and also was president of the general merchandising establishment of Blount Brothers. Successful in his efforts because he had the self-reliance necessary to the propagation of business courage, he piled success upon success, acquiring ever new tracts of land until he became one of the largest owners of land in his district of the State of Georgia. At the same time he won high position as a business man. He owned property in the counties of Burke, Oconee, Fulton, Jenkins and Clarke.

He was also interested in still other phases of Georgia life. Banking groups in whose affairs he was interested reflected his health-giving optimism and cheer, and the First National Bank of Waynesboro was deeply grateful for his work as vice-president of the institution. In his capacity as a member of the board of tax assessors of Burke County, he made use of his financial ability and astuteness in behalf of the general public. He was also a trustee of the Georgia Normal School, at Statesboro, and a member of the board of trustees of Waynesboro High School. Through his membership on the executive committee of the Georgia Cooperative Association he lent his efforts to still another kind of civic work. He was also a trustee of the Georgia Experiment Station, at Griffin, Georgia, and was one of three life members of the Waynesboro Ice Association.

Though he never cared for public office and never held any, he did take a lively interest in civic affairs and always stood ready to make his stand clear on any public question. His political alignment was with the Southern Democracy. Early in life he began to be concerned with fraternal activities, which gave him a means of outward expression of his own warm spirit of brotherhood. In the Free and Accepted Masons he belonged to the Knights Templar Commandery and Alee Temple, Ancient Arabic Order Nobles of the Mystic Shrine. He was also a member of the Exchange Club of Waynesboro and was affiliated with the National Civic Club. He held membership in the First Baptist Church of Waynesboro, in which he was a member of the finance board. As one publication described his religious life at the time of his demise:

> Mr. Blount was one of the most faithful and zealous members of the Baptist Church in his town and the entire community mourns his death. For twenty years he had manifested his interest in

missions by supporting missionaries in foreign lands. He supported one or more missionaries in China during that period. On Sunday before his death, Mr. Blount sent proceeds of five acres of cotton as a gift to the church toward a building fund and a contribution to missions. This Christian gentleman was held in high esteem by all who knew him.

Not only did he give to foreign missions, as noted in the above quotation, but he also gave extensively of time, energy and material resources to local charities, including an orphanage in Macon.

Always reserved in manner and action, Mr. Blount was none the less ready to express his opinion when he believed that such expression would be of value. Though slow to admit new persons to his circle of friendship, which he regarded as a sacred thing in life, he was extremely popular among those whose privilege it was to be close to him. They knew him as a genial and loyal friend and an individual upon whose judgment they might at all times rely. Farming constituted his main interest, both as a business and as a hobby and his many friends liked nothing better than to avail themselves of the Blount hospitality in city or country. Georgia planters recognized him as an authority on agricultural methods and procedure, and often relied upon his extensive and valuable experience in cultivation of the soil.

Above all else in life he enjoyed the time that he was able to spend in companionship of home and family groups. Edward Hosea Blount married, at Bogart, Georgia, on Nov. 25, 1914, Nina Thompson, d/o Robert and Levie (Griffith) Thompson. Her father, who was born on Sept. 5, 1885, at Bogart, Ga., retired from his active endeavors and made his home in Bogart until his death on Aug. 25, 1936; he was for many years a prominent planter and merchant in Oconee County, as well as postmaster of Bogart. His wife, Mrs. Blount's mother, was born Sept. 22, 1856, in Oconee County, Ga., and still resides in Bogart, with which place the Thompson family has long been associated. To Edward Hosea and Nina (Thompson) Blount three children were born: 1. Mildred Grace Blount, who died in infancy; 2. Edward Hosea Blount II, who graduated from the Univ. of Ga., class of 1937, with a Bachelor of Science degree; 3. Georgia Cates Blount, a graduate of the W.H.S. and now a student of Sumter College, Rome, Ga.

The death of Edward Hosea Blount occurred in Sept. 10, 1931, at Waynesboro, Ga. and was a loss to the entire Waynesboro community and the State of Ga. Many citizens and institutions were the richer, however, for his having lived, and his influence, which was felt as a living force in his lifetime, will be so felt through future years.

HUGH M. BLOUNT - During the past twenty years, Hugh M. Blount has served as clerk of the Superior Court at Waynesboro. He has been a resident of this community since boyhood and is well known both through his public service and his earlier career in business.

Mr. Blount was born in Burke County on Jan. 16, 1881, a son of William A. Blount, who died in 1909, and Georgia (Cates) Blount, who died in 1912. His father was a farmer, but his own interest turned to commercial pursuits and after completing his education in local public schools he entered the grocery business at Waynesboro. Later he became a partner in the Waynesboro Mercantile

Company and so continued until 1917, when he was elected clerk of the Superior Court of Waynesboro. He has served with fidelity and efficiency in this office during the intervening years. For several years he served as a member of the board of trustees of Georgia State Teachers College at Statesboro, Georgia.

Mr. Blount is also active fraternally as a member of the Free and Accepted Masons - Blue Lodge and Royal Arch Chapter - and the Knights of Pythias. He is a member of the Baptist Church. He has interested himself in various civic and community movements with whose aims he is in sympathy and has a wide circle of acquaintances throughout all Burke County, where he is held in the warmest regard.

On October 10, 1918, in Waynesboro, Mr. Blount married Emma Smith of Bartow, Jefferson County, Georgia, a daughter of Le Roy and Sallie (Stapleton) Smith, the former a prominent merchant of Bartow.[1]

STEPHEN W. BLOUNT, Col. Stephen W. Blount, honored and distinguished delegate to the Convention, was no ordinary man. His grandfather was a renowned soldier in the Revolutionary War. He lost a leg at the siege of Savannah. He also held the place of Customs Collector at Savannah during President Washington's second administration.

Stephen W. was born Feb. 3, 1808. Was sheriff of Burke County, Ga. He served on the staff of Governor Schley of his native state.

In the summer of 1835 Blount made a business trip to Montgomery Ala. While there he became acquainted with Capt. Archibald Hotchkiss, a distinguished man of Nacogdoches who gave him a glowing account of Texas. "Mr. Hotchkiss' description of Texas was so fascinating to me", said Col. Blount to the writer, "that I once made up my mind to go to Texas".

Col. Blount reached San Augustine in the fall of 1835 and very soon thereafter arranged to make it his permanent home. Soon after he married Miss Mary Landon, who was a native of Vermont, but came to Texas with her parents and settled at San Augustine prior to his coming.

Blount soon was known as a man of unusual intelligence, judgment and strength of character, and his advice was sought. At Old Washington on March 1, 1836, Blount was one of the delegates representing the municipality of San Augustine. Texas must separate from Mexico. But the delegates did not shake their duty.

From Eastern Texas they joined other delegates on their way to Old Washington, a three (3) day journey. The vote of the delegates was unanimous. Sam Houston signed first; the next name was David Numos, who afterward became Attorney General in Mr. Burnet's Cabinet. A writer on "Texas and Texas" tells us that while Colonel Blount was returning for Old Washington to San Augustine he met a company of troops under the command of Captain Hatecliff, which he

---

[1]
The Story of Georgia, p. 555.

joined on their march to join General Houston's army, but only those of this Company who had good horses were enabled to reach San Jacinto in time for the battle.

When San Augustine County was organized in 1837, Colonel Blount was elected its first County Clerk. He served as Postmaster of San Augustine under the administration of President Taylor, taking office early in 1848. In 1832, he was a delegate to the Democratic State Convention at Waco. During the War Between the States he was fiscal agent of the Confederate states. In 1876 he was a delegate to the Democratic National Convention in Cincinnati. Col. Blount was a charter member of the Red Land Lodge No. 3 of Masons. He reared a family of six children, three sons and three daughters. His sons all became prominent and influential citizens of West Texas.

Col. Blount was an admirable companion. His heart grew mellow in his declining years. The writer spent 10 days in an almost daily association with him at one of Texas' most famous watering places about 10 years before his death, and during this period had many opportunities to hear from his own lips accounts of interesting events which enlive the pages of Texas history. XXX He was a close observer of the personal characteristics of the delegates to the convention which declared Texas independent of Mexico and the writer received from him valuable information regarding many of them. Those reminiscences, the writer has preserved. But for this they would have been lost.

Col. Blount died in 1890, Mrs. Blount followed him in 1892.[1]

MARCUS P. BOROM, Ph.D., s/o Mr. & Mrs. J. Winston Borom of Waynesboro, Ga. He was graduated from the Georgia Institute of Technology, where he received a B.S. degree in ceramic engineering, and from the University of California at Berkeley where he received a Ph.D. in materials science. Prior to completing his graduate studies, he spent a year at the Swiss Federal Institute of Technology at Zurich as a World Student Fund Fellow.

The author of 20 technical publications, Dr. Borom holds ten patents. In addition to the American Ceramic Society, he is a member of the National Institute of Ceramic Engineers.

In 1977 Dr. Borom was presented the Ross Coffie Purdy Award by the Ceramic Society. He is a ceramist at the General Electric Research and Development Center.

He received the special recognition for an "Outstanding contribution to ceramic literature of the year", at the Society's 79th Annual Meeting in Chicago. The three co-authored the award-winning paper, "Strength and Microstructure in Lithium Disilicate Glass Ceramics" deals with materials formed into glass and converted by heat treatment to partically crystalline products with imprismed properties.

He married Maxine Hoerner, d/o Martha and Fred Hoerner. Her parents live at Richarton, N.D. The Boroms live at 2171 Fox Hill Drive in Schenectady, N.Y.

---

[1] By Sam Houston Dixon in the Houston (Texas) Chronicle.

Children:
1. Michael, a sophomore at Colgate University.
2. Jay Winston, Hamilton, N.Y., a High School Senior.
3. Fredric Hoerner ("Ric") 10th grade in School
4. Andrew Hicks, 9th grade in School

Part of this sketch was found in T.C., May 25, 1977.

REV. EDMUND BOTSFORD - The book, Charles D. Mallary, Memoirs of Elder Edmund Botsford, Charleston, S.C., W. Riley, 110 Church Street, 1832. 240 pp. was found in the Georgia State University Library, Atlanta, Ga.

Written by his son-in-law, also a minister, Mallary refers to "some brief and hasty Memoirs which Botsford wrote of himself in the year 1807," and to the imperfect state of the manuscript. Mallary allows Botsford "as far as practicable, to speak for himself."

Edmund Botsford, the second son of Edmund and Mary Botsford, was born Nov. 1, 1745 in the town of Woodburn, Bedfordshire, England. His father was reputably employed, for many years, as a grocer and ironmonger, and at one time was considered wealthy. (page 2) On January 28, 1766 he arrived in Charleston; heard a Baptist minister (Oliver Hart) preach, and on March 13, 1767, was baptized and joined the church. (27, 30, 33) He first indented himself to learn the carpenter's trade. (34). In Feb. 1769 he entered upon his preparatory studies for the ministry under the care of Mr. Hart. Was licensed to preach Feb. 1771. (34, 37, 38).

In June 1771 he went into the Province of Georgia to preach the Gospel. At that date there was no regularly constituted Baptist church in Georgia and only one ordained Baptist minister, Daniel Marshall, who had just recently moved there. (38-39).

"In the same summer (1772) with Mr. Savidge, he preached at the Courthouse in Burke County. The assembly at first paid a decent attention; but towards the close of the sermon, one of them bawled out with a great oath, "the rum is come." Out he rushed; others followed; the assembly was soon left small, and by the time Mr. Botsford got out to his horse, he had the unhappiness to find many of his hearers intoxicated, and fighting. An old gentleman came up to him, took his horse by the bridle, and in his profane dialect, most highly extolled both him and his discourse, swore he must drink with him, and come and preach in his neighborhood. It was now no time to reason, or reprove; and as preaching was Mr. Botsford's business, he accepted the old man's invitation, and made an appointment. His first sermon was blessed to the awakening of his wife; one of his sons also became religious, and others in the settlement to the number of fifteen, were in a short time hopefully brought to the knowledge of the truth; and the old man himself became sober and attentive to religion, although he never made a public profession of it."
*Benedict's History of the Baptists, 2nd Vol. p. 181, 182. (44-45)

On March 14, 1773, in Charleston, Botsford was ordained by the Charleston Church; Oliver Hart and Francis Belot, assisted on that occasion. (45) Soon after his ordination, he commenced baptizing, and by the middle of the following November, he had baptized 45. "In the month of August, 1773," says

Mr. Botsford, "I rode 650 miles, preached 42 sermons, baptized 21 persons, and administered the Lord's Supper twice. Indeed, I travelled so much this year, that some used to call me the 'flying preacher.'" (45)

In May, 1774 he purchased some land in Burke County and built a house on Briar Creek. (48)

In November, 1773, the persons who had received baptism from the hands of Mr. Botsford, were constituted a church. It was first called New Savannah, but afterwards was known as Botsford's Old Meeting-house. It was the second oldest Baptist church in Georgia; Kiokee was constituted the year before, viz. 1772 (46-47).

Botsford married in 1773, at Augusta, Miss Susanna Nun, a native of Cork, Ireland, but who had lived in America from her childhood. Previous to her marriage she had commenced a religious life, and had been baptized by Daniel Marshall. They had six living children, and two still born. His marriage was a source of much domestic happiness. (47) She died at age 39 years, on March 9, 1790. (70)

In the spring of 1779, the horrors of the Revolutionary War began to be seriously felt in Georgia. At length Savannah was taken by the enemy; Sunbury surrendered; Gen. Ash was defeated on Briar Creek, and the whole state was brought under the power of the British arms. On the defeat of General Ash, Botsford found it necessary to betake himself to flight. There was no time to be lost. He took with him his wife and three children, the youngest (a daughter) being not then two months old, and a Negro man. So precipitate was their flight, that they had only time to snatch off with them two horses and a cart, containing a single bed, one blanket and a sheet, thrown in for the children to sit upon. Thus, after having carried the gospel into many benighted neighborhoods, sown much precious seed, baptized 148 persons, reared upon a flourishing church, and prepared the materials for future churches, so that he might justly be regarded (if we except the indefatigable Marshall) as the principal founder of the Baptist interest in Georgia, Rev. Botsford hurried from the state, an unprotected fugitive, no more to find a permanent abode in the region of his early labors. (51)

Soon after Botsford fled from Georgia, he received an invitation from General Williamson, to join his brigade as a chaplain; this invitation was accepted, and he continued in the army several months. (53)

After settlement in South Carolina, he was connected with the Charleston Baptist Association, and was esteemed as one of its most pious, valuable and efficient members. Several times he served as Moderator of the Association. (216)

The Faculty of Brown University, several years before his death, conferred upon him the degree of Master in the Liberal Arts. (239)

He died at Georgetown, S.C., Dec. 25, 1819, in the 75th year of his age. (233)

BRASWELL FAMILY, Lillian Osee Fulcher was born in Burke County, Ga. on Jan. 15, 1894. Educated at the Waynesboro High School and Agnes Scott College. Married on April 5, 1917, Albert Monroe Braswell, Sr., born June 9, 1888, at Elberton, Ga., son of Emma Hyslop and Bartow Braswell.

Mr. Braswell began his business career in Waynesboro and was well liked and successful. But in 1932 he decided to have his own business. With his two sons he established Braswell Foods, Inc. at Statesboro, Ga. The firm has been highly successful. His foods are found in chain stores as far north as Washington, D.C. Watermelon rind pickles and many other delicious brands have a large following.

He died on May 8, 1971 at age 83 and is interred at Statesboro.

Children and Grandchildren:
1. Albert M. Braswell, Jr. b. Mar. 16, 1919. Married Dorothy Hoefel, the daughter of Edna and Carl Hoefel. Their children:
    (1) Albert Monroe Braswell, III
    (2) Bonnie Ann Braswell
    (3) Susie Braswell
2. Edwin Fulcher Braswell, b. Jul. 28, 1923, d. Oct., 1924.
3. Belton Braswell, b. Sept. 11, 1924. Married Jean Starr, d/o Annie Nell and Col. Jack Starr. Their children:
    (1) Danny Edwin Braswell
    (2) Kay Ann Braswell

JUDGE EDWARD L. BRINSON was born in Burke County, April 10, 1854. He had unusual advantages in the way of preparation for his career. He attended that great school, in fact one of the greatest in its day, the Hephzebah High School, and its influence of the masters, men like Washington Kilpatrick and William H. Davis. They impressed his life at that formative period which tells so largely in the future activities of the man. Having finished high school he entered the Univ. of Ga. and graduated with the class of 1874, receiving the A.B. degree. His record at the Univ. was the highest standing throughout each year. He was trained for the practice of law at the Law Department of Cumberland Univ. at Lebanon, Tenn., and graduated in 1877, receiving the degree of Bachelor of Laws.

Immediately after receiving his degree, E. L. Brinson came back to Waynesboro where he began the practice of law, and his success was well known. He was always a staunch Democrat and served his county in offices of prominence for a long term of years. For eight (8) years he was Ordinary of Burke County. He represented the 17th Senatorial district in the State Senate, and in 1892 he was elected Judge of the Superior Courts in the Augusta Circuit (1899-1903).

In addition to his interest in the public life of the county he was a prominent member and a trustee of the Methodist Church. He was also an active Mason, belonging to both the Chapter and the Blue Lodge of Masons. In several years Judge Brinson was associated in the newspaper firm of the Herald & Expositor, published in Waynesboro by Brinson and Lovelt. He was also faithful in his church. For many years he consecrated his best efforts for the men who joined his Sunday School Class. As a lawyer he was sound and clear.

On Dec. 14, 1887 he married Miss Annie Hearne of Franklin, Tenn. They had no children. Both are interred in the Waynesboro Magnolia Cemetery. He died July 17, 1922; his wife followed him in 1926.

Judge Brinson was highly honored and respected for his splendid character and ability. He was endowed with a studious mind and in his youth cultivated a desire for extensive reading. In fact, all his life the study habit with him was strong and dominant. He liked the seclusion of his office and library where he could enjoy for hours the wonderful storehouse of the world's great minds.

WILLIAM LESLIE BRINSON, son of Frank L. and Sarah McElmurray Brinson. Born 11 March 1921. Early life was spent in Waynesboro. Graduating with the high school class of 1938, of which he was president, he continued his education for the next three years at Emory at Oxford and the Univ. of Ga., where he was a member of the Sigma Alpha Epsiolon Fraternity.

Volunteering as a flying cadet in the Army Air Corps in the summer of 1941, he completed his flight training and was commissioned in May, 1942. Departed the U. S. the following Oct. and served in England, the Mediterranean area, France and Germany as a pilot in the 8th and 9th Air Forces until the end of the European war, participating in seven campaigns. Took part in the D-Day operations in Normandy on 6 June 1944 as deputy leader of a flying group airlifting paratroops. Served in the Caribbean following the war in Europe.

Returned to Germany in 1948 as the operations officer for a troop carrier group, which moved from Texas when the Soviets blockaded the ground routes to Berlin, and flew the "Berlin Airlift". Moved from Europe to the Pacific Northwest at the beginning of the Korean War and engaged in flying troops to the Far East via Alaska and the Aleutian Islands. Other assignments included duty in Alabama at the Air Command and Staff School, and various staff and command positions in California, Maryland, Hawaii, and the Marshall Islands, where, in 1958, he was a member of Joint Task Force Seven, engaged in nuclear tests in the Pacific.

Organized and commanded the first fan jet (C-135B) air transport squadron in the USAF. Selected to attend the Naval War College, where he received his promotion to colonel, he graduated in 1963, and subsequently received from George Washington University a masters degree in International Relations. Following duty at Headquarters, USAF, was named Chief of the U.S. Military Assistance Group to the Kingdom of Morocco and served there from 1966 to 1969. Concluded his military career at the same military airfield (Maxwell Air Force Base, Alabama) where he began thirty years earlier, as Commander of the Academic Instructor and Allied Officer School of the Air University. Command Pilot with over 7000 military flying hours.

Awards include the Legion of Merit with Oak Leaf Cluster, Air Medal with five clusters, Presidential Unit Citation, Medal for Humane Action, Commander of the Alouite Order of the Kingdom of Morocco, various campaign ribbons.

In 1947, married Alice Gray Reynolds, daughter of Joseph J. and Tommie Quinney Reynolds, both of Waynesboro.

Following retirement from active military duty, lived in England for a year. Presently resides in Jacksonville, Fla. but is a frequent visitor to Waynesboro.

WILLIAM HARRISON BRYAN, SR., M.D., the son of Richard and Rose Bryan was born June 3, 1872, near Sylvania, Ga. He was educated in the Gisting secondary school. He worked first as a brick layer and school teacher. He studied later at Clark College in Atlanta and graduated in 1906 from Meharry Medical College, Nashville, Tenn.

He practiced medicine in Waynesboro and Burke County, Ga., until his death on Oct. 6, 1933.

WILLIAM H. BRYAN, JR., M.D., was born at 1001 Main Street in Waynesboro, Ga., on Oct. 17, 1913, the s/o Lila Norton and W. H. Bryan, Sr., M.D.

Education: grade school (United Presbyterian School); the Augusta Payne High School and Fort Valley High School (1934). College graduate, Talladega College, A.B. (1939), and Meharry Medical College, M.D. (1944)

Residencies: Homer Phillips Hospital (St. Louis); General Hospital at University of Pennsylvania, Residency (1947-51) and graduate surgery Oct. 1950-June 1951 (included in Residency). Married Claudia Jackson, June 16, 1957; American Board of Surgery Diplomate (Dec., 1952). Major, served in Japan. Has practiced surgery in Kansas City, Mo., since 1956-58.

In 1968 elected Coroner, Jackson County, Mo.; term expired Dec. 31, 1972.

Also has the title "Industrial Surgeon", Branch Medical Director, for one of five branches of Montgomery Ward in the United States.

THOMAS BURTON, planter and Patriot, was probably the son of William A. Burton whom the Rev. George White listed as one of the earliest settlers of St. George's Parish.[1] As a member of the third delegation,[2] one in 1774 and two in 1775, which the Parish sent to the Revolutionary meetings in Savannah, Burton holds a place among the first eight of St. George's Revolutionary representatives.

He was also recognized by the Council of Safety in Jul. 2, 1776 as a Magistrate under the new Provisional government.[3] Again, on Jul. 8, 1776, Archibald Bullock, who as President of the Council of Safety was Provisional Governor, recognized Burton's standing in the Parish by appointing him as executor of the estate of the late William McDaniel. All units had ceased to function and in the confusion as protector of the estate was needed. Already the estate had been plundered by Quinton Poole, a Savannah merchant and the remaining assets were in danger.

Burton apparently lost no time in living up to his trust. When the Provost Marshal of the Province did not move swiftly and successfully against the Savannah merchant who had taken some slaves from the McDaniel plantation, Burton, on July 25, presented a petition to the Council. Forthwith the Council ordered Colonel Stick of the provisional troops to assist the Provost Marshal in taking Poole into custody and also the slaves belonging to the said estate which the merchant had in possession.[4]

Thomas Burton was still living in 1786. His name appears as one of the Grand Jurors in the Oct. 1786 term of the Burke Superior Court.[5]

---

[1] Knight, Georgia's Landmarks, etc., p. 342.
[2] C. C. Jones, Jr., The History of Georgia, Vol. II, p. 184; G. G. Smith, op. cit., p. 77.
[3] Collections of the Georgia Historical Society, Vol. V, Part 1, p. 69.
[4] Proceedings of the Council of Safety, p. 76, Jul. 8, 1776; ibid, 83. Proceedings of the Council of Safety, Jul 25, 1776.
[5] The Georgia State Gazette and Independent Register, Nov. 25, 1786.

ADELE JOHNSTON BUSSEY, the d/o Lena Penelope (Shewmake) and Philip P. Johnston, was b. Jul. 13, 1890 in Waynesboro. She earned the A.B. and M.A. degrees at Oglethorpe Univ.; also studied drama at the Univ. of Ga. and Columbia Univ. She married Henson Estes Bussey, an electrical engineer. A sketch of him appears in Who's Who In America (1938-39).

Mrs. Bussey was both a poet and playwright. Several of her poems were published in Driftwood and Bozart and Contemporary Verse. Others appeared in The Atlanta Journal and The Atlanta Constitution. One, "The Protestant", was included in Frank L. Stanton's column. Among her best poems are "To My Mother" and an "Ode to Full Memoire".

Her plays include "They Shall Not Perish", "L+2=5", "Miss Millie's Story", and "The Man With the Hoe". All have been produced in Atlanta or in Athens. The second mentioned has also been published.

The Bussey family lived in Atlanta at 2793 Peachtree Rd., Nth Atlanta. They had one son, William Wallace Bussey in 1912. They had two grandsons:
1. William Wallace Bussey, Jr., born 1942.
2. Charles Estes Bussey, born 1946.

To My Mother (1858-1934)

Sweet Pilgrim to the glimmering dawn beyond
Letheran shores, none seems to know the way
What I may find it, asking you to stay
A longer while with me. The argent bond
Is sent that bound to earth your rare noblesse
And beauty, whose affinity with good
Discovered me a God I understood
Reflected in your quiet loveliness.

His truth became in you a living creed:
Each work a lamp of heaven finely wrought
Caught up the Master's holy flame of thought
And shed its light upon my every need.
You taught me how to spell the word, True.
Believed --- you blazed the trail!
I'll follow through.

The alive tribute entitled "To My Mother" first appeared in The Atlanta Journal on May 12, 1940 by Adele Johnston Bussey (Mrs. Henson Estes Bussey). Such literary production greatly enriches one's family record, and recalls the memory of our greatest earthly friend.

The Maryland Historical and Genealogical Bulletin Vol. 19, January, 1948, No. 1, page 3 Editor reproduced this poem.

NEEDHAM A. BUXTON, merchant and farmer, Girard, Ga., was born in Burke county in 1835, and is the son of William and Mary (Wimberly) Buxton, and the grandson of Samuel Buxton. His mother was a daughter of Needham Wimberly, a successful farmer and native of Burke county, but a man who did not own any slaves, though operating a large estate. Receiving a good common-school education, the subject of this sketch studied assiduously and fitted himself for teaching, a vocation he followed for ten years. In 1864 he enlisted in the state militia and was engaged in the battles of Atlanta and Griswoldville. In 1875 he married Anna E. Oliver, daughter of Thomas and Elizabeth (Mims) Oliver. Mr. Oliver now lives in Screven county and is a leading citizen there. This union was blessed by the birth of two children now living: William O. and Julian A. The mother was born in Screven county in 1848, and died in 1878. She was a member of the Methodist church south, as is her husband now. He belongs to the masonic order and in 1889 represented Burke county in the legislature, serving with credit to himself on the following committees: Banks, manufacturing, lunatic asylum and agriculture. Upon his return from the war Mr. Buxton began teaching school, but in a few years he engaged in a mercantile business and farming. For twenty-five years he was in partnership with his brother, Samuel H. Buxton. He is at present in business for himself. Mr. Buxton is a man of strict integrity, and his word is as good as his bond. His business career has been as honorable as it has been fortunate.[1]

SAMUEL BUXTON, grandfather of Mr. S. H. Buxton, was a Virginian and came to Georgia just after the revolutionary war, when he married Nancy Plummer. Mr. S. H. Buxton attended the old log cabin schools, and received instruction from private tutors, and for several years after reaching manhood taught school. In 1841 he married Elizabeth Godbee, daughter of James and Martha (Mulkey) Godbee. Mr. Godbee was a native of Burke county and a highly esteemed citizen. To this union three children were born, now living:

---

[1] Memoires of Georgia, Vol. II, p. 365.

Lenora, Samuel D., and Green C. The mother was born in Burke county in 1817 and died in 1858. She was an honored Christian lady, belonging to the Methodist church. In 1862 Mr. Buxton married Josephine Dixon, a daughter of Robert J. and Rosanna (Hurst) Dixon. Mr. Dixon was an old resident of Burke county and a well known citizen. By the second marriage Mr. Buxton has eight children living: William R., Glover B., Charles W., Joseph J., Preston B., Edna, Thomas P., and Judith P.B. The mother was born in Burke county in 1842. Husband and wife are members of the Methodist church. Mr. Buxton has always been a farmer, and had the accumulation of the first half century of his life swept away by the war. But with "never-say-die" pluck he jumped into active life again and has builded up his fortunate. In 1869 he engaged in the mercantile business with his brother and the same was continued until 1895. He owns about 1,600 acres of land near Girard, and is one of the most highly respected citizens of the county.[1]

---

[1] Memoirs of Georgia, Vol. II, p. 365

[1]
EDMUND BYNE, Revolutionary soldier, minister, and public-spirited citizen of Burke County, was a native of King & Queen County. He had married Ann Lewis, of Huguenot descent, in Virginia and brought with them a large family of children. They moved to Burke County shortly before 1785, locating on the north side of Brier Creek.[2] According to one account, they sailed from Yorktown, Va., with some other emigrants from Virginia on the little brig "Nancy". Landing at Savannah the group proceeded in wagons to northern Burke. This journey took five weeks, their route having taken them through a part of Wilkes County.[3]

Soon after his arrival he was ordained a Baptist minister by David Tinsley and Loveless Savage.[4] For some twenty-nine years he was very active in preaching the Gospel, his labors being bestowed chiefly upon the Rocky Creek Baptist Church, and in preparing the material which afterwards became Hopeful Baptist Church. The latter church began its religious life in 1815. Dying the year before, Rev. Byne failed to witness the full fruition of his labors, but the first service was dedicated to him in recognition that the church's establishment was largely his work.[6]

At the October term, 1786, of the Burke Superior Court, he was Foreman of the Grand Jury.[7] On this nineteen-man body were serving such men as Amos Whitehead, Batt Jones, William Martin and Thomas Burton. In 1787 he

---

[1] He does not appear in the index of Georgia's Roster of the Revolution because he had served in Virginia.
[2] Minutes of the Ninety-Seventh Anniversary of the Hephzebah Baptist Association, Oct. 20-22, 1891, pp. 24-25.
[3] The True Citizen, June 21, 1961.
[4] Minutes, supra, pp. 24-25.
[5] Ibid.
[6] "Hopeful Baptist Church", The Augusta Chronicle, Oct. 31, 1937; The True Citizen, Aug. 5, 1970.
[7] The Georgia State Gazette or Independent Register, Nov. 25, 1786.

was elected as a Representative of Burke in the Assembly, and his colleagues elevated him to membership in the Executive Council.[8] Again in 1788 he was returned to the Assembly, and in 1789 his son, Edward, was elected.[9] He also appeared in 1788 as one of the administrators of Dr. Henry Todd's estate.[10]

He died on his farm in Burke County, February, 1814 and was buried in the vicinity of Hopeful Church but his grave has not been found.[11] A more extended notice of Rev. Byne's life appears in Campbell's Georgia Baptists. One of his sons, Deacon Thomas Byne, became one of the outstanding leaders of the mission cause in the Hephzibah Baptist Association.[12]

---

[8] OR, 1961/62, pp. 1220 and 1009.
[9] OR 1961/62, p. 1220.
[10] William H. Dumont, Some Early Residents, Burke County, Ga., (1969) p. 9.
[11] Minutes supra, pp. 24-25. See also Dumont, op.cit., p. 8.
[12] Ibid.

JAMES MILLER BYNE, M.D., s/o John S. and Margaret J. (Murphree) Byne, was born in Hephzibah, Richmond County, Ga., on Mar. 17, 1879. Both of his parents were born in Burke County and both are deceased. His father was a planter by vocation. Their son studied first at the Hephzibah High School; then entered Gordon Institute at Barnesville, Ga., where he continued his academic discipline. He then entered the Medical College of Augusta and graduated in the Class of 1900. Received the Doctor of Medicine and was well prepared for the practical work of his profession.

Soon after graduation he opened an office in Waynesboro, where he has since continued as a physician and surgeon. In 1902 he completed a course in the New York post graduate medical school and hospital. He is a member of the Medical Association of Georgia and is a close and appreciative student in both departments of his profession.

The doctor is a loyal supporter of the Democratic Party and he and his wife are members of the Baptist Church. On Feb. 24, 1901, he married Miss Mary W. Heggie of Georgetown, Columbia County. They have two sons, James Miller, Jr. (b. May 30, 1905) and Edward*Gordon Byne (b. Sept. 1, 1917). Dr. Byne died May 3, 1961. His wife preceded him on June 16, 1959. Both rest in the Waynesboro Magnolia Cemetery.

*(or Edmund)

Cyc.of Georgia, Vol. I, pp. 283-284, with additional information.

JAMES MILLER BYNE, JR., M.D., s/o Mary W. Heggie and James Miller Byne, Sr. (M.D.), was born May 30, 1905 in Waynesboro, Ga. Attended the Waynesboro High School and G.M.A.; University of Georgia (Athens) 1922-24; Phi Delta Theta Fraternity, Medical College of Georgia in Augusta (1924-1928); M.D. Interned in the University Hospital (1928-1929).

On July 3, 1929, he married Mary Elizabeth Jones (b. May 23, 1905) at the Waynesboro Presbyterian Church. On July 15, 1929, he began the practice of medicine in Waynesboro and Burke County, and his active and highly successful practice has spanned 50 years. In 1978 he closed his office, but still serves three retirement homes, three clinics, and physical examinations of workers at the Georgia Power Company's Nuclear Plant in progress.

He was long a member of the Burke County Medical Society, First District Medical Society, the Georgia Medical Assn. and the American Medical Assn.

In 1943 he was made a F.A.C.P. (Fellow of American College of Physicians); served as Associate Professor of Medicine at the Medical College of Georgia. In 1950 he was elected to Alpha Omega Alpha, Honor Medical Fraternity.

He was an active member of the State Board of Health for seventeen years, and was chairman of two of those years. He has been President of the Alumni Society of the Medical College of Georgia. For twenty-eight years he was Chief of Staff of the Burke County Hospital, and until his retirement in 1978.

He is a Director of the Bank of Waynesboro; a Rotarian and was president of the local club, 1938-39. Since 1931 he has been a faithful Deacon of the First Baptist Church. He is also a member of the Christian Medical Society (national organization). He is highly regarded as a citizen, but best known for his dedication to medicine.

The Bynes have a son, James Miller Byne, III (b. Apr. 2, 1933). He graduated at Davidson College; is in business in Charlotte, N.C., and married a Charlotte girl, Sarah Irene Harrington (b. Mar. 19, 1941). They married Mar. 12, 1966, and have a daughter, Elizabeth Jones Byne (b. April 5, 1968).

ENOCH HOWARD CALLAWAY, was born July 19, 1862 at the old Callaway homestead in Wilkes County, the s/o Lucy B. Howard and Rev. Brantley M. Callaway, D.D., a Baptist Minister. In Jan., 1879, he entered the sophomore class at the Univ. of Ga. at Athens. He graduated, B.A. with third honor in the class of 1881.

After his graduation he taught as Assistant in the Waynesboro Academy until Jan., 1883. In the fall of 1884 he abandoned teaching and studied in the law office of Wm. & M. P. Reese in January, 1885, and was admitted to the Bar in the fall of the same year. He then moved to Waynesboro (Burke County), and began the practice of his profession in Oct., 1885. There he formed a partnership with Judge E. F. Lawson, which continued until 1893 when he retired from the firm and formed a partnership with his younger brother, W. R. Callaway, who had read law in his office. He rose rapidly to prominence in his profession and acquired a large practice, which continued until 1894, when he was elected by the legislature Judge of the Superior Courts of the Augusta Circuit at the age of thirty-two years. In Jan., 1897, he removed to the city of Augusta where he has since maintained his home. He retired from the Superior Court bench in Jan., 1899, and resumed the active practice of his profession in Augusta. In April, 1905, he entered into a professional partnership with Judge Joseph R. Lamar upon the latter's retirement from the bench of the State Supereme Court. This partnership lasted until Judge Lamar was appointed to the United States Supreme Court in 1910 by President Taft.

Judge Callaway has been and remains a leader in the councils of the Democratic Party in his state. He was Chairman of the Democratic Executive Committee of Burke County for six years; several times a member of the Democratic State Committee, and in 1888 was a presidential elector on the party ticket. He served as Mayor of Waynesboro in 1890; represented the seventeenth district in the State Senate in 1890 and 1891; as a Director of the Georgia Normal and Industrial College for Girls, at Milledgeville, from 1899 to 1901; was a Trustee of Mercer University in the city of Macon from 1900 to 1901; and was a Trustee of the Shorter Baptist Female College, the Univ. of Ga., the Ga. Medical College, and the Augusta Orphan Asylum, and is President of the Alumni Society of the Univ. of Ga. He is a Deacon in the Baptist Church and is affiliated with the Masonic fraternity.

On Feb. 23, 1888, Judge Callaway was united in marriage to Miss Mary Eugenia Jones, d/o of Maj. George and Catharine (Calhoun) Jones, of Newnan, Ga. Mrs. Callaway departed this life Dec. 3, 1901, leaving three children, viz.: Catherine, Brantley, and Gena J. Callaway.

Perhaps Judge Callaway's most distinguised public service was on the bench of the Superior Court. His administration was characterized by extraordinary diligence and promptness in the trial of cases and the discharge of public business. His rulings and decisions, expressed always in clear and vigorous language, evinced not only a high sense of fairness and justice, but a thorough and comprehensive knowledge of the law. He is an earnest advocate of efficiency and supremacy in government and the suppression of all forms of lawlessness, especially mob law, and is proud of the fact that during the four years he was on the bench there was not a successful act of mob violence within his circuit.

Since his appointment as a trustee of the state university in 1901, he was most active and zealous in aiding all measures directed to the enlargement and development of the university. He was elected President of the University Alumni Society in June, 1905.

JOHN WRIGHT CARSWELL, SR., was born Oct. 7, 1806, the s/o Sarah Wright and John Carswell and the grandson of Alexander Carswell and Isabella Brown who came to America from Ireland about 1776 or 1770.

He was a large man, standing six feet three or four inches in height, weighing 225 pounds or more, and of markedly erect bearing he was a fine speciman of physical manhood.

He married Sarah Ann Devine on Jan. 28, 1835. She was born Sept. 9, 1811 and lived to Nov. 21, 1869. They had two children:
1. Anne Eliza Moselle Carswell, b. Jul. 27, 1839 (who married Maj. Wm. Archibald Wilkins). The Wilkins' children were his grandchildren.
2. John Devine Carswell, b. Jul. 16, 1841. Md. Linda Royall (b. Oct. 30, 1844). He was captured in the Civil War and was in a Federal prison. He lived only to Feb. 28, 1868. Through Linda Royall and John Devine they had two grandsons, Porter W. Carswell and John D. Carswell.

John W. Carswell was known as a "Judge" for the reason that his long and honorable associations with Joseph A. Shewmake, William W. Hughes,

Jerry Inman and others, members of the Old Inferior Court bench in Burke County. For his long years of service on the Court his associates gave him a beautiful silver pitcher, which now belongs to John Wright Carswell, his namesake, in Savannah.

Judge Carswell ably handled the large "Bellevue" plantation which came from his wife, Sarah Ann Devine. He had good judgment and often he was placed in wills. For one example, Edmund B. Gresham and the Judge were in Dr. B. B. Miller's will. Gresham died before Dr. Miller so the "Judge" handled Dr. Miller's plantations until the young men in the Miller family had the "know-how".

During a visit to his home in the heated term he said: "I don't like to admit that I'm lazy, but I must confess to an indisposition to doing anything this hot weather."

He died May 21, 1885 and is interred in the Old Church Cemetery.

ARABELLA WALKER CARSWELL, was born Mar. 3, 1868 in Augusta, Ga., the d/o Lucy Pearson and Col. Clarence Valentine Walker. She graduated from Tubman High School in Augusta and Millersburg Female College, Millersburg, Ky., with the A.B.S. degree in 1889. While there she was a member of the Upsilon Phi sorority.

On April 3, 1895, she married Porter Wilkins Carswell, s/o Linda Royal and John Devine Carswell, b. Jan. 7, 1867. They lived at the beautiful plantation home at "Bellevue". She was widely loved by friends in Augusta, Waynesboro, Atlanta and Savannah.

She was active in the Waynesboro Methodist Church, and an ardent worker in the Daughers of the Confederacy in which she held an honorary life-time membership. Their first son, Clarence Valentine Carswell, died in infancy. The other two sons, however, John Wright Carswell and Porter Wilkins Carswell have made their work in the world.

She was widowed shortly about ten years after the marriage, in Sept., 1905. Her husband was tragically caught in a gin on his plantation which mangled his arm and he died before doctors could get him to a hospital.

When the two boys were old enough to go to the Waynesboro schools, she moved into town on Water Street. Later when the sons were in college she

lived for a time in Atlanta. One of her special friends was Mrs. J. H. Roberts, the wife of the Superintendent of the Burke County Schools.

Funeral service was held at the Methodist Church, and interment in the Waynesboro Magnolia Cemetery.

Surviving her were her two sons; two sisters, Mrs. Z. E. Miller of Atlanta and Mrs. Walter C. Davidson of Greensboro, Ga.; one brother, John D. Walker of Atlanta; one brother-in-law, John Devine Carswell of Savannah, and one grandson, John Devine Carswell, Jr. of Savannah.

JOHN DEVINE CARSWELL was born in Burke County, Feb. 28, 1868, s/o Linda Royal (Carswell) and John Devine Carswell. He graduated from the Univ. of Ga. in 1886, a member of the Sigma Alpha Epsilon fraternity and he was one of its most active alumni.

He moved to Savannah in 1888. He started as a clerk in the office of Maj. George A. Whitehead, who was general passenger agent of the old Central Railroad and Banking Company of Georgia. From that position Mr. Carswell entered the insurance business, becoming an outstanding figure in that line during the more than 40 years he was engaged in it. Mr. Carswell became associated with the late W. A. Daniels, who was carrying on the insurance business founded by Gen. Joseph E. Johnston. At the time of his death, Mr. Carswell was president of the John D. Carswell Company, one of the most prominent and largest insurance companies in the South. He had served as president of the Savannah Board of Fire Underwriters.

Active in business and a genial figure socially, Mr. Carswell gave of his time and money to charitable enterprises, taking a personal interest in the work. He was a communicant of Christ Episcopal Church. He was also actively identified with Bethesda, serving on the board of managers, and with the Fresh Air Home at Tybee.

His other activities were varied. Besides his insurance business, he was a member of the Savannah Cotton Exchange, a director of the Savannah Bank & Trust Company, a director of the Citizens and Southern Company, and a member of the Savannah Chamber of Commerce, serving as a director from 1915-18 when the organization was known as the Savanah Board of Trade. He was a member of the Oglethorpe Club, serving as its president in 1927 and 1928, and a member of the Savannah Golf Club.

When the Savannah Yacht Club existed and was one of the features of Savannah life, Mr. Carswell was a member and had filled the office of commodore of the club. He was at one time an officer and active in the affairs of the Savannah Volunteer Guards.

Mr. Carswell never married. He was loyal in every way to his business trusts and to his personal friends. There was something gentle, lovable, and true about John Carswell. Everyone who knew him liked him. He died in March, 1932, and was interred in Bonaventure Cemetery. When his death was announced the flags on the Cotton Exchange were placed at half-mast.

He was survived by nephews, John Wright Carswell and Porter Wilkins Carswell, and a grand nephew, John Devine Carswell, the second.

JOHN WRIGHT CARSWELL, born Sept. 18, 1901, on family plantation in Burke County, Ga., which was one of the original land grants from the King of England, and is now the oldest grant in Ga. still in the same family name.

Attended grammar school in Waynesboro, Ga., Preparatory School in Winchester, Va., and Richmond Academy in Augusta, Ga., graduated from Georgia Tech with a B.S. in Electrical Engineering June, 1924.

Worked for Retail Credit Company in Atlanta and Chicago as District Sales Manager for five and one-half years, and moved to Savannah on Apr. 15, 1930, to enter John D. Carswell Co. Insurance Agency with his uncle, John Devine Carswell.

Upon the death of Mr. Carswell, on March 14, 1932, he succeeds his uncle in the ownership and management of the Agency.

Mr. Carswell's family consists of his wife, the former Elizabeth Putnam, a son, John Devine Carswell (President of John D. Carswell Co.), and daugher, Mrs. Archie L. Morris, and six granddaughters.

Mr. Carswell has been very active in business, civic and charity organizations. Presently, in partial retirement, he has reduced his activities:

Member: Christ Episcopal Church, Chatham Club (honorary), Georgia Tech Alumni Association, Oglethorpe Club, S.A.E. Alumni Club, Solomen's Lodge F & AM (life member since Dec. 18, 1952), and Union Society of Savannah. Director: Piggly Wiggly Southern, Inc.

Formerly, when he was very active, his responsibilities included:
Chairman: Cotillion Club, John D. Carswell Co., Park and Tree Commission, United Community Appeal.
President: Chatham Club, The Desoto, Inc., Georgia Assn. of Insurance Agents, Hosonny Club, Oglethorpe Club, Savannah Assn. of Insurance Agents, Savannah Benevolent Society, Savannah Family Welfare Dept., Savannah Golf Club.
District Manager: Office of Price Administration (WW-II)
Road Commissioner: Chatham County
Director: Savannah Steel Company, Steel Erectors, Inc., C.& S Banks in Savannah, Ga. Golfer's Assn., Kings Appliance & Electronics, Savannah Jr. Chamber of Commerce, Savannah Newspapers, Inc., Savannah Symphony Society, Twin City Mfg. Co., United Community Services, Wadley Mfg. Co.
Vestryman: Christ Episcopal Church. Trustee: Memorial Hospital of Chatham County. Member: Century Club, and Sons of Colonial Wars.
Alderman: City of Savannah.

He died at the age of 79 on December 21, 1980. Graveside services were held on December 23 at the Bonaventure Cemetery in Savannah. He leaves his wife, the former Elizabeth Putnam, a son, John D. Carswell, one daughter, Mrs. Archie L. Morris, six granddaughters, and a brother, Porter W. Carswell in Burke County.

PORTER WILKINS CARSWELL, s/o Arabella Walker and Porter Wilkins Carswell, Sr. was born March 8, 1904 at Bellevue Plantation, Burke County. His father died in 1905.

Porter studied in the Waynesboro school, Richmond Academy, Emory Academy and the Univ. of Ga. where he was a member of the S.A.E. Fraternity.

On June 15, 1932 he married Elizabeth McMaster (Macaulay) in New York at the Little Church Around the Corner. There were no attendants; the only guests were Mr. & Mrs. John Wright Carswell (Savannah), Mr. & Mrs. L. P. Hillyer, Maj. A. C. Sanderford and Mr. & Mrs. Frank Tanham. The wedded couple left for an extensive European tour.

The Carswells live at Bellevue Plantation in Burke County. He has improved the plantation; began a museum of old agricultural machinery and artifacts. Mr. Carswell helped to organize the Planters Electric Corporation and was the first president of the Corporation and has served on the board of directors since the first meeting in 1936. He served as first chairman of the Buckhead Watershed Project and is still serving on its board of directors. He is board chairman of the Farmers Production Credit Assn. and the Louisville Federal Land Bank Assn. He is chairman of the Trust Committee and a member of the Advisory Committees of the Federal Land Bank and the Intermediate Credit Bank of Columbia, S. C. He is former chairman of the State Advisory Committee of the Farmers Home Administration. He has served as president of the Burke County Farm Bureau and as vice-president of the Ga. Forestry Assn.

He is a member of the Administrative Board and a certified lay speaker of the Waynesboro Methodist Church, where he has also been teaching a Bible Class for more than 40 years. He is president of Methodist Restoration, Inc. and editor of the monthly publication, "Methodist Observer." He is a former member of the National Council of the Boy Scouts of America and is past president of the Georgia-Carolina Boy Scout Council. He holds the Silver Beaver award for outstanding service to boyhood. He is past president of the Ga. Div. of the American Cancer Society and is presently serving on the State Board of Directors. He has been active in the fight on cancer for the past 28 years, including a term as State Crusade Chairman. He has also served as sponsor and county chairman of the Ga. Crippled Children's Society.

Mr. Carswell has been a member of the Rotary Club of Waynesboro since 1933 and is a past president of that club. He has served Rotary International as district governor, director, and as chairman or member of numerous committees. He has personally organized seventeen (17) Rotary clubs in Ga., S. C., and Ill., as well as assisting in the organization of several others.

Mr. Carswell served eight years in the General Assembly of Ga., as a member of both the Senate and the House of Representatives.

He helped to organized and served as first president of the Burke County Chamber of Commerce and also helped to organize the Ga. State Chamber of Commerce and served on the original board of directors and on the Industrial Council of that organization. He has also served as Southeastern Counselor of the U. S. Chamber of Commerce. He has served as president of the Burke County Historical Society and as president of the Ga. Citizens Road League.

In 1938 while Henry Manau was the proprietor of The True Citizen, Porter served for a time as Editor. In later years, Porter W. Carswell, Jr., his son, worked for the paper.

Porter William Carswell has proved himself as a man of many talents. He is urbane and "Wilkins" conjures up an earlier "Major Wilkins", his great-uncle. He has traveled extensively and has spoken to numerous groups in the U. S., in Canada, and in Australia. His membership in clubs and societies include: Gridiron Club, the Pinnacle Club of Augusta, the Society of Colonial Wars, the Sons of Confederate Veterans, and the Masonic order (Blue Lodge, Scottish Rite, York Rite, Shrine).

PATRICK CARR,[1] the scavenger and terror of the Tories, who had in battle or in cold blood, killed more than one hundred men with his own hand. One day, on being praised for his soldier like conduct, he cooly replied that he would have made a good soldier but nature had formed his heart too tender and compassionate. "He was a very singular person; he was never known to utter blasphemy or an oathe and was never agitated by passion."

A fellow soldier whose name is given as Carter, in one occasion, determined to put Carr's personal bravery and firmness to the test. Carr had said that he had never felt fear. A key of gunpowder was placed near a chair, Carr was asked to sit in the chair. He sat down with the utmost apathy and composure. Then Carter applied a lighted candle to the powder. Carr sat still and composed, seemingly indifferent and unafraid. Fortunately, the providence of God interposed and prevented a calamity. Somebody passing by and seeing the danger snatched away the powder and destroyed it. In the meanwhile, Carr calmly surveyed the men who had saved him from death turning to Carter, he asked if he was now convinced that Patrick Carr was invincible to fear.

Patrick Carr was an ardent patriot, so ardent was he in the cause of America that he hated the Tories with a hatred both dreadful and implacable. Their destructions of principles which he held so sacred, entitled them to no mercy. Therefore, as prisoner or as enemy in battle, he gave them no mercy. He hunted them down like wild beast and permitted no asylum to protect them. He was a brave and gallant soldier in his nature, he was amiable and benevolent.

He was captain of the Burke County Rangers in 1781-1782. At this time, Burke County included parts of Jefferson, Screven and Jenkins counties. Hence, the Burke County Rangers included men from these counties. Roster includes names of Hatcher, Moore, Jones, Hurst, Evans, Ballard, Burch and consisted of forty-eight (48) men.[2,3]

1.
  Capt. Patrick Carr is not to be confused with "Paddy" Carr, a half Indian.
2
  After the Revolutionary War, Cap. Carr was killed by someone whose relative had been killed by Carr during the War.
3
  An "Historical Sketch" by Annie Mackenzie Humphrey for the True Citizen, Oct. 6, 1955.

BRIG.-GEN. JOHN CARPENTER CARTER, s/o Dr. Edward J. and Angelina M. (Carpenter) Carter, distinguished himself as a soldier in the Army of Miss. and later the Army of Tenn. After attending the Univ. of Va., 1854-56, he studied law under Judge Abram Caruthers at Cumberland Univ., Lebanon, Tenn., married the judge's daughter, and for a time was an instructor in the Cumberland Law School. In 1861 when the War began, Carter was practicing law in Memphis. He entered the Confederate Army as a captain in the 38th Tenn. Regt. (Inf.)[1] The first official report of his bravery appeared in a report by his regimental commander on the Battle of Shiloh, Aprl 6-7 in Mississippi.

> Capt. John C. Carter deserves the highest praise for his great coolness and high courage displayed throughout the entire engagement. At one time he took the flag, and urging his men forward, rendered me great assistance in moving forward the entire regiment.[2]

By Aug., 1862, he was a colonel in charge of the 38th Tenn. Regt. His valuable services at Perryville, Murfreesboro, and Chickamauga are a matter of record. During the Chattanooga campaign, which followed, his regiment was on a dangerous detached duty. He served as a brigade commander in the Atlanta campaign, and was formally promoted to Brigadier-General, to rank from July 7, 1864. He was then only twenty-six years old. At the battle of Jonesboro, Ga., Carter was temporarily in command of Cheatham's division, the div. to which his brigade and former regiment belonged.

On Nov. 30, 1864 he was mortally wounded leading his brigade in an assault against the Federal breastworks at Franklin, Tenn. Parenthetically it should be noted that this was the same day that Sherman personally first set foot on Burke soil at Station 9½ (Midville) in the county where Carter was born. Carter died on Dec. 10 in the Harrison home, three miles south of the battlefield, and was interred in the Rose Hill Cemetery at Columbia, Tenn.[3]

The battle of Franklin was an ill-fated venture. After Atlanta was captured, Gen. John B. Hood with about 25,000 men moved to Florence, Ala. and from there headed northward toward Nashville, which was his objective. Gen. John Schofield of the Union Army with a force of about the same size, but with heavier artillery, was similarly moving toward Nashville to reinforce Gen. George H. Thomas there. Within two days Hood attacked Shofield in two successive battles, at Spring Hill Pike and against Franklin. Schofield picked his own ground for the second battle. On high ground he had a full complement of artillery field pieces which could sweep the plain below, and his entire infantry force was ensconced behind breastworks. The slaughter of the Confederates at Franklin has been compared to Pickett's charge at Gettysburg. "The ground passed over at Franklin to the enemy's works was two and a quarter miles; at Gettysburg, sixteen hundred yards"[4]

---

[1] Ezra J. Warner, Generals In Gray - Lives of the Confederate Commanders, 45.

[2] War of the Rebellion, Official Records, Series II, Vol. X., Part I, 526; report of Col. R. F. Looney.

[3] Warner, op. cit., 45

[4] John W. DuBose, General Joseph Wheeler and the Army of Tennessee, Neale Pub. Co., N.Y., 1912, 401

Twenty thousand gallant Confederates, infantry and cavalry with but little artillery support, at the word moved proudly over the open plain with banners floating. The enemy's artillery mowed the men down. The battle was an utter disaster. Twelve of Hood's generals were killed, wounded or captured, and among them was John C. Carter. After losses in two battles, Hood was in no condition to meet Thomas and Schofield at nearby Nashville. There, in Dec., 1864, the Union forces routed Hood's army, and according to one historian, "only the want of energy in the enemy saved it from immediate annihilation."[5] Since leaving Atlanta Hood had lost 10,000 men, two-fifths of his original force. At Tupelo, Miss. he turned over the remnants of his command to Lieut.-Gen. Taylor, and went to Richmond a broken and agonized man.[6]

---

[5] Ibid, 402-03

[6] Ibid, 403-04

FRANCIS MARION CATES, SR., was born Mar. 25, 1854, s/o Robert H. Cates and Mary Ann Rebecca Knight. He was a native of Burke County, educated at Fairhaven School in Burke County and Hephzibah High School in Richmond Co. He married Julia Boyd Cates who died Nov. 22, 1929. They had three sons: Robert Boyd Cates who died June 22, 1937; Francis Marion Cates, Jr., was born Sept. 10, 1890; Paul Davis Cates who died Oct. 15, 1938, and one daughter, Mary Rogers Cates, who died Mar. 14, 1896.

In 1890 Mr. Cates was elected as County Commissioner and served for a short time and then was elected County Treasurer in 1894 and served for two terms. He was again elected as County Commissioner a few years later, serving as Chairman of the Board. He was elected Mayor of the City of Waynesboro and served in 1912 as a Senator in the General Assembly. He began setting out pecans in 1904--the first commercial orchard in this section of the State.

He was Chairman of the Board of Deacons in the First Baptist Church for 25 years. One of the greatest tributes that his family always thought was made about him by one of the colored citizens in an article. The writer said that Mr. Cates was a lovable man; that no man was more careful, and that when he spoke the whole County stopped and took notice.

He bought half-interest in what is known as McCullough's Mill about 1902, later acquiring full ownership of this property. It was famous for barbecue and fish dinners that he gave to his friends. He later gave this to one of his sons, Paul Davis Cates, and built on Buckhead a Grist Mill and Club House that was famous for the dinners and suppers that he gave there. He built this mill, engineering it himself, naming it after his granddaughter, Mary's Mill. It was later destroyed by high water after his death. His residence in Waynesboro was started in 1899 in what was then an old field and what is now one of the most prominent residential sections of the town. His home was the first one started but the Presbyterian Manse was finished before his home was finished. He moved into this home in the Spring of 1900. Mr. "FM" died Jan. 21, 1931 and is interred in the Waynesboro Magnolia Cemetery.

FRANCIS MARION CATES, JR., was born in Burke County on Sept. 10, 1890, s/o Francis Marion Cates, Sr. and Julia Boyd Cates. Attended Waynesboro H.S. and Orsborn's Business College in Augusta, Ga.

He was County Commissioner of Burke County for 18 years, Chairman of the Board from 1924 to 1932 and again serving from 1941 through 1944 and was Chairman from 1945 through 1948; member of the House of Representatives from 1943 to 1952; Senator in 1953 and 1954, back in House in 1955 and 1956. His father, Francis Marion Cates, Sr. was a Senator from the same district. His great grandfather, Jonathan Lewis, was a Senator when Capital was at Milledgeville, Ga. and died there.

He sponsored the Burke County Hospital beginning in 1942, which was finally erected in 1951. He was its first Chairman and continued as Chairman of the Hospital Authority.

He was presented an honor placque by the Woodmen of the World in 1952, as well as an honor award citation for service to the county and State. Subsequently he was consultant to Phil Campbell, Commissioner of Agriculture of Ga. He was a Mason and Deacon of the First Baptist Church of Waynesboro.

He was married Jan. 10, 1910 to Susan Douglas Cates. They had one daughter, Mrs. S. A. Griffin of Waynesboro, three grandchildren: Frank Cates Griffin, Lieut. in the Marines; Shelley A. Griffin, Jr., M.D. and Mary Susan Griffin.

Mr. Francis ("Frank") M. Cates, Jr. died on July 27, 1959 and is interred in the Magnolia Cemetery in Waynesboro, Ga.

CATES AND HODGES FAMILIES

A. CATES FAMILIES

Three Cates brothers came to Ga.: 1. James Cates; 2. William Cates (he dropped the "s"); 3. John Cates.

I. <u>James Cates</u>, ancestor of Frank M. Cates (father and son) was born Sept. 12, 1789.

James Cates and Mary McCroan (the McCroans came to Queensborough) were the parents of Robert H. Cates.

Robert H. Cates and Mary Ann Rebecca Knight were the parents of Francis Marion Cates, Sr. (i.e., F.M. Cates, Sr.)

F.M. Cates, Sr. and Julia Boyd had three sons, F.M. Cates, Jr., Robert Boyd Cates and Paul Davis Cates.

Francis Marion Cates, Jr. (i.e., F.M. Cates, Jr.) md. Susan Douglas Cates ("Miss Sue") had a daughter, Mary Cates (md. Shelley Griffin) and a grandson, Shelly A Griffin, M.D., practicing in Waynesboro.

I-A The F.M. Cates, Sr. family is also descended from Jonathan Reese Lewis <u>via</u> Julia Boyd.

Julia Boyd was the d/o Mary Virginia Scott and John Boyd.
John Boyd was the s/o Stephen Boyd and Betsey Lewis
Betsey Lewis was the d/o Jonathan Reese Lewis and _____.

Jonathan Reese Lewis, for some years represented Burke County in the Legislature. There is an historic cemetery on the old Capitol grounds in Milledgeville, Ga. "By legislative vote there were tablets erected to ten people in this burial ground, and on one of these in memory of Jonathan Lewis, legislator from Burke County, who died in 1831, are these lines:

A wit's a feather and a chief's a rod
An honest man is the noblest work of God." [1]

II. <u>John Cates</u> received a headright grant of 100 acres in Burke County, Ga., Apr., 1796 (or 1797). He married Presilla Lloyd[2] on Nov. 21, 1797.

III. <u>Joseph Cates</u>, born probably before 1800, married Araminta Hodges (born 1808). Joseph Cates died before the Census of 1850. Their children were:[3]
1. Hosea Berrien Cates, born 1824, married 1842 at Louisville, Ga. to Susan Douglas Addison (born 1830).
2. Sarah Ann Cates, md. Henry White.
3. Allie Augusta Cates, md. 1st _____ Hughes; and second, Augustus Franklin (ancestor of Judge Malcolm Jones of Macon, Ga.)
4. Araminta Cates, born 1830, md. Ezekiel Attaway.
5. Nancy Cates, b. Sept. 13, 1831, md. 1st _____ Davenport (both were under age when they were married. A guardian was appointed.);

---

[1] *A Treasure Album of Milledgeville and Baldwin County, Georgia*, compiled and edited by Nelle Womack Hines, The J. W. Burke Company, 1936, at page eleven tells of the Jonathan Lewis grave at Milledgeville. Jonathan Reese Lewis (Rev. War soldier). Jonathan was born 1774.

[2] Information received in 1937 by Mr. F.M. Cates, Jr. from a genealogist, State Archives, Raleigh, N.C.

[3] The U.S. Census of 1850 for Burke County at p. 492 lists Araminta Hodges Cates and her children, giving children's ages. From these the year of birth for several were derived.

    2nd, in 1854, Jethro Thomas (b. Mar. 4, 1823)[4]
  6. Huldah Cates, md. 1st, Walter Seegar; 2nd, Dr. William B. Sikes.
  7. Assenath (or Asenath) Cates, b. 1836, md. Dr. Robert E. J. Thompson (b. 1825).
  8. Almira Cates, b. 1842, md. _____.

William Joseph Cates, b. Feb. 12, 1850; d. June 26, 1903.
(graduate of the Hephzibah High School), 2nd Margaret MacKenzie.[5]
 (1) Susan Douglas Cates ("Miss Sue")
 (2) Mrs. John Applewhite
 (3) Mrs. Linwood Herrington [6]

  The farms of several of the above (Henry White and his wife; Hosea B. Cates; Jethro Thomas and wife; and Araminta Cates Attaway) adjoined, or were close by. The Cates-Hodges land holdings were on the Waynesboro to Louisville highway (road). The post office was originally "Drone", but later, "Catesville".

B. HODGES FAMILY

  Mr. F. M. Cates, Jr. found in the Ga. State Archives a Joseph Hodges. Joseph Hodges . . . in a return of officers of the 2nd Battalion of Burke County Militia, or the 11th or 7th Company, Horse Creek, Ogeechee County, Ga. 1st Lieut. Received Commission, Feb. 22, 1798. Delayed Commission.
  Francis Hodges received a Ga. land grant in 1792.[7]

 [8]Will of Nancy Hodges in old Deed Book, 10-111, Burke County, Waynesboro, Ga. She was born in 1790 and lived at least until 1848.

  "Know all men by these present that I, Nancy Hodges, of the State and County aforesaid for and in consideration of the love, good will and affection I have and bear toward my Grandson, Hosea B. Cates, and for givers other good causes and considerations, we hereunto moving, do freely give unto him, the said Hosea B. Cates, the plantation whereon I now reside, lying immediately on the Road leading from Waynesboro to Louisville, containing one hundred and forty-five acres more or less, bounded North and East by lands of Francis M. Forth and on all other sides by lands belonging to the estate of Joseph Cates, Deed being a part of surveys granted to Francis Hodges the other to John Whitlaw, to have and to hold the above described Lot and parcel of land unto him, the said Hosea B. Cates, his heirs and assigns, reserving unto myself, however, the free use and benefit of the same during my lifetime. In Witness whereof I have hereunto set my hand and affixed my seal this 15th day of April 1848. (signed) Nancy Hodges"

---

[4]Jethro Thomas died Sept. 8, 1885; Nancy died Oct. 2, 1911.

[5]"Miss Sue" Cates is a granddaughter of Mrs. Mary Ann Campbell MacKenzie who had a large hand in the Wayside Home Center for wounded and sick Confederate soldiers at the Millen railroad Junction. The Campbells in her family were from Montgomery, Ala. The grave of Sir Alexander MacKenzie of Scotland is on "the Hill" near the Bon Air Hotel, Augusta, Ga.

[6]Mrs. Herrington's son is an M.D., a practicing physician and professor at the Vanderbilt Univ. Med. School.

[7]Mrs. F. M. Cates, Jr. ("Miss Sue") provided the author the above valuable information during two or three conferences in July, 1964.

[8] Troup B. Hodges, b. Jan. 6, 1851; d. Oct. 3, 1902. He married Sophronia Inman and from this marriage they had three daughters, but none of them married. In the Bark Camp Cemetery, Maud Estelle, Leslie Inman, and Rosa D. Troup, all three are buried there. Miss Maud E. Hodges of Midville, but also lived for a time in Atlanta. The Georgia State Archives no doubt would supply more details in the Hodges family in Burke County.

ALEXANDER CARTER, Esq., was born in 1751. Family tradition is that he had three wives, but their names are not now known. Hetty Carter, a daughter, md. Maj. George Poythress from Virginia. Their son, John Carter Poythress, was Alexander's only grandchild. Both Alexander and Isaiah Carter were believed to be the sons of Thomas Carter who had earlier grants.

Alexander Carter was living in St. George's Parish during the Revolution and his estate in 1783 was confiscated. He was banished from the State, because he sold food and other needs to the British forces. Later the ban was lifted and he was pardoned by the State and his citizenship and lands were restored.

In 1783 the General Assembly, meeting in Augusta, July 31, passed "an Act for laying out a town on the reserved, or public lands of Burke, into one-acre lots and disposing of same at public outcry". Thomas Lewis, Sr., Thomas Lewis Jr., John Duhart, Edward Telfair, and John Jones were appointed commissioners of "said land on the waters of McIntosh Creek", but there was no record of lots sold.

In 1791, eight years after the sale of lots, President George Washington visited Waynesboro. At the time he wrote that there were only six or eight dwelling houses. They were probably those of Alexander Carter and Isaiah Carter. Peter and David Robinson, Edward Trittle and John Davis. The Robinsons were merchants from Philadelphia. Davis was sheriff of the county, 1785. Alexander Carter was the host of President Washington. The President's Aid had placed Waynesboro on the Tour for a stop. Alexander's house was within a half block (south and west) to the crossing of Liberty and Peace Streets.

Later when Waynesborough was officially incorporated as a town, two of the five commissioners elected, January 1813, were Alexader Carter and William Stone.[1] This was the first town governing body. Alexander was also named a correspondent of The Augusta Chronicle and Gazetteer of The State.[2]

Alexander Carter was one of the organizers at the Old Church near Waynesborough (1790) and later the Congregation Church in Waynesboro.[3]

He is buried in the Old Cemetery (known now as Waynesboro Confederate Memorial Cemetery.) When he lived his house was the Alexander Carter House; later it was the Carter-Poythress House and ultimately the Munnerlyn House. At one time his gravestone bore this inscription:
"This Modest Stone, What Few Vain Marbles Can,
May Say - here lies an honest Man"
To date his grave shows that he died June 24, 1821.

Ann Carter, age 21 y, Jan. 21, 1801 was believed to be the unmarried daughter of Alexander. She is buried in a section with him and his grandson, John Carter Poythress.[4]

---

[1] The True Citizen, Jan. 18, 1884

[2] The Augusta Chronicle, May 23, 1789 edition.

[3] Agerton, p. 5.

[4] This is the oldest marker in this cemetery (ed).

ISAIAH CARTER I, was born 1764, the younger brother of Alexander Carter. He md. first on Apr. 27, 1792, Esther Walker, d/o Mary Gerhardt Duhart and Georgia Walker. Esther and Isaiah had two children:
1. Mary Carter and William Stone of Milford, Conn. He was first a teacher and then a Waynesboro merchant, and member of the first town council. The first meeting was in his home.
2. Margaret Carter and Welcome Allen, a native of New Hampshire. They lived in Augusta where he was a prosperous merchant.

Carter built a house on Liberty Street on the East side and about half of the block from the Liberty and Peace Streets intersection. Esther Carter died on Nov. 13, 1810. In time he married again Sarah Redd or Reid (the widow Tuttle). They had two sons:
1. Isaiah Carter, II was born Aug. 11, 1811. He md. first Emily Carpenter; 2nd Johanna Shewmake (a sister/o John Troup Shewmake) and 3rd Electra Varner. Isaiah II was the elder of his brother, Dr. Edward J. Carter (M.D.).
2. Edward J. Carter was born Oct. 4, 1814, s/o Sarah Redd (or Reid) (the widow Tuttle). Edw. J. and Isaiah II were full brothers. Dr. Carter (M.D.) was an intellectual and a fine physician. He studied in the Jefferson Med. College in Phila.

Many years later a Receipt which read "Rec'd. of Mr. James Brown six dollars and three cents in full of all demands, 2nd November, 1779. Isaiah Carter". So his signature has been preserved.

Isaiah Carter I died on Jan. 8, 1817. His elder brother lived four more years (June 24, 1821). Both are interred in the Old Cemetery, but the name has recently been named the "Waynesboro Confederate Memorial Cemetery".

DR. WILLIAM CHANDLER was born in Burke County. He received his medical degree from Univ. School of Med. at Augusta, Ga. He lived and practiced at Girth, Ga. He was a general practitioner.

He was married to Miss Norma Wimberly of Waynesboro. They had a family of thirteen children. His oldest daughter married a Dr. McMaster, brother of Dr. H. B. McMaster.

Dr. Chandler worked to devise a cure for typhoid fever which was so prevalent in that part of the country.

Dr. Chandler was a very remarkable man when he was confronted with problems of finances. He kept books in a most peculiar fashion. He never worked on his books until Saturday night, then he would sit down and ask his wife, "Norma, where did I go Wednesday morning or was it Wednesday night. Whom did I seen?" If she could remember, she would tell him and then he would ask her how much should he charge. Although he kept his books in this manner, he educated twelve of his children during his lifetime, and when he died he left money for the thirteenth child's education.

He had five sisters, who were some of Waynesboro's earliest citizens. They were: Mrs. C. W. Hurst, Mrs. McCathran, Mrs. Mary McElmurray, Mrs. Callie Wimberley, and Mrs. Emma Bell.

G. FRANK CHERRY. Dentist. Born April 8, 1894, Waynesboro, Ga. s/o Fannie Thompson and Stark O. Cherry. Married Louise Perryman, Feb. 8, 1919; two children, Dorothy Louise, b. Dec. 18, 1919 and Gertrude Alice, b. May 21, 1921.

Education: Haines Inst., 1911; A.B., Lincoln Univ., 1915; D.D.S., Temple Univ., (Philadelphia), 1918; Dentist, 1918-present.

Memberships: National Med. Assn.; Penn State Med.; Dental and Pharm. Assn.; Odontological Assn. of W. Penn.; Republican; Methodist; Office 6221, Frankstown Ave.; Resident, 7331 Montacello St., Pittsburgh, Pa.[1]

---

[1] Who's Who In Colored America (5th Ed., 1938-40), p. 119; ibid, (2nd ed.-1928-29), 74.

KENNEDY CANTY CHILDERS, SR., the second child of five sons and four daughters was b. to Joe and Pearliner Childers in Bullock County, Ga. The s/o a farmer and turpentine tapper, he lived and grew into manhood in the Mt. Zion rural community of the county. He attended the community school that had been built primarily through his father's efforts and completed the fifth grade, the highest grade offered by the school. At an early age he became affiliated with the Mt. Zion A.M.E. Church and it was there that he was inspired to continue his education by the presiding elders and ministers who visited the church of special occasions.

After completing the fifth grade, K.C. remained on the farm as his father's second plowhand until his twenth-first birthday. His father recognizing that he had attained manhood offered him a choice of a suit or $30.00. K.C. accepted the last and left for Savannah, where he applied for admission to the sixth grade of the boarding school of Ga. State College (now Savannah State College). He was informed that the seventh was the lowest grade at the school but after being tested he was admitted to that class. Working his way through high school at odd jobs and receiving no financial assistance, he finished high school and earned a certificate in the shoemaking trade in 1929. In the eighth grade, K.C. was elected president of his class, a position which he retained until he graduated from college.

While in college he supported himself, and helped a younger sister through high school with earning from his shoemaking practice and summer work in Asbury Park, N.J.

In 1932 he married his high school sweetheart, Eunice Walker, a native of Moultrie, Ga. and also an alumna of Ga. State College. To this union, after 16 years of marriage were born a daughter, Bettieanne and later a son, K.C., Jr.

After graduation, he accepted a job as principal and superintendent of the Masonic Orphan Home and School in Americus, Ga. He remained there until 1937 when he accepted the position of Agricultural Extension Agent in Burke County where he served for fourteen years. He chose Burke County, over another area, because of its immense land area and the potential for improvement and innovation among its Black farmers. The young agent worked diligently with the farmers of the area for 14 years, from 1937 to 1951, bringing numerous programs and ideas into the area. He organized one of its first farmer's organizations, the Burke County Planning Board, to plan and co-ordinate activities and farm clubs in various sections of the county. He worked with youth in the 4-H Club and along with his former classmate and principal of the local school, R. E. Blakeney, formed the first Boy Scout Troop for Black youth in the county.

His experience on the farm and later his work earned him a reputation as meat cutting specialist and resulted in his promotion in 1951 to State Director for Ham and Egg production, and later to the position of Associate Agricultural Supervisor for Negro Agents, which he held until his retirement in 1967. He was cited for 30 years of service to the farmers of Georgia upon his retirement, and for 28 years service to the 4-H Club.

After one year in retirement, K. C. Childers' love for his people and his continuing desire to be of service led him to give up his leisure and assume the full-time position of Director of Eastern Georgia Farmers' Cooperative. This was another endeavor to pull together the resources of Burke County and upgrade the economic level of the area farmers. Under his leadership have been established and organizaed the Eastern Georgia Farmers Cooperative, Inc. and to date, a service station, employing three full-time men, a sewing cooperating, a discount food store, and an experimental co-op farm employing a new concept in farming for the area.

His return to the county also gave K.C. the opportunity to become involved in numerous civic activities and organizations which he had supported but had not actively participated in because of his absence from the county. Through these acitivites he continues his endeavor to be of service to mankind.

PAUL COALSON, was b. in Burke County, Ga., Aug. 19, 1799. After passing through the primary schools, he was sent to Eatonton where he was placed under the tuition of Rev. Alonzo Church until he was prepared to enter college. He then went to Athens to Franklin College. He graduated in Aug., 1824. In the last year or two of his collegiate course he devoted his leisure moments to the study of law under Judge Clayton, and shortly after graduation, was admitted to the Bar at Athens.

He married Miss Elizabeth G. Blackshear in the spring of 1825, the s/o Edward Blackshear, Esq. of Thomas County. He continued to reside at Athens the balance of that year. He moved the next year to Thomas County where he opened a law office. At Lowndes the bar was joined by Mr. Coalson.

By his marriage, he secured a large family influence, which was of great advantage to him in the profession in Thomas County. On the 23rd day of March, 1830, the warm-hearted Paul Coalson, breathed his last in the 31st year of his age. His eldest son, Edward B. Coalson, became a wealthy planter in Thomas County, having married a niece of the late Major John Young of Macon County.[1]

---

[1] Stephen F. Miller, The Bench and Bar of Georgia, Vol. I, Lippincott, Co., Phila., 1858, pp. 193-195.

JOSEPH E. COOLEY, D.D.S.[1] Since coming to Waynesboro, Ga., in 1920, to engage in the practice of dentistry, Joseph E. Cooley, D.D.S., has not only been eminently successful in his profession, but is one of the outstanding citizens of the place. To his broad general training in dentistry he has added the results of intensive study and keeps in touch with all that research brings to light in the field of scientific knowledge by memberships in local, State and the American Dental associations. The various aspects of civic and social life engage a great deal of his attention and he gives generously of his time and means to the measures and organizations intended for the public welfare.

Dr. Cooley was born at Cleveland, Ga., Nov. 30, 1887, s/o Joseph and Martha (Dean) Cooley, his father was a merchant and substantial citizen. After attending local schools, he studied at Young Harris College, and then entered Emory Univ. Dental College. He was a Psi Omega. He graduated with the class of 1908, a Doctor of Dental Surgery. After practicing at Young Harris, Ga., for 12 years, he opened offices in Waynesboro, where he had a large clientele. Fraternally Dr. Cooley was affiliated with the Masonic Order, being a thirty-second degree Mason, and member of the Temple, Ancient Arabic Order Nobles of the Mystic Shrine. He is also a member of the Junior Order of American Mechanics, and is a steward in the Waynesboro Methodist Church.

At Waynesboro, Ga. in 1921, Joseph E. Cooley, D.D.S., married Alice Fulcher, d/o Osee Herrington and Edwing Fucher, Sr. They had two children:
1. Joseph Dillard Cooley, Jr., was born Jan. 29, 1922. He graduated at the Emory Univ. Dental College. He has not married. Practices in Waynesboro.
2. Lamar Fulcher Cooley was born March 4, 1926. He graduated at the Univ. of Ga. in Pharmacy. He married Alice Amelia Bartlett, d/o Beulah Crowe and Lewis Bartlett. They have three children:
(1) Alice Kimberly Cooley; (2) Joseph Dillard Cooley; (3) Amelia Kay Cooley.

Dr. Joseph E. Cooley, Sr. died on Jan. 12, 1974, and is interred in the Magnolia Cemetery in Waynesboro.

---

[1] A sketch of Dr. Cooley appeared in The Story of Georgia, p. 778 and now has been brought up to date. Editor.

FRANK G. CORKER was b. in Waynesboro, 63 years ago, the s/o of the late Mr. & Mrs. Stephen A. Corker. He was a graduate of the Univ. of Ga. and the Emory Law School where he was a classmate of Major Key. He was a member of the Alpha Tau Omega fraternity and helped organize the Ga. Tech. chapter of the fraternity.

He was one of the most prominent citizens of Dublin, Ga. He was a leading banker in Dublin. After his retirement he moved to Atlanta in 1919. He was found dead at his home, 1347 Fairview Road, N.E. The doctors pronounced the result of either apoplexy or heart failure.

PALMER L. CORKER, was b. in Waynesboro, Ga., Aug. 7, 1860, the s/o Margaret M. (Palmer) and Capt. Stephen A. Corker. Palmer L. received his education in the Richmond Academy at Augusta, Ga. and the Virginia Military Institute. Upon leaving school he became a clerk in the mercantile establishment of Maj. William A. Wilkens in Waynesboro. At the age of 20 years he embarked in a mercantile venture for himself with a few hundred dollars, which he had inherited from his father's estate. But by close application to business and the excuse of sound judgment he has won a place among the foremost business men of his native city.

In 1898 he was chosen Vice-President of The Citizens Bank of Waynesboro, and held this position until in Sept., 1905, when he resigned to accept the presidency of the First National Bank of Waynesboro, which had just been organized.

In addition to his banking and mercantile interests he owned several farms in Burke County, and was made President of the Waynesboro Grocery Co.

In his political views he is a consistent advocate of Democratic principles; served as a member of the Board of County Commissioners for 10 years; a member of the City Council for 16 years; and for 10 years was the Treasurer of Waynesboro. In his youth he was for a time a member of the "Stonewall Rifles". In 1880 he married Miss Melrose Attaway d/o Mary V. Parrish and John Attaway, formerly of Waynesboro. They had three children: Stephen A., Mamie, and Palmer L. Corker, Jr. Mr. Palmer L., Sr. died Feb. 11, 1920. His wife lived until Dec. 29, 1935. Both are interred in the Waynesboro Magnolia Cemetery.

STEPHEN A. CORKER, was b. May 7, 1830 in Burke County, studied law and was admitted to the Bar. At the beginning of the Civil War he resigned the office of Ordinary and joined the Confederate Army as Orderly Sergeant of Co. A, Third Ga. Regt., Wright Brigade, ANV, (the Burke Guards). This was the second company to depart from Waynesboro (April 29, 1860). Subsequently he became Capt. of his company. He was captured at Gettysburg at the head of his company and was sent to Johnson's Island, where he remained a prisoner until the end of hostilities.

He married Margaret M. Palmer, d/o Jane Allen and Edmund Palmer (a sister of Prof. James E. Palmer of Emory College). They had three sons: Palmer L. Corker (founder of the First National Bank of Waynesboro; Frank G. Corker (a successful banker in Dublin, Ga.), and Stephen A. Corker, Jr. (a broker in New Orleans).

After the War he resumed the practice of law at Waynesboro, served several terms in the State Legislature, and was elected a Representative in the Forty-first U. S. Congress, but owing to a contest did not take his seat until the close of the term. He died on Oct. 18, 1879 (at the age of 49 years), and is interred in the Waynesboro Confederate Memorial Cemetery.[1]

After his death, his wife married Judge Weaver, Madison, Ga. She is buried at Madison.

---

[1] See Memorial to him in *Minutes of the Burke Superior Court, Bk H., 1877-1880*, 433-34.

GEORGE F. COX, JR., s/o Mary Toombs Jones and George F. Cox, Sr., was b. in Oct., 1904. Following attending Waynesboro H.S. (T.J. Lance, Principal), he graduated from the Univ. of Va. and shortly thereafter was employed by the Insurance Co. of North America in Atlanta. He was with North America four years serving in Philadelphia, New York, and New Orleans before moving to Dallas in the early thirties to open a Marine branch office for the Royal-Globe Group of Insurance Companies.

In 1942 he became a local independent insurance agent, operating as George F. Cox & Co. where is is still active. Mr. Cox is a past president of the Dallas Assn. of Insurance Agents and a former Director of Texas Assn. of Insurance Agents. For some years he was active in Boy Scout work. He is a former president of the Men's Bible Class, "Kitchen Cabinet", of the Church of Incarnation. Currently, he is president of the Dallas Chapter of the English-Speaking Union. He is a member of the Dallas County Club and Civitan International. Social Club memberships past and present include Rondo, Calyx and Terpsichorean.

In 1938 he married Aylett Royall, a third generation Dallasite (unusual in this city). With degrees from Univ. of Texas and East Texas State Univ., she is currently working on her doctorate while training teachers. She pioneered in teaching school teachers' techniques of alphabetic phonics to enable them to teach children how better to read and write and spell. She is Director of teacher training at Dean Memorial Learning Center where teachers from many states and countries come for training. Her writings and professional honors sustain a demand for her services, lecturing teacher groups around the country.

Children:
1. Weldon Royall Cox is the older son; a physicist, a Duke graduate who completed his doctoral work at the Univ. of Texas and "post-doctorate" at Rice and Western Reserve. His first employment was with Texas Instruments Central Research Lab. He resides in Santa Roas, Ca., where he has recently started his own company making "memory chips" for

P. DUNCAN COX, The subject of this sketch enjoys the honor of being the youngest member in the House, having been born in Burke County on the 14th of March, 1847. He received a private education, and since attaining to manhood has followed the profession of a planter. In 1864, being then only seventeen years of age, he volunteered in defense of the Confederacy, joining the Fifth Ga. Cavalry, and served until the surrender of Wheeler's Corps. On returning home he engaged in politics, becoming prominent and popular among the Democrats of his county. In 1868, having then attained his majority, Mr. Cox was nominated by the Democracy for the Legislature and was defeated. In 1870 he was again the nominee of the party and was elected by 470 majority. Since taking his seat he has made an excellent member, and may be regarded as one of the promising young men in politics in Ga. He is a man of ability and will yet make his work. Mr. Cox was married in 1867 to Miss Fletcher of Burke County, and is a member of the Methodist Episcopal Church, South.[1]

---

[1] A. St. Clair - Abrams, <u>Manual and Brozynheal Register - State of Ga. For 1871-2</u>. Atlanta, 1872, p. 45.

SIDNEY C. COX, III was b. July 10, 1936, in Augusta, Ga. His roots and heritage are in Burke County, Ga. His is the son of Sidney C. Cox, Jr. of Waynesboro and Emily Elliott Cox of Covington, Ga. His grandfather, Sidney C. Cox, Sr. was a Burke County native who farmed in Burke County for many years and also had a drug store which he operated as "Cox Drug Store", which he opened in about 1916. A successful drug store, now known as "Burke Drugs", is still in operation at the same location at 620 Liberty Street. Sidney attended Waynesboro Grammar School and was graduated from Waynesboro H. S. in 1954. While in High School he was on the debate team, football team and a charter member of the Waynesboro H. S. band, in which he played trumpet, and also a dance band. He also was a solo vocalist and a member of the Male Quartet.

He attended Davidson College in Davidson, N. C.. While there he participated in cross country running and the Davidson Choir. He was a member of the Sigma Alpha Epsilon fraternity and was voted Outstanding Pledge in 1955. He majored in Economics with a minor in Business Administration, and was graduated in 1958. After graduation he served in the U. S. Army in Ft. Bragg, N. C., and Ft. Bliss, Tex., in an anti-aircraft artillery unit.

He began his insurance career in 1960 by obtaining a management training position with the Aetna Casualty & Surety Company of Hartford, Conn. After the job training in various departments in the company's Atlanta office, he attended the company's Management & Sales Training School in Hartford, Conn. for four months, and was then assigned to the branch office in Jacksonville, Fla. for the next four years. He was in charge of securing and training agents for Aetna in the north Florida area, as well as expanding production from existing agents.

While in Jacksonville, he met his wife, the former Nell Revels of Mayo, Fla., who was employed by a Jacksonville insurance agency, Harry E. James, Inc. They were married Oct. 13, 1963. In 1965, Sidney was offered a position as

Assistant Branch Manager in Orlando, Fla., with the Employers Commercial Union Insurance Co., and he and Nell moved to Winter Park, Fla., where they spent the next two years, and where their first child was born in 1966.

In 1967 Sidney received the shocking news that his younger and only brother, Jack, had been killed in Vietnam. He moved back to his hometown of Waynesboro, where he joined his father, Sidney C. Cox, Jr., and W. F. Evans, in the insurance and real estate business. His father had started this business in 1934. Under Sidney's direction, the business was incorporated in 1969 as Sidney C. Cox Insurance and Real Estate, Inc. In 1970 the company moved from its location of many years at 640 Liberty Street to 205 East Sixth Street upon purchasing the old First National Bank Building at that location. His company also purchased the Herrington Insurance Agency, formerly Fulcher-Herrington Agency, which was operating from that location.

Sidney became President of the company upon his father's death in 1974. In 1979, due to further expansion of the insurance and real estate business to the point that it was the largest in Burke County, and also due to the need for modern office space with ample parking for employees and clients, the company purchased a new office building from Paul Stone, just south of the Waynesboro Motor Court on Liberty Street, across from the City Lake. The site has been improved by extensive landscaping with a sprinkler system for shrubbery and a large paved parking lot.

Since returning to Waynesboro, Sidney has been active in the First Presbyterian Church as a choir member and has served on the pulpit committee. He has been a member of the Exchange Club and served as a director for the Waynesboro Rotary Club, and is presently serving as a director and sponsor of the Waynesboro-Burke County Community Concert Assn. He is also the Co-Chairman of the Waynesboro Citizens Advisory Committee, which advises and co-ordinates recommendations regarding the allocation and expenditures of Federal funds for urban renewal, to provide for adequate housing and recreational facilities for citizens of Waynesboro, especially minority or disadvantaged groups. Being designated a Certified Senior Appraisor (CSA) by the American Society of Certified Appraisors, he was engaged by the City Council to appraise sustandard residential properties being torn down in slum areas to make certain that the owners were adequately and fairly compensated. Sidney is a broker member of the Nat'l Assn. of Realtors. He is a member of the state and national Assn. of Independent Insurance Agents, and currently serves on a State Committee for Agency Evaluation and Perpetuation. Under his direction as President and Chairman of Sidney C. Cox Insurance & Real Estate, Inc., the organization has grown to eight (8) employees and associates. Since 1975, he has constructed and continues to make available on cost basis, new facilities for vital community social services, among which are two all metal buildings on Council Street across from City Hall; one of which houses the Augusta Rescue Mission, Inc., a non-profit organization, which distributes clothing on a cost basis to the economically disadvantaged, and the other, which houses the Job Training Center to train unemployed youths in new skills. He also built, and continues to make available, a new brick building on Dogwood Drive for the Dept. of Family & Children's Services. The south wing of his new office building is occupied by Health Help, Inc. which provides out-patient care for elderly indigent persons.

He is an enthusiastic sportsman and likes quail, deer, dove and duck hunting, which he enjoys on the 2,000 acre Jones tract, adjoining his home, which he leases for that purpose. He has allowed the Ga. Field Trial Assn. to use his leased land for their trials. He also enjoys fresh water fishing in the ponds and streams of Burke County, and time permitting, an occasional salt water trip, for cobia, king mackeral or dolphin, from his cottage at Frigg Island, S. C.

Sidney has four children, Sidney Elliott Cox; Maria Revels Cox; Jackson Elliott Cox, II; all students at Edmund Burke Academy, and Stepehn Cox, a junior at Furman Univ. He, his wife and children, reside on Pine Cone Road, in Waynesboro.

WILLIAM D'ANTIGNAC, M.D. Dr. Wm. D.'Antignac had served in the Confederate Army as a Captain. This was learned from an incident recorded in Brig. Gen. Sorrel's memories. During the Sharpsburg (Antielem) Campaign, Sorrel (then a Lt. Col.) was wounded and placed, for recovery, in the Hamtrammock family's home at Shepherdstown, Va. The nurses were two of the daughters in the family and an aunt, Miss Shepard.

To quote from Sorrel:
There was a Georgian in the house, Capt. Wm. D'Antignac, badly wounded in the head, and in the charge of Miss Shepard. She would sometimes rush into our room laughing immoderately; the poor fellow was out of his head and talking all sorts of nonsense.[1]

He later owned the land which had belonged to Dr. Lyman Hall in the Savannah River. He also practiced as a medical doctor.

---

[1] Gen. G. Moxley Sorrell, Recollections of a Confederate Staff Officer, McCowat-Mercer Press, Inc., Jackson, Tenn., 1958, p. 111

HENRY CARLTON DANIEL, SR., was born Dec. 24, 1875, the s/o Annie Blanton and Col. Charles Pope Daniel at Brooks Station, Ga.[1] His father was one of the youngest Colonels in the Confederate Army. A snapshot of the momument showing where the Col. had his Ga. 5th Infantry at 5:30 P.M., Sept. 20, 1863 ready for the Battle of Chickamauga. The Confederates won that battle.

In 1903 C. P. Daniel & Sons was ready for expanding. One of his sons, Bert P. Daniel, would stay and run the store at Senoia, Ga., while the other three sons: Emory; C. Ross, and Henry Carlton Daniel would go to Waynesboro for opening up a store. At the beginning Henry C. agreed to leave the other two to run the store so he could pick up a little more needed cash. People in Girard had talked Henry C. to come there to teach, because they were unable to get a good teacher.

After he returned to the store after teaching, his father often told his son about driving his horse and buggy from Waynesboro to Girard and back to enable him to court his "wife-to-be".

Henry Carlton Daniel married Lena Houston (b. March 19, 1888) in 1905, the d/o Savannah Heath and Joseph W. Houston. The C.P. Daniel & Sons began business in 1902 & 1903. This was a good time to enter the competition in Waynesboro. Maj. W. A. Wilkins retired from Wilkins & Jones in 1902 and dissolved the partnership. On July 27, 1904 Col. W. Everett Jones died from apoplexy. William Wilkes Jones died on Oct. 3, 1908. Maj. Wilkins died Nov. 14, 1907; and his son, W. A. Wilkins, Jr. wanted to, and did, get out of merchandising and live in New Orleans. C. P. Daniel & Sons, the Goldbergs and one or two others bought out bargain merchandise. For a time C.P. Daniel & Sons did business at the W. A. Wilkins Old Store. These new merchandisers in Waynesboro vied with each other with one or two big spaces each week in The True Citizen. In 1905 C. Ross Daniel was made a Director of the Bank of Waynesboro.

Henry C. and his wife had two children:
1. Helen Daniel was born July 22, 1906. She married H. H. Chandler, Jr. and lived in Augusta. She died on Sept. 6, 1977.
2. Henry C. Daniel, Jr. was b. Nov. 19, 1910.

Professor T. J. Lance and the Daniels lived side-by-side on Whitaker Street. They were devoted to the First Methodist Episcopal Church; both taught Sunday School and Mr. Daniel became a member of the Board of Trustees of the Waynesboro schools. Mr. Daniel ran for the post of Superintendent of the Burke County Schools. The term was four years. He ran again but was defeated. Henry, Jr. remembered that his father began spending much time buying cowpeas, corn, scrap cotton, etc. and Parnell's Drygood Store. From that time on the C. P. Daniel & Son has never been out of business and has been solely wholesale and retail seeds until this day.

Mr. Daniel died June 22, 1929. He was a fine man and a good citizen. He was interred in the Waynesboro Magnolia Cemetery.

---

[1] Brooks Station, Ga. is just a few miles from Senoia, Ga. and about 20 miles west of Griffin, Ga.

HENRY CARLTON DANIEL, JR. was born Nov. 19, 1910 at Waynesboro, Ga., the s/o Lena Houston and Henry Carlton Daniel, Sr. He grew up on Whitaker Street, graduated at the Waynesboro H. S. and went to the Univ. of Ala. in the fall of 1927. He was a member of the Pi Kappa Alpha fraternity.

When his father died on June 22, 1929, Henry, Jr. had to make a difficult decision. He had spent two full years at the Univ. He would have to stay in the Univ. two more years for his degree and that meant that he would have to sell the business. He finally opted leaving the Univ. in order to hold on to the business built up by his father.

On March 17, 1932, he married Emily (known as "Lou") Applewhite, the d/o Emily Cates and John Owen Applewhite. On her mother's side, she is connected with the Cates, Attaways, and MacKenzies, prominent in early Burke history.

She is a granddaughter of Margaret MacKenzie and William Joseph Cates. Mrs. MacKenzie was the first president of the Burke County Wayside Home in Millen during the Civil War. Mr. Daniel's grandfather was Col. Charles Pope Daniel who lead the 5th Ga. Regiment in the Battle of Chicamauga, and one of the youngest Confederate Colonels.

Mr. Daniel has a going concern under the old name of C. P. Daniel & Sons, Inc. His business is wholesale and retail seeds. He has been a member of the Rotary Club twice. He has been a Deacon at the First Baptist Church and served one term of the Chairman of the Board of Deacons. He has been a Director of the Bank of Waynesboro since 1934 and has served as Chairman of the Board of Directors since C. W. Skinner, Jr. retired.

They have three children:
1. Billie Applewhite Daniel, b. May 8, 1933. Married Michael B. Parker. They have one son, Michael, Jr. who was b. Apr. 30, 1964.
2. Sara Ann Daniel, b. Feb. 14, 1936; married W. H. Shepard of Griffin, Ga. Sara Ann died Apr. 4, 1975. The three children live with their father in Griffin: Sally Ann Shepard, age 18; Emily Daniel Shepard, age 16; and W. H. Shepard, Jr., age 14.
3. Henry C. Daniel, Jr., b. May 16, 1949, was married and divorced. No children.

---

[1] Henry Carlton Daniel, Jr. is correct; and his son is third (III) and correct. But the father will let his son talk him into being Daniel, Jr. So now the father is incorrect, using Henry Carlton Daniel only. The Editor.

J. H. DANIEL, merchant at Millen, was b. in Burke County in 1831, and was the s/o of Zack and Lydia (Griffin) Daniel. His father was a native of, and followed farming, all his life in Burke County, and grandfather, a native of N. C., first settled in Burke County about 1800. The parents of the mother of Mr. Daniel were born in S. C., and moving to Ga., died in this state. He was educated at the public schools and in 1858 married Mary H. Gray, d/o Robert H. Gray. Mr. Gray was b. in Columbia, S.C., and moved to Waynesboro, Ga. He was tax receiver for a number of years and afterward moved to Millen, where he died in 1870. To this union were born four children, now living: Robert G., engaged in business with his father, now in England; James H., also in business with his father; and Grover Stanley. The mother was b. in Waynesboro in 1840. They are both active members of the Methodist Episcopal church, and he is a member of the Masonic Fraternity. In 1855 he was made Tax Receiver of Burke County and held the office two years. He was then employed as a mail clerk for two years and was then promoted to conductor, and afterward became a railroad agent at Millen. He also established a general mercantile business in 1876, which has since been continued. He is a partner in the firm of Daniel Sons & Palmer, and owns large family interests in both Burke and Screven counties. Mr. Daniel has about 20,000 acres of land, a large number being in clutivation, in tilling which he runs about 130 plows; his cotton production being about 1,500 bales annually. Mr. Daniel is one of the best business men in Screven County, and handles the reins of his vast interests without any apparent responsibility. He lives in a fine residence near Millen.[1]

---

[1] Memoirs of Georgia, Vol. II, (1895), pp. 824-825.

MYRICK DAVIES, a martyr of the Revolutionary War, was a miller on Brier Creek. He did not rush into the Revolution; in fact his name appears among the 114 signatories who rejected the signing by Henry Jones and William Lord of the Resolutions of Aug. 10, 1774.[1] But in July, 1776, he was approved as one of the Magistrates in the lower district of St. George's Parish,[2] and during 1779 to late 1781, after the British had over run Ga. and Tory activities were running high, he braved the dangers of serving as a member of the Supreme Executive Council. This was the new State government "in exile", meeting when and where it could find relatively safe places. He first represented Burke on the Council in the second half of 1779; the Council consisted then of nine members. Again he served in 1780 and in 1781. Meetings were held in Augusta, Heards' Fort in Wilkes County and at Harvell's Plantation in Burke.[3] These were dark days when the American Cause in Ga. seemed all but lost. From Aug. 19, 1781, to his death in Dec., 1781, he was President of the Council, and Dr. Nathan Brownson was Governor.[4] It was during his presidency that the seat of the Council briefly was in Burke at Harvell's Plantation. Tragically, Davies was captured in the county by a band of Tories in Dec., 1781, and murdered by, or upon the orders of, Capt. Brantley. See p. _____ for the Resolution of the Council upon his death. Myrick Street in Waynesboro seems to be the only memorial to his brave patriot and martyr.

---

[1] White's Historical Collections of Georgia, p. 284.
[2] Proceedings of the Council of Safety, July 2, 1776 in Collections of the Georgia Historical Society, Vol. V., Part I, p. 69.
[3] Official Register, 1961/62, pp. 1004 and 1005.
[4] Ibid., pp. 1005 and 995.

MARION TRACY DAVIS, M.D., s/o Kate MacKenzie (Davis) and his father _____ Davis.[1] Dr. Davis died at his home in Atlanta on June 26, 1920.

Dr. Davis was prominent in medical circles in Atlanta and elsewhere. He was a member of the Fulton County Medical Association. He was also active in fraternal orders, the Masons and the Knights of Pythias.

Dr. Davis was about 55 years of age and is the last member of his immediate family. He was a first cousin of Mr. J. Hope MacKenzie and some of the Cates family. He with his mother, was a resident of Waynesboro some forty or more years until they moved to Atlanta. He was remembered by some of our older citizens.

His remains were escorted to Waynesboro by Mr. Fred Turner of the Atlanta Lodge No. 20 of the Knights of Pythias of which Dr. Davis was an honored member. The Waynesboro Lodge No. 96 took charge of the burial which was with Pythian honors. Dr. J. P. McFerrin of the Waynesboro Methodist Church assisted.

---

[1] The marker of his mother and father, and his own, have been removed from the Old Cemetery (now the Waynesboro Confederate Memorial Cemetery).

WILLIAM HUDSON DAVIS was b. Feb. 2, 1865, on the Burke County plantation of his parents, William Hudson Davis and Mrs. Sarah Kilpatrick Davis.

Judge Davis' father, William Hudson Davis, was b. in Jsaper County, Ga. Upon his marriage to Sarah Kilpatrick he moved in 1858 to the ancestral lands of his wife in Burke County. His father was a distinguished Baptist minister and educator and was one of the trustees of Mercer Univ. from 1877 to the date of his death.

Soon after the birth of William H. Davis his father left Burke County and moved to Hephzibah, where he and his brother-in-law, Washington L. Kilpatrick, were co-principals of the Hephzibah H. S. William H. Davis, the elder, was connected with this school, either in the capacity of trustee or teacher from the date of its organization to the date of his death, which occurred in 1879.

William H. Davis received his elementary education at this school under the direction of his able father and uncle, and subsequently entered Mercer Univ., from which he was graduated in 1885. After graduating from Mercer Univ., Judge Davis returned to his native county where he was principal of the Waynesboro Academy for two years. He then took up the study of law in the office of Robert O. Lovett and was admitted to the bar in Burke County, Ga., on June 6, 1889; but even before his admission to the bar, he evidenced an interest in public affairs and was elected to the House of Representatives in 1888, and served as a member of the General Assembly until 1891. At the session of the General Assembly of 1892 he was elected as Solicitor General of the Augusta Circuit, which position he occupied from Jan. 1, 1893, to Dec., 1900. Upon his admission to the bar he formed a partnership with Judge R. O. Lovett, with whom he practiced at Waynesboro until his election as Solicitor General. After retiring as Solicitor General in 1901, he formed a partnership with the late Judge E. L. Brinson, with whom he practiced in Waynesboro until 1908. At the Nov. election of 1908 he was elected as Judge of the City Court of Waynesboro, succeeding Judge Phil P. Johnston, and went into office Jan., 1909, which office he occupied continuously from that date until the date of his death, Feb. 4, 1928. Just prior to his death he had been renominated for his sixth term as Judge of the City Court of Waynesboro. Judge Davis had the distinction of having held numerous public offices over a period of 40 years, and had never been defeated for any office for which he had ever offered. After his services as Solicitor General of the Augusta Circuit he served in 1902-3-4 as Senator from the 17th Senatorial District and in 1906-06 was elected as a representative of the General Assembly from Burke County. At these sessions of the Legislature he was chairman of the appropriation committee.

On Nov. 24, 1899, he was married to Miss Marie Porter Wilkins, daughter of Joseph H. Wilkins and Fannie Warren Wilkins. His wife lived only a short while after their marriage, and their only child died in infancy.

Judge Davis was deeply interested in the cause of education and served as president of the Board of Trustees of Mercer Univ. from 1913 until, on account of his declining health, in June, 1927, he retired as president, but continued as a member of the Board.

He served as a member of the Board of Directors of the Ga. State College for Women at Milledgeville from 1910 until the date of his death.

He was also a Trustee of the Ga. Training School for Girls.

Judge Davis was a member of the Baptist Church of Waynesboro, in which church he had served as deacon for years. He was deeply interested in his church and in all of its activities, and for a number of years was teacher of the Men's Bible Class of the Baptist Sunday School.

Of late years Judge Davis had discontinued the active practice of law and devoted his time exclusively to the performance of his duties as Judge of the City Court of Waynesboro and as President of the First National Bank, as well as looking after his large farming interests.

In personal appearance, Judge Davis was handsome and of heroic mould. He was over six feet tall and weighed over two hundred pounds. He was possessed of a vigorous constitution and untiring energy. His shapely and massive head and shoulders and his erect and easy carriage compelled attention in any group or assembly. By inheritance Judge Davis was endowed with splendid physical appearance and a high degree of intellect, far beyond the average man. He was a ten-talent man, and by training and mastery of himself and his talents he became one of the ablest leaders of the state.

With only four years' experience as a practicing attorney he became Solicitor General of the Augusta Circuit, and from the start was one of the most vigorous and successful prosecutors in the history of the state. By his keen insight he had no difficulty in getting to the heart of any case, and presented his cases to the jury with such logic, fairness, eloquence and power that it is said that "Rarely did the guilty escape." After he retired as prosecutor these same attributes he most successfully employed in the general practice of law, and before his retirement from general practice his services were sought in every case of importance in the courts of Burke and adjoining counties.

As a Judge he was endowed with the fundamental characteristics of the good Judge. He had discernment to weigh facts carefully in their proper relations to the entire case. His fairness, sense of justice, and integrity were so unquestioned that litigants most frequently preferred him to be the trior of the facts as well as the law, and his judgments were so just that large numbers of cases and many important ones were submitted to him for determination without the intervention of a jury.

He was most obliging, patient and considerate in his dealings with the members of the bar and in the conduct of his court, and all practitioners in his court respected and loved him.

In the bigness of his heart in passing sentence on the criminal side of the court, he was always deeply concerned with the past and future of the unfortunate who happened to be before him. He had a broad sympathy for the frailties of mankind, and always sought to apply a sentence that would not only protect society, but convince the defendant that he had received justice but tempered with mercy. His heart was big, and he sought to lift men up, rather than to permit them to be dragged deeper.

Judge Davis touched the life of his community and state in many places. He was deeply interested in every civic enterprise of the betterment of the community and its citizens. His benefactions were many and made without ostentation. He loved to help people in need and especially deserving young men and young women who were trying to better themselves in life. He gave unstintedly of himself and his means to every worthy enterprise that was presented to him. He was of a deeply religious nature and devoted to the church of which he was a member, but he was not sectarian in his views. All good enterprises of any denomination were assured of his cooperation and hearty support.

He loved his community and stood for the highest things in it, and always strove to maintain the highest standards in the citizenry of Burke County.

This man of intellect, physical strength, power, influence and affluence, in an age when the world is beset with doubts instilled by false prophets, relied not on human reason and things of this world, but put his trust reverently, humbly and triumphantly in the eternal verities of the Living Word. In temporal matters his vision was comprehensive and he kept step with the age in which he lived, but in spiritual matters he clung unalterably to the simple faith of his fathers.[1]

---

[1] 45 Annual Report (1928), Ga. Bar Ass'n., pp. 180-183, by F. S. Burney and P. B. Lewis, Jr., of Waynesboro, Ga.

JOHN MARSHALL DENT, M.D. was b. July 16, 1834, the s/o Sarah McIntosh and Dr. John Dent. His father, an Augusta physician, was a member of the first State Board (1825) to license physicians; a Trustee of the Medical Academy of Ga. (1828), which ultimately became the Medical College of Ga. in Augusta.

The son graduated at the Medical School (1853). He served in the Confederate Army as a surgeon, with Co. A, 12th Ga. BN, and practiced medicine for 50 years. He married Maria Harper, d/o Mary Ann Cashin and William Harper. They had three sons: Edwin G.; Charles A.; and William Harper Dent, and three daughters: Sarah (Sadie) Crawford Dent (Fulcher), d. 1934; Caroline Elizabeth Dent, d. 1947; and Marian Dent (Cox), d. 1952.

He died at the home of his daughter (Mrs. Wm. Fulcher) on Nov. 20, 1922 and was interred in the Waynesboro Magnolia Cemetery. He was long an Elder of the Waynesboro Presbyterian Church.

CAPTAIN WM. HENRY DICKINSON, was b. Oct. 5, 1839. He was reared in the atmosphere of the old true Ga. days, finishing his school days in the Ga. Military Institute at Marietta. He was the s/o that distinguished gentleman, Maj. Dickinson, whose memory is esteemed by all who knew him to this day although he died many years ago.

It has been the good fortune of the writer to have known him from early years. In all that time, and side-by-side in war where men are tried most severely not an instance ever happened in which the true, brave, modest, refined gentleman was not present in his conduct.

In the Civil War he was one among the first to the front. He went April 19, 1861, with the Burke Sharpshooters, which afterwards became Co. D in the Ga. Regt., the flag company out there directly under the banner of the South. He stayed until disabled at Gettysburg by the loss of his right arm. He had risen to be Capt. of this famous company.

In the Battle of Chicamauga, the bloodiest in proportion to numbers of the whole war, there happened an incident which we mention to show what character of man he was. It was late in the evening of the 19th of Sept. while our left wing being pressed, the 2d. Ga. Regt. was hastened forward. It ran suddenly on a large body of the enemy and was in close quarters. A Federal soldier was loading his gun, the ramrod being partly down the barrel. He fired the ramrod at Capt. Dickinson in a few feet of him. It passed through the breast and he fell. Immediately the Federal fell mortally wounded. The enemy were driven back, and Capt. Dickinson and his assailant lay in a few feet of each other. With the assistance of a wounded Confederate the ramrod was pulled out. In a few minutes the wounded Capt. of Co. D was by the side of the brave Fed. soldier giving him water from his canteen, the Federal having none on that sultry day upon the dustiest, dryist field ever fought over. Capt. Dickinson left him and struggled back to the hospital. He survived, the other died where he lay.

His widow was the daughter of Hon. Alexander C. Walker of Richmond County, who was a prominent man throughout the state. He leaves her and five children bereft of a tender loving husband and father. He was about 58 years of age, respected by all and died honored for the purity of his life for the many virtues of his life and for the many virtues he possessed and practiced to the last hour of his sentence. His body rests in the Brothersville Cemetery near Hephzibah. He died Oct. 1, 1897.

<u>EVA WALKER ARMSTRONG DIXON</u>, was b. at Windsor, S.C., Apr. 22, 1886, the youngest of the five charming daughters of Mr. & Mrs. Robert Rhett Armstrong. The family moved to Aiken, S.C. when she was quite young. There she was educated. She married first Olive W. Buxton, s/o Needham A. Buxton, prominent in Girard, Ga. as a leading farmer and merchant. Her husband died in 1914 and she married secondly in 1916, Mr. Bonnie M. Dixon, a prosperous farmer and a leading Burke County citizen in Girard. They were married at the home of her sister, Mrs. Mike Usher, in Hephzebah, Ga.

In 1933 she was drafted to run for Mayor in Girard and won. On Mar. 28, 1933 she earned the distinction of being the first woman chief executor in Burke County's long history She was elected almost in spite of her own wishes, but took pride in such honor since Girard was a progressive community. Serving with the first woman mayor were Councilmen Malabar Dixon, Will Chandler, Frank Odon, and J. B. Buxton. The last name was the recorder and town clerk.

She had long been recognized as one of the most public spirited citizens and four years before had been voted Girard's "Best Woman". Doing thing was right in her line. Being the Mayor was just another job. She was already the President of the W.C.T.U., head of the Woman's Club, Assistant Superintendent of Sunday School, and General Supervisor of Senior League.

Death came on Sept. 21, 1957, leaving no children. Interment was in the Bethany Methodist Church Cemetery in Girard. Her death was a great loss to the Girard community, but left behind an example for other women to aspire to municipal leadership.

ARNOLD JOSEPH DOLINSKY was b. June 30, 1914 in New York City, and in Waynesboro from age of eight months. His parents were Sarah Goldberg and Samuel Dolinsky.

Educated at Richmond Academy (Augusta) and Georgia Tech. (Institute of Technology) at Atlanta.

During WW II he was rejected because of arthritic gout. He married Celentha, d/o Anna Waldstreicher and Max Weingarten.

His stores kept him busy: President of Goldberg's Furniture, Inc.; President of Goldberg's, Inc. (Dept. Store); Managing Partner of Goldberg Bros. & Dolinsky (Holding Company).

Club: Rotary, Past President; Director; Rotary Man of the Year, 1978.

Past Public Services: Scoutmaster; Chairman of Scouting in Burke County. Presently: President of the Waynesboro Development Corp.; Chairman of Burke County Development Authority; Director of Augusta Symphony.

His Church: Walton Way Temple (Augusta, Ga.).

TROY DREW of Medville, Ga., the s/o Laura E. and W. B. Drew, entered the Army Air Corps in Feb., 1941 and was a Cadet at Jackson, Miss., Maxwell Field, Ala. and Albuquerque, N.M. where he received his commission as 2nd Lt. His first operational assignment was overseas in the China-Burma-Indian Theater as a bombardier with the 7th Bomb G.P., 10th Air Force. There he totaled 255 hours of combat missions. While flying a B-25 and B-24 bomber in June, 1942, 2nd Lt. Drew was shot down in the Bay of Bengal. He and his crew remained on a life raft for several days and nights, finally landing on the coast of Burma. For four days they evaded capture, and were rescued. Capt. Drew returned to the States in Aug, 1943 and was assigned to the Army Air Force Tactical Center, Orlando, Fla., and there went on to Ft. Leavenworth, Kan. to attend the Command and General Staff School in 1944.

After completion of the Ft. Leavenworth School, he was stationed at the Hq - USAF Pentagon, and held rank of Major at the end of the War. The Army Air Corps became a part of a separate Air Force in 1947. In 1951 he was made a Lieut-Colonel and in March, 1963, a full Colonel.

He remained in the Air Corps, retiring with the rank of full Colonel.

DAVID EMANUEL. Something is known of David Emanuel who was Governor of Ga. for a few months from the resignation of Gen. Jackson as Governor in March, 1801, until Nov. of the same year when Joseph Tattnall was elected Gov.

Adiel Sherwood in his <u>Gazeteer for Georgia</u> said that David Emanuel was of German descent and was born in Pa. in 1744; that he came to Ga. before the Revolution, married Ann Lewis and several children were born to them. George White in his <u>Statistics of Georgia</u> states that David Emanuel came to Ga. about

1768 or 1770 and settled in Walnut Branch near Waynesboro from which place he moved to the head of Beaver Dam Creek. He endured many hardships during the Rev. War and near the end of it his family and 30 others built cabins below Augusta and the Tories called it "Rebel Town".

David Emanuel was a sturdy youth when the Revolution began. His family was prominent in Burke County and he took part in the War. He was later taken prisoner by the British and with two others, Rev. Josiah Lewis and Myrick Davies.[1] They were condemned to be shot. Most of their clothes were taken from them, and when they were ready for the execution, Davies asked permission to pray, which was granted and he offered a fervent prayer. The three condemned were placed between the fire and the executioners. The signal was given and Lewis and Davies dropped dead, but the shot at Emanuel missed him and he jumped over the fire and escaped. Emanuel ran to the swamp and sank up to his neck, and when all had passed him in the darkness, and when all was quiet, he crept out and in the morning made his way to the army of Col. Twiggs, who was his brother-in-law.

A slightly different version of what happened was that Emanuel jumped onto the group of horses and got away while the loyalists were trying to catch their horses. It has also been written that Emanuel's executioner was a mulatto Negro.

Other members of his family were involved in the bitter struggle. John Duhart (listed as Dukart), a brother-in-law, and Levi Emanuel, a brother, were commissioned by the Council of Safety in Jul., 1776 as Capt. and 2nd Lt., respectively in the militia.[2] Another brother, Asa, became a Col. in 1781 of the Burke Militia.[3]

After the War David Emanuel became a leading citizen of Burke County. "He was a man of fine character, who was fully trusted by his fellow citizens."[4] Locally, at various times, he held such posts as Justice of the Peace and Receiver of Tax Returns,[5] but more often he represented Burke in the State Legislature and at state conventions. Between 1782 and 1796 he was an Assemblyman from Burke for six terms, and in 1786 was elected to the Executive Council.[6] In 1787 he was the State's Commissary-General. This we know because he was denied an Assembly seat that year for this reason.[7] With Thomas Lewis he represented Burke in the State Constitutional Convention of Jan., 1789.[8] In 1796 he was active in the Assembly Committee which examined and reported against the Yazoo land grants.[9] From 1797 to 1804 he served seven terms in the State Senate from Burke, and was three times President of the Senate. He became Governor of Ga. in 1801 by virtue of his office as President of the Senate; his term as Governor was an interim period, March 3 to Nov. 7,

---

[1] Myrick Davies of Burke had been President of the Executive Council that year. See Charles C. Jones, Jr., Vol. II, pp. 502-503.

[2] Proceedings of the Georgia Council of Safety (Jul. 2, 1776) in Vol. V, Collection of the Ga. Historical Society, Part I, p. 70.

[3] Jones, op.cit., Vol. II, pp. 436-437.

[4] George G. Smith, The Story of Georgia and The Georgia People, 1732-1860. (2d ed.), p. 228.

[5] The Augusta Chronicle and Gazette of the State, Dec. 26, 1789, Feb. 20, 1790.

[6] Official Register, 1961/62, pp. 1219-1220.

[7] Ibid, p. 1220.

[8] The Georgia State Gazette or Independent Register, Dec. 6, 1788 & Jan. 24, 1789.

[9] Cyc. of Georgia, Vol. I, p. 666.

before an election could be held to fill a vacancy after Gen. James Jackson resigned as Gov. to accept a Senatorship in Congress.[10]

His brother-in-law, John Duhart, was also an Assemblyman from Burke in 1782, and later County Coroner.[11] Levi Emanuel, a brother, was Clerk of the Land Court in 1788 and a member of the Grand Jury, Oct. term, 1788.[12]

We know something about David Emanuel's life and family. David's "little son" was mentioned in brother John's will which was probated June 16, 1768.[13] This son may have been John Emanuel who appears in 1787 as a deputy surveyor and in 1790 as Capt. of one of Burke's militia district, or Eli Emanuel who represented in the Gen. Assembly seven terms from 1810 to 1816, and once in the State Senate, 1817.[14] Both may have been sons or nephews. Col. John Twiggs of the Rev. War was another brother-in-law of David Emanuel.[15] The Civil War General, David Emanuel Twiggs, born in 1790 in Richmond County, was a nephew of David Emanuel. David's religion is a matter upon which sources differ. He has been referred to as the first American of the Jewish faith to become chief executor of a State. Lucian Lamar Knight, Georgia's Landmarks, Memorials and Legends, Vol. I (1913), p. 542 states that he may have been of "Israelitish origin". Adiel Sherwood, A Gazetter of the State of Georgia (1837), p. 275 refers to Emanuel as a "Colonel", "of German extraction", and "by profession a Presbyterian", and his residence as having been ten miles northwest of Waynesboro. David Emanuel died on Feb. 19, 1808 at age 65.[16] Today his grave can no longer be identified. Only Emanuel County remains on his monument.

---

[10] Official Register, 1961/62, p. 996. Smith, op.cit, pp. 228 and 645.

[11] The Georgia State Gazette or Independent, Dec. 16, 1786, and Official Register, 1961/62, p. 1219.

[12] Ibid., Jul 26, 1788; Nov. 1, 1788.

[13] Abstract of Col. Wills of the State of Georgia, (1733-1777), p. 45.

[14] The Augusta Chronicle and Gazette of the State, Nov. 6, 1790; Official Register, 1961/62, pp. 1221 and 1044.

[15] Twiggs may have married Ruth, David's sister, or David may have married Col. Twigg's sister.

[16] William H. Dumont, Some Early Residents of Burke County, 1786-1819, (196), p. 8.

ARTHUR FORTE EVANS, SR. was b. in Burke County Sept. 13, 1881, the s/o Sarah Holleyman and Joshua K. Evans. He married Elizabeth Macaulay of Chester, S.C., b. Oct. 4, 1890, the d/o Sallie McMaster and David J. Macaulay.

A native of Burke County, Arthur Evans had lived in Waynesboro all his life and was prominent in business, civic, fraternal and church circles. Until his retirement he operated a successful wholesale grocery business.

A life-long member of the Methodist Church, he had served for many years as a member and as Chairman of the official board. He was a Mason and a Shriner and a charter member of the Rotary Club of Waynesboro.

An ardent sportsman, he played golf almost daily in many tournaments for elder golfers, both in this country and abroad. He was a familiar figure for years at the Augusta Country Club, as well as at the course in Waynesboro. He was also an excellent tennis player and continued the sport up to a good age.

His wife preceded him in death some 15 years and is interred in the Magnolia Cemetery. They had two sons, Arthur Forte Evans, Jr. at Bluefield, W. Va., and Hugh Macaulay Evans at Eau Gallie, Fla. and seven grandchildren.

Mr. Evans d. Nov. 1, 1968 at Bluefield, W. Va., at the home of his son. The funeral service took place at the Waynesboro Methodist Church on Nov. 4. He is also interred in the Magnolia Cemetery.

THOMAS B. FELDER, JR., the well known attorney of Atlanta, Ga. was b. Oct. 6, 1863 in Burke County, Ga. and in this and Emanuel County passed his boyhood days. He received his early education in the Waynesboro H.S., from which institution he was graduated in June, 1879, taking highest available honors and receiving the first prize of declamation. From here he went to the North Ga. Agricultural and Military Academy, Dahlonega, Ga., remaining a member of the same for a year, deriving much benefit from both the classic and military branches of the school. Leaving after the expiration of the first term, he entered the law department of the Univ. of Ga., received his diploma in 1883, and after locating in Dublin, Ga., was admitted to the bar during the same year. Six months later, having given great attention to his practice, had gained a broad popularity in this section, he was made solicitor of the County Court of Lauren County, Ga., and served as such for six years. He resigned in 1889 to accept the higher office of Mayor of Dublin, holding this place creditably for one year, and was re-elected for a second term, but declined in order to serve as presidential elector on the Cleveland ticket. Mr. Felder moved to Atlanta early in 1890, and continued in this city the practice of his profession. Mr. Felder is a business man of much ability and it did not require long for his associates and acquaintances to recognize this fact. In June of 1892 he was elected president of the Atlanta Traction Company, and filled this position until May, 1893, when he resigned. Mr. Felder was married on Aug. 12, 1886, to Charlotte, d/o Grafton Johnson. They have no children. He is a Royal Arch Mason and chairman of the committee of laws and appeals of the Elks, and is also a member of the Improved Order of Red Men, the Knights of Pythias and the Methodist Church. Besides these secret societies and religious organizations he is a director in the State Savings Bank, president of the Union Loan and Trust Company, and a director of the Southern Exchange Bank. He has manifested a versatility that is seldom surpassed; and his efforts in the many different enterprises in which he has been engaged have never met with disappointment or failure.

His father is Thomas B. Felder, a native of Sumter S.C., who served as colonel in the late war and conducted himself chivalrously in a great number of campaigns. When the war was over he returned to his home in the palmetto state and followed the profession of law until a few years ago, when he retired permanently from active work. He now resides at Dublin, Ga. Mr. Felder is the worthy scion of an old, illustrious southern family, and by dint of perseverance is advancing rapidly to the front.[1]

---

[1] Memoirs of Georgia, Vol. I (1895) p. 779.

In 1917 Col. Felder was admitted to practice in New York after he had come from Ga., where he had made a notable record as a criminal lawyer. But on May 15, 1925, Col. Thomas B. Felder Jr., who <u>with</u> Gasten B. Means, former Department of Justice Agent, was convicted at Federal Court last Jan. of conspiring to bribe high government officers, was disbarred that day in the appellate division of the New York Supreme Court. Justice Clark in presenting the court's opinion, asserted that the conviction of Col. Felder for a felony made it mandatory that he be disbarred. Witnesses at this trial testified that Felder, Means and the latter's secretary, Elmer W. Jarnecke, had received $65,000 from numerous defendants in the Glass Casket-Cragen System mail fraud case to influence former Attorney General of Harry M. Daugherty to present prosecution of indictments in the case.[2]

---
[1]
T.C., May 23, 1925.

LEWIS R. FORD, M.D. was born in Augusta, Ga. Nov. 22, 1843. His father, Dr. Lewis D. Ford, was one of the early professors in the Medical Academy (Institute) in Augusta which developed into the Medical College of the Univ. of Ga.

During the Civil War, Lewis R. was a soldier and finished his medical training in Augusta. He moved to Waynesboro and practiced there during his life. He married Fannie Blount (b. Mar. 30, 1854), the d/o Abbie Attaway and Thomas H. Blount. They had one son, Frank G. Ford (b. Nov. 23, 1874; d. May 30, 1927). The son never married. The father was a Shriner. Frank was a trained musician, added a lot to the concerts and church music in the community, and taught many students.

The family lived on Liberty Street, opposite the house known as the Scales, MacKenzie, and C. W. Skinner house (now a funeral home). Dr. Ford died June 26, 1903, and his wife, Nov. 29, 1925. All three of the family were interred in the Waynesboro Magnolia Cemetery.

ALONZO LEE FRANKLIN - As judge of the Superior Courts of the Augusta district, comprising the counties of Burke, Columbia and Richmond, the Hon. Alonzo Lee Franklin has performed a work of value to this State. He has come to be widely and favorably known as a practitioner of   law, an official and a public-spirited citizen.

Judge Franklin was b. Dec. 16, 1873, on a farm in Burke County, Ga., s/o John and Emma (Youngblood) Franklin. His father was an ardent Southern patriot who joined the Confederate Army at the age of sixteen years, serving a four-year term and losing an eye at the battle of Gettysburg. After the war he made his strong personality felt in important public affairs. Settling in Burke County, his native community, he engaged in teaching as his first vocational activity. He was, moreover, deeply interested in civic affairs in his community, and was, along with his other activities, tax collector for Burke County. In 1881 he removed to Richmond County, where he became associated with Augusta's extensive commercial life, there continuing his labors until his death, in 1895, at the age of 56 years. After his death, his wife, Judge Franklin's mother, made her home in Matthews, Ga. The Youngblood family, of whom she was a member, were natives of Jefferson County, Ga., and of English origin. Judge Franklin's maternal grandfather was Augustus Youngblood who was born in Jefferson County, Ga., and was a soldier in the Confederate Army during the War Between the States. Mrs. Emma (Youngblood) Franklin today makes her home with her son, Judge Franklin. There were two children in the family: 1. Benjamin Franklin, who died in Augusta in 1896; 2. Alonzo Lee Franklin, of further mention.

Alonzo Lee Franklin was eight years of age when he was brought by his parents to live in the city of Augusta, where he grew to manhood and attended the public schools. Later he went to the Kimberlin Heights School in Tenn., there spending two years, at the conclusion of which he entered Milligan College for a four-year course. Graduated from Milligan College with a Bachelor of Arts degree in 1900, he then returned to Augusta and began to read law under the guidance of Judge Henry C. Hammond, of Augusta. In the autumn of 1901 he was admitted to the bar of the State of Ga., immediately thereafter taking up his practice of law in Augusta and continuing it until, in 1913, when he was elected to the office of solicitor-general for the Augusta district. For ten years he filled this position of public trust, continuing in it without opposition until he finally resigned.

His was the distinction of working his way upward through school and college, as well as through the more difficult phases of practical life, wholly by his own unaided efforts. Politically he held to the views of the Democratic party, and at an early period in life he began to do everything in his power to advance the civic interests of his community and district. He is a member of the Christian Church, of Augusta, in which he has filled the office of deacon for a number of years and is a member of the board of trustees. At the same time he is active in the work of the Disciples', or Christian, Church, serving for years as teacher and lecturer in the Bible class of this congregation. His wife has shared his enthusiasms for the church, and is active in numerous movements of the church society and a teacher in the Sunday School.

He is a member of the Ga. State Bar Assn., the Augusta Bar Assn., and other professional groups. In the Free and Accepted Masons he is affiliated with the Knights Templar and Alee Temple of the Ancient Arabic Order Nobles of the Mystic Shrine (at Savannah), and is also active in the work of the Order of Eastern Star. Other fraternities with which he is associated are the Junior Order United American Mechanics, the Fraternal Order of Eagles, the Knights of Pythias, the Independent Order of Odd Fellows, the Improved Order of Red Men, and the Benevolent and Protective Order of Elks.

He was elected judge of the Superior Courts of the Augusta Circuit in 1923 without opposition and still holds this office. In his work as judge he has sought to carry his splendid Christian principles into action in every-day life, so demonstrating the practicability of real idealism. He is a member of the Augusta Country Club. Judge Franklin was toastmaster at the banquet tendered President Harding at the Partridge Inn on April 6, 1923. He also had the honor of being a member of the committee representing the city of Augusta at the christening of the U.S.S. Cruiser "Augusta", in Newport News, Va. His niece, Evelyn McDanile, performed the ceremony.

Judge Franklin, on Dec. 22, 1902, married Katherine N. McDaniel, of Edgefield, S.C., d/o of Wm. H. McDaniel and Mrs. Lucinda McDaniel Hughes. The McDaniels are one of the old S.C. families. She is also descended from the Van Swearingen family of S.C., renowned for their services during the Revolutionary War. The Franklin home is one of distinctive atmosphere, reflecting always its outsanding hospitality and friendliness and so revealing the inner nature of its occupants. Judge Franklin himself is one of Augusta's very popular judges and men.[1]

---
[1] The Story of Georgia, p. 818.

GEORGE W. FRYHOFER was b. March 8, 1927 at Washington, D.C. Education: Vanderbilt Univ. (1944); N.C. State College of Agric. & Eng. (1945); A.B. degree Emory Univ. (1949); LLB, Emory Univ. Law School (1950); Doctor of Law Degree (J.D. 1970)

Military Service: Active duty, U.S Army, 1944-45; American Theatre Ribbon and WW II Vretary Medal.

On April 2, 1955 md. Ellen Hodges, d/o Mattie Mae Hodges and Eugene Hodges, deceased at Oconee, Washington County, Ga.

Member of the Official Board, First United Methodist Church of Waynesboro; former Sunday School teacher; former Chairman of the Board of Trustees and Official Board; Certified Lay Speaker.

Professional Activities: Member of State Bank of Ga.; practiced law with Fulcher Law Firm, Augusta, Ga. (1951-54); Solicitor of State Court of Burke County (1961-63); member of American Trial Lawyers Assn.; member of Augusta Area Trial Lawyers Assn.; member of Grievance Committee State Bar of Ga.; member and former President (1968) Ga. Trial Lawyers Assn.; member of American Bar Assn.; Judge of State Court of Burke County 1963 to date; member, Inner Circle of Advocates, 1977 (a rational legal organization limited to 100 lawyers who have obtained a jury verdict of $1,000,000).

Civic-Social and Political Organizations: Business Manager of Emory Glee Club; Alpha Tau Omega Social Fraternity; Phi Delta Phi Legal Fraternity; O.D.K. honorary Leadership Fraternity; Commander of Waynesboro American Legion Post; member of Waynesboro Country Club; President of Waynesboro Exchange Club; President of Augusta Choral Society; member of Pinnacle Club of Augusta; Charter member of Sea Pines Plantation Club, Hilton Head Island, S.C.

Children:
1. George W. Fryhofer, III, b. May 29, 1959. Graduated from Emory Univ. with a major in History and minor in Political Science, member of Phi Beta Kappa and graduated with honors. During the past year he has been attending the Univ. of St. Andrews in Scotland as a Robert Tyre Jones Jr. exchange scholar from Emory to St. Andrews.
2. Vera Lynn Fryhofer, b. June 16, 1960. She has finished her sophomore year at Emory University.

EDWIN FULCHER, SR. was b. Sept. 30, 1856, the s/o Melvina and Valentine Fulcher. He married, first, Osee Herrington, b. July 4, 1863, d/o Frances L. and Barry Herrington.

Before he was married he kept good hound dogs to trail and catch foxes. On one occasion his dogs chased the fox into the business district of Waynesboro. That was an exciting chase!

From his uncle John Fulcher, he inherited land and money ($15,000 to $20,000). From early years he loved farming and was one of the best farmers in Burke County, and one of the wealthiest and extensive plantations.

When the First National Bank of Waynesboro, Ga. was established, he was made Vice-President and a Director. Other than farming he was much interested in the Waynesboro Methodist Church and he gladly served on the Board of Trustees of the Waynesboro Academy. He was also a member of the Waynesboro Masonic Lodge.

When he first married they lived in the country on the old road to Augusta. There they lost their two little boys, Cleveland Fulcher (he lived only two months) and Whitney Fulcher, lived almost seven years.[1] The family later moved to town when the children began to go to school. The house stood opposite where the Maj. W. A. Wilkins was to build his new home.

In 1910 Pres. William Howard Taft visited Waynesboro for an afternoon as the guest of Mr. & Mrs. R. C Neely, Sr. The tea was given at the home of Capt. W. A. and Mrs. Wilkins, Jr. As the long, black limousine stopped in front of the Wilkins' home, secret service men formed a protective circle around the presidential party. The President was in the process of walking toward the home when a tall angry man strode across the street and into the party, calmly but completely disregarding the secret service and any protesting efforts. He was heard to say, "I've always wanted to shake hands with a President. Figured that this was as good a chance as any. Ed Fulcher is the name." Taft, who was a good-natured person and loved people, waved the secret service aside and chatted amicably with his unexpected guest before retiring to the house for tea.

Eight children grew to full adulthood: Roger Edwin, Lamar L., George Glenn, Heywood E., Mary Osee, William, Florence and Alice. Two of the sons served in WW I: Lamar L., Ga. Pvt. 161 Infy. Co., and Heywood E., Calif. Cpl. 78 Field Arty. 6 Div. Heywood E. md. Elizabeth McElmurray and Roger E. md. Mary S. Moffett.

The four daughters of Osee and Edwin all married: Mary Osee md. Wm. Gordon and Lillian md. A.M. Braswell. Florence md., first, Atty. Evans V. Heath and a State Senator. He died Aug. 8, 1926. They had one son, Evans V. Heath, Jr. of Wyckoff, N.J., and one daughter, Mary Heath Massie of Glasgow, Va. Florence md. again: James H. Oliver, Sr. They had one son, James H. Oliver, Jr. He is a Ph.D. and Prof. of Biology at Georgian Southern College. Alice Fulcher md. Joseph E. Cooley, D.D.S. They have two sons.

Edwin Fulcher, Sr. lost his first wife who lived to the age of 42. (Dec. 2, 1904). He md., second, on July 19, 1905, Margaret Bell Herrington, the niece of his deceased wife. They had children: Margaret was b. Mar. 1, 1920 but she lived only until Oct. 19 of the same year. Their second child was

---

[1] Both Cleveland and Whitney Fulcher are buried in the Fulcher Cemetery just across in Richmond County.

Edwin Fulcher, Jr.[2] Mr. Edwin Fulcher, Sr. died Sept. 8, 1924 and is interred in the Waynesboro Magnolia Cemetery.

---

[2] See Edwin Fulcher, Jr. now deceased.

EDWIN FULCHER, JR. was b. Aug. 28, 1906, the s/o Margaret Bell Herrington and Edwin Fulcher, Sr. His father had remarried on July 19, 1905, the niece of his deceased wife (Osee Herrington). Edwin Jr. was the s/o a young lady about 21 years of age. Edwin Jr. was the only child of the second marriage who lived. His sister, Margaret was b. March 1, 1920, but lived only until Oct. 19. of the same year.

So Edwin, Jr. grew up with his half brothers and half sisters. At his birth there were two sons in the 18-20 age range, Lamar and Roger. The younger ones were Alice, age 5; Florence 7, Heywood 9, Lillian 11 and Glenn, 13.

Edwin, Jr. graduated from the Waynesboro H.S.; studied at Emory Univ. and the Univ. of N. C. His fraternity was Phi Delta Theta. His father d. on Sept. 8, 1924 and his mother remarried. Her husband was Alexander Oliver Butts, a retired shipyard worker in Va. She died at age 82 on Oct. 3, 1967 in Miami.

Edwin, Jr. married on Jan. 4, 1928, Mildred Hill, d/o Lillian Dicks and Levi Walker Hill. They had one son, Edwin Fulcher, III of Waynesboro and one daughter, Joanne Fulcher Davidson of Hilton Head, S.C.

During his life of 73 years he was a farmer and later an insurance agent. He had a number of interests: was a member of the Official Board of the First United Methodist Church, the Brinson Bible Class, Methodist Men's Club, Wed. morning prayer group, Waynesboro Rotary Club and the Waynesboro Field Trial Assn. He was a Mason and a York Rite Shriner, a past president of the Burke County Historical Society. He d. on Jan. 3, 1980. Burial was in the Magnolia Cemetery.

Besides his wife, one son and one daughter, four sisters, and three grandchildren, Jim Davidson of Atlanta; JoDelle Davidson of Kansas City, Mo.; and Margaret Ann Calleran of Hilton Head, S.C., and one great-grandson.

EDWIN DENT FULCHER, s/o Sarah (Sadie) Crawford Dent and William Marcus Fulcher, Sr., was b. Sept. 2, 1906 at Waynesboro, Ga. Graduated at the Waynesboro H.S. (1923) and the Univ. of Ga. with the L.L.B. degree (1927). Fraternal orders: Sigma Alpha Epsilon, Phi Delta Phi (legal) and later, BPOE.

He began practice in Augusta, Ga. on July 1, 1927, with the firm of Hull, Barrett, and Willingham. In 1933 he joined a law partnership, Bussey & Fulcher (Feb. 1, 1933). On Oct. 1, 1946, the two brothers formed a partnership which became the firm of Fulcher, Fulcher, Hagler, Harper and Reed.

On Jan. 16, 1932, he married Rachel Buchanan McMaster, d/o Rosa Moore and Hugh Buchanan McMaster, M.D. They have no children. Rachel graduated from Brenau College and has served as President of the Jr. League of Augusta and President of the Garden Club of Ga.

He is a Fellow of the American College of Trial Lawyers and has served as President of the Augusta Circuit Bar Assn. His denomination is Methodist and his party, Democrat.

During WW II he distinguished himself. He began with Capt., Sept. 9, 1942; a Maj., Oct. 11, 1943; and Lieut-Col. Sept. 6, 1945. Legion of Merit (Feb. 28, 1946); General Order #78, Gen. Hq. USAF Pacific; Asiatic Pacific Theater Medal with two bronze stars for Northern Solomons Luzon Campaigns; Phillipine Liberation Medal with 1 bronze star; Amer. Theater Medal, Victory Medal, Distinguished Unit Badge (USAFFE).

From Jan. 1, 1944 to Mar. 19, 1945 he was on duty at the Staff Judge Advocate, Sol IS.; Hq. USAFFE, Asst. Chief War Crimes Branch, J.A. Section (Mar. 20 - June 30, 1945), Manila, Phil IS.; Gen. Hq. AFPAC, Executive Officer Legal Section (July 1, 1945 to Dec. 31, 1945), Phil IS. and Tokyo, Japan, Gen. Hq. SCAP, Executive Officer Legal Section, Tokyo, Japan (returned to States). Relieved active duty, June 26, 1946.

Before his appointment as a Superior Court Judge he had served as Augusta City Attorney under five administrations over a 23-year record. After his Army duty he returned to Augusta and to his practice. In 1971 he was appointed Judge of the Superior Court in the Augusta Circuit by Governor Jimmy Carter. His circuit covered Burke, Columbia and Richmond counties. He was a Fellow of the American College of Trial Lawyers and a member of the American and Georgia Bar Association.

At age 73 he died at his Augusta home on Saturday, July 12, 1980 after a prolonged illness. Funeral services for the Waynesboro natives were on Sunday, July 13 at St. John United Methodist Church with the Rev. Eugene Dunn officiating. Burial was in Magnolia Cemetery in Waynesboro.

His wife followed him over a lengthy illness and died on January 2, 1981 and was also buried at Magnolia Cemetery.

CAPT. WILLIAM MARCUS FULCHER, SR. was b. Dec. 3, 1858, s/o Louisa Wimberly and Vincent Warren Fulcher. He was handsome and energetic and soon became a highly respected man in civic matters and business. He established a wholesale grocery store, competing with the Waynesboro Wholesale Grocerty Co. He served the public in various ways and capacities. He and J. K. Evans in 1897 formed a partnership under the name of Evans & Fulcher (general insurance). Until his death he was in the insurance business. In 1892 he was a 1st Lieut. in the Burke Light Infantry, and subsequently was made Capt. of his company. In 1897 he was appointed Receiver of the Receiver sale of J.A. Joyner & Co.

He was interested in education and was Sec. of the local Board of Trustees, and was made Chairman of the local Board for several years. In 1921 the Grand Jury in session elected him a member of the County Board of Education.

He married Sarah (Sadie) Crawford Dent and they had three children: William Marcus Fulcher, Jr.; Edwin Dent Fulcher; and Sadie Dent Fulcher. They grew up in the beautiful home directly opposite the Waynesboro Presbyterian Church and on the block where the Methodist Church stands.

He was a Shriner; was one of four delegates that attended the Shriner's Convention in Portland, Ore.; at one time he was Ambassador of the Burke County Shriners; a Trustee and one of the largest contributors to the beautiful Masonic Temple which was created. He was President of the Luncheon Club and when the Rotary Club was established in Waynesboro, Capt. Fulcher was the first President.

He owned a plantation near Briar Creek and became the President of the 66th and 67th Dist. Agric. Club. And when the Burke Natl. Farm Loan Assn. was created, he was one of the Board of Directors and was President. He was also the founder of the Peoples Savings Bank of Waynesboro and was the President.

His wife d. Jan. 27, 1934 and his death followed on Nov. 30, 1935. Both are interred in the Waynesboro Magnolia Cemetery.

WILLIAM MARCUS FULCHER, JR. s/o Sarah (Sadie) Crawford Dent and William Marcus Fulcher, Sr. was b. Sept. 23, 1902, at Waynesboro, Ga. Graduated at the Waynesboro H.S. (1920) and the Univ. of Ga. (1924) with the L.L.B. degree. Member of the S.A.E. fraternity, and the legal fraternity, Phi Delta Phi.

He began the practice of law in Waynesboro but moved to Augusta in Nov., 1925 to become an associate with the firm of Lee and Congdon. He became a member of that firm in 1927 which became Lee, Congdon & Fulcher.

In 1946 he established the partnership, Fulcher & Fulcher, with Edwin Dent Fulcher, his brother. That firm became Fulcher, Fulcher, Hagler, Harper & Reed. But after his brother was appointed Judge of the Superior Courts of the Augusta Circuit by Gov. Jimmy Carter, the firm name changed to Fulcher, Hagler, Harper and Reed.

Attorney Fulcher has served as President of the Augusta Bar Assn. for one term; Fellow of the American College of Trial Lawyers, and Fellow of the American College of Probate Council.

He is the former member of the Advisory Board of the Citizens & Southern National Bank. He presently is a member of the Board of the Tuttle Newton Home and served one term as President. He is also Trustee of J. B. White Foundation and of the Augusta Free School. He is a member of St. John United Methodist Church and a former Chairman of the Official board; member of the Augusta National Golf Club; also the Kiwanis Club.

He married Mary Bell on July 14, 1932, also of Burke County. She graduated at the Waynesboro H.S. in 1927. Graduated from Randolph-Macon Woman's College in 1931 where she was a Phi Mu and earned a Phi Beta Kappa Key. At one time she was President of the Jr. League of Augusta.

Children: William Marcus Fulcher, III who is a real estate salesman with Sherman & Hamstreet in Augusta and an executive in the Augusta Racquetball Center. The second son is Rev. Simeon Bell Fulcher who is the Assoc. Pastor of the Calvin Presbyterian Church in Louisville, Ky.

GEORGE GALPHIN (pronounced Golfin) came to America from Northern Ireland, probably Armagh County sometime before 1743, the year he first appeared in the Creek Indian trade.[2] He established a home and Indian trading post at Silver Bluff (in present Aiken County, S.C.) about 12 miles below Augusta on the South Carolina side of the Savannah River. Here he bought land which had originally been surveyed for Archibald McGillivray and Co., in 1737.[3] In time he expanded his trading to the Chickasaws, Uchees and Cherokees, as well as the Creeks. At one point in time he was a partner in Brown, Rae and Co. of Augusta.[4] Since he was a man whom the Indians early learned to trust, his power and influence with their Indian chiefs grew steadily. By 1750 he had only 400 acres in Ga., but subsequently his holdings increased. It is known that he secured in 1764 a large grant of land around Andrew Lambert's former settlement. The same year he was granted 500 acres and bought out Lambert's interest completely when he acquired another 1,000 acres. On this grant he established a cowpen and later a trading post, which came to be known as Old Town or Galphin's Old Town,[5] located about ten miles south of what is now Louisville, Ga.

Even before the Royal Governor, James Wright, appointed Galphin Superintendent of Indian Affairs, many Indians brought matters of controversy to him for settlement. He also was asked to intervene when any serious trouble arose between the settlers and the Indians. In one incident where an Indian had murdered a settler who had offended the Indian hospitality for the night, such was Galphin's influence with the Indians that they took the unprecedented action of putting the culprit to death in the presence of several Indian traders.[6]

In 1765 Galphin was associated with Lachlan McGillvray and John Rae in the promotion of Imigration from Northern Island to Queensborough Twnshp., St. George's Parish. At this point it is worth noting that in 1765 or 1766 John Bartram, botanist to King George III, accompanied by his son, William, visited Galphin at Silver Bluff. John Bartram referred to Silver Bluff as "a very celebrated place" with "a beautiful villa", and Galphin as "a gentleman of very distinguished talents and great liberality"[7]. Besides his reputation for fair dealings with the Indians, his willingness to permit the establishment on his plantation of a Negro Baptist Church, the first in S.C., stands as further proof of his humaneness. One author has paid him this tribute:

> The spirit of justice and kindness, it appears, was manifest in all his dealings with the peoples of the weaker races, who were daily about him. The red man and the black man alike saw in him a man of kindly soul. David George, who was ever a British subject, described his former master as an "anti-loyalist." N. W. Jones, speaking as an American, pronounced him a "patriot." Neither spoke of him except to praise. A master less humane, less considerate of the hapiness and moral weal of his dependents, less tolerant in spirit, would never have consented to the establishment of a Negro church on his estate. He might have put an end to the enterprise in its very incipiency, but he did not. He fostered the work from the beginning. It was by his consent that the gospel was preached to slaves who resided at Silver Bluff. It was by his permission that the Silver Bluff Church was established. It was he who permitted David George to be ordained to the work of the ministry. It was he who provided the Silver Bluff Church with a house of worship, by permitting

his mill to be used in that capacity. And it was he who gave the little flock a baptistry, by placing his mill-stream at their disposal on baptizing occasions. But we are satisfied that he had no conception of the far-reaching influence of these deeds of kindness.[8]

During the Rev. War, Galphin, despite his former close connection with the Royal Gov. as Superintendent of Indian Affairs, sided with the Patriots. For this, Gov. Wright, subsequent to the British recapture of Savannah, placed him upon the Act of Attainder and Confiscation.[9]

Galphin d. at his residence, Silver Bluff, on Dec. 2, 1782, in his 71st year.[10] His son, Thomas Galphin, succeeded him at Silver Bluff. One daughter, Anne, m. Barna McKinnie, whose granddaughter, or great granddaughter, was Catherine B. Whitehead. Another daughter married John Milledge. Milledge had inherited a sizeable estate from his father, but his wife brought even larger properties to the marriage. He became one of the rich men of Ga.; served in Congress as both a Representative and twice as a U. S. Senator, and was elected Gov. A grandson, Milledge Galphin, pursued to successful conclusion in 1848 the claim of the heirs of George Galphin against the U. S. The heirs were awarded $200,000. Under the Treaty of 1773 with the Indians, the had received vast cessions of land in Ga., and in return had agreed to pay to Galphin and other traders the large debts which the Indians owed them. Since after the War the lands belonged to the U. S., the Fed. gov't. finally accepted the subrogation.

---

[1] During his promotion of emigration to Queensborough Twnshp., St. George's Parish, 1766, he referred prospective emigrants to his sister, Judith Galphin, and his cousin, Robert Pooler, in Armagh County. E.R.R. Green, "Queensborough Township: Scotch-Irish Emigration and the Expansion of Georgia, 1763-1776", William and Mary Quarterly, 3rd Series, Vol. XVII, No. 2, April, 1960, p. 187.

[2] Green, op. cit., p. 184.

[3] Robert L. Meriwether, The Expansion of S.C., 1729-1765, Kingsport, Tenn, 1940, pp. 69-70

[4] Green, op. cit., p. 184.

[5] Green, op. cit., p. 186.

[6] Green, op. cit., p. 194.

[7] For further remarks on Galphin and his settlement at Silver Bluff, see John Bartram's Diary of 1765-1766 (1942), pp. 64-66, annotated by Francis Harper.

[8] Walter H. Brooks, "The Priority of the Silver Bluff and its Promoters", Journal of Negro History, Vol. VII (Apr., 1922), pp. 181-182.

[9] George G. Smith, The Story of Ga. and the Ga. People, 1732-1860, (2nd. ed.), pp. 93-94.

[10] White's History of Georgia, pp. 246-247.

CARROLL BLOUNT GARLICK, was. b. July 10, 1882, the s/o Julia Blount and Edgar S. Garlick. Studied at the Waynesboro H.S. Took a business and commercial course in Atlanta. Entered the office of Brinson & Dans; studied law with the firm; passed the Bar, and practiced in Burke County. In 1921 he was elected to the State Senate. In 1923 he was forced to give up his practice on account of his wife's health. They moved to St. Simeon's Island. He is survived by his wife, Mrs. Mary Boyd Garlick; his mother, Mrs. Julia Blount Garlick, his sisters: Miss Lucy Garlick, Miss Rosa Garlick and Mrs. Annie Garlick Cox, and one brother, McClesky Garlick.

He d. in Burnswick, Ga. The body came by train. Dr. J. B. Johnston and Dr. J. P. McFerran were in charge of the service. He was buried in the Magnolia Cemetery. He died July 13, 1925.

His great, great grandfather was Stephen W. Blount, who came to this country from England; fought under Gen. Elbert in the Rev. War. Lost an arm at the Battle of Cowpen and later suffered the loss of a leg. Stephen W. Blount, jr. was his great-grandfather (b. 1786 and d. in 1853). His grandfather was H. V. Blount (b. in 1812 and d. in 1875). His grandfather on his father's side, was Judge Edward Garlick, one of the lawyers and jurists of his time. His father was in the Civil War (1861-1865).

CICERO GARNER, D.D.S., s/o Franklin and Margaret Garner, was b. in Liberty, N.C. in 1895, and attended preparatory school at Whitsett Institute, Whitsett, N.C. Before he had the opportunity to continue his education, he was called to serve his country in WW-I (1917) at the age of 22. When Pres. Woodrow Wilson was in London after the Armistice, Garner served on the honor guard for the President.

After his two-year service he attended Elon College in N. C. and the Atlanta Southern Dental College in Atlanta. Fresh out of dental school, he "didn't have a penny to his name". He went to the Atlanta Dental Supply Co. and told them if they would find him a job he would set up his practice there. They sent him to Waynesboro. He moved in the Jones building and began his practice in 1924 and retired after 53 years in 1977.

On Oct. 1, 1973 he was presented a plaque for 50 years of service at the Ga. Dental Assn. meeting in Atlanta. He held life membership in the GDA, the Eastern District Dental Society and the American Dental Assn. He was a member of the Alumni Assn. of Emory Univ., Atlanta.

Dr. Garner was a member of the Waynesboro First United Methodist Church where he served as a steward and on the administrative board. He had been a member of the Waynesboro Rotary Club for 52 years.

He was a member of the Waynesboro Country Club, a Veteran of WW-I, Barracks No. 1049 and the American Legion.

He died on Aug. 8, 1977. He was survived by his wife, Mrs. Bernice Welch of Bartow, Ga., three sons: Cicero Garner, Jr. and Claude F. Garner, Atlanta; C. C. Garner, Silver City, N.C.; and a daughter, Mrs. Emma Russell, High Point, N. C. He was interred in the Waynesboro Magnolia Cemetery.

EVELYN WARD GAY. This Burke County author established herself in 1967 with the fine biography of Lucian Lamar Knight - The Story of One Man's Dream, (1967), 562 pp. Vantage Press, Inc., New York, NY. Earlier writing had appeared in several Georgia newspapers, among them the Waynesboro True Citizen, the Augusta Chronicle and the Atlanta Georgian.

A native of Girard, Burke County, she was, during WW-II, on the editorial staff of the public relations office of the War Bond Division of the U. S. Gov't in Atlanta, where she was assistant editor of the War Bond News. Later she edited the Auxiliary News, official publication of the 2,000 member women's group of the Medical Assn. of Ga. She has also served as medical sec. in the Dept. of Anatomy at the Emory Univ. School of Med.

Active in PTA groups, the Emory Univ. Woman's Club, auxiliaries to the Fulton County Medical Society, the Medical Assn. of Ga., the American Med. Assn., and the Henrietta Egleston Hospital for Children, she frequently participates in fund drives for organizations engaged in medical research. She is a member of the Atlanta Art Assn. and Arts Alliance, the Arts Festival of Atlanta, and the Atlanta Historical Society.

Early in her research for this book, Mrs. Gay discovered that Lucian Lamar Knight was - and still is - a controversial figure in Ga. In this, her first full-length biography, drawn from years of meticulous research, the proud son of Ga. emerges in clear, revealing light...and it is up to the reader to judge him for what he was, and what his eventful life signified.

HOWARD WASHINGTON GIVENS, Clergyman, b. in Waynesboro Ga., Aug 5, 1904, s/o of Ada Handkerson and Howard W. Givens. Md. Helen Bampfield of Beaufort, S.C., 1935. One child was adopted, Lois Givens.

Education: Grad. Boggs Academy (1928) Keysville, Ga.; A.B., Johnson C. Smith Univ., Charlotte, N.C. (1932); B.D. (1935); D.D. (1950); A.M. Columbia Univ., (1949).

Pastor, Biddleville Presbyterian Church, Charlotte, N.C., 1940-present; pastor Ben Salem Presbyterian Ch. and Lloyd Pres. Ch., 1935-40; Clerk, Presbytery of Catawba, 1945-48; President, Interdenominational Ministerial Alliance, 1949; Pres., Comm. Political Social Club, 1940-present; member, Masons, K of P, NAACP, Phi Beta Sigma, Presbytery, Democrat; 401 Camprist St., Charlotte, N.C.[1]

---
[1] Who's Who In Colored America (7th ed., 1950) p. 212.

A. HOLLAND GNANN was b. at Stillwell, Ga., July 26, 1899, the s/o Lena Gnann and A. O. Gnann. He attended Mt. Pleasant Collegiate Institute (a Jr. Col) and graduated. He earned next an A.B. degree from Newberry Col. in S.C., and and M.A. degree from the Univ. of S.C.

He married on June 27, 1928, Miss Pearl Frick of Chapin, S.C., the d/o Minnie Frick and Paul M. Frick. They had three children: 1. Elaine (Gnann) Smith at Millen, Ga.; 2. Heyward Gnann at Sardis, Ga.; 3. Shirley (Gnann)

Whitley at Sardis, Ga.

Mr. Gnann is a descendant of the Salzburghers who settled many years ago in Effingham County, Ga. They came from Salzburg Austria: Their church built there is still standing and active.

Mr. Gnann, the educator, covered 47 years. He came first to the Sardis High School and later moved to Waynesboro as the County School Superintendent. He had six years of experience as a teacher and principal when he came to the Burke County School System. He served Burke County as the County School Superintendent for 24 years, 1945 until 1969. He then served a period as Principal of the Waynesboro Jr. H.S. after his term ended Jan., 1969. This gave him a total of 47 years in the educational field.

At one time the State Board of Educ. appointed him on a committee to work with the State Dept. of Educ. to develop a new State Curriculum.

He was an active Sunday School Teacher for over 50 years. He also was once active with the Boy Scouts, and the Easter Seal and Red Cross. He was a charter member and first president of the Sardis Lions Club, a former president of the Waynesboro Curtan Club and the Waynesboro Rotary Club. He served as Sec. of the Rotary Club for approximately seven-and-a-half years.

FRANCIS ROBERT GOULDING, who was b. in 1810 and d. in 1881, was the s/o Dr. Thomas Goulding, the first native-born Presbyterian minister. He came from the celebrated Midway Colony of Liberty County, Ga., which produced 83 clergymen and a number of lawyers, doctors, authors, statesmen, soldiers, and scientists. His father was eminent in the Pres. Ch. and one of the founders of the Theological Seminary at Columbia, S.C., which in recent years was moved to Decatur, Ga.

Francis R. Goulding had good educational advantages and graduated from the Univ. of Ga. in 1830. He then entered the Theological Seminary at Columbia, S.C., and after two years graduated there and became a Presby. minister. He married Mary Wallace Howard, of Savannah.

Francis Goulding served the Church at Sumter, S.C., for two years and them became an agent for the Amer. Bible Society.

In 1842, to relieve his wife of a great deal of sewing, he invented a sewing machine, several years before Howe's machine was patented, but not having in mind any profit he did not take the trouble to patent the machine. In 1843 he was pastor of a little church at Bath, Ga.,[1] where his duties were light and he devoted his leisure time to writing a story which was published by the American Sunday School Union. Then he began writing the book, "The Young Marooners", on which he made his reputation as a writer. He spent three years writing, revising, and correcting it before sending it to a N.Y. publis. house which rejected it. He then sent it to a Phila. publ. whose reviewer gave the manuscript to his little girl and she literally devoured it. Seeing this, the reviewer took it up himself and read it. The interest so absorbed him that he did not lay it down until he had finished it, and it was published. The book was printed in many editions in this country and reprinted by six different publishers in Great Britain, rivaling Robinson Crusoe in its interest for young and old.

---

[1] He was also the pastor of the Waynesboro Presbyterian Church in Burke County.

After this Mr. Goulding moved to Kingston, Ga., where he taught school and in leisure hours wrote his book, "The Instinct of Birds and Beasts."

In 1853 Dr. Goulding's wife died, leaving him six children. In 1855 he was married again to Matilda Reeves, who owned a beautiful home at Darien, Ga. They moved there and he resumed pastoral work, but gave some time to literary pursuits.

On the outbreak of the war in 1861, he became a chaplain in the Conf. Army and gave much time to the sick and wounded. In 1862 when Darien was evacuated by the Confederates, his beautiful home was burned and his library with valuable manuscripts was destroyed. At the end of the war he was an old man without means, and resumed his writings to support his family. He wrote several popular books, "The Marooners Island," "Woodruff's Stories," "Frank Gordon," "Cousin Aleck," "Adventurers Among the Indians," and "Boy Life on the Water."

Dr. Goulding died at Roswell, Ga., Aug. 22, 1881, in his 71st year, after a ministry of 48 years, with a record of a useful life, many good deeds, and a literary reputation which has stood the test of time.[2]

---

[2] The Story of Georgia, pp. 727-728.

SIMEON ALEXANDER GRAY. The first "S.A. Gray" was b. near Waynesboro, Ga. on Nov. 3, 1829, the s/o of Minch Gray and Nancy Warnock. He md. Elizabeth Blount d/o Axalina Clark (Thomas), (Robinson) and Stephen William Blount. They had five children who survived to maturity: Alice, Charles, Emma, Clifford and Frank.

Prior to the Civil War, "Mr. S.A." was the leading merchant in Waynesboro, owning and operating an emporium which was located on the east side of Liberty Street, in the block just north of the public square (courthouse), and where Palmer Hardware Co. is now located. All stores in Waynesboro were then wooden and one-storied. Just north of the emporium was the Gray residence. A garden separated his property from the next home to the north, that of his brother-in-law, Jethro Thomas.[1]

During the Civil War Gray was old for military duty, but on Oct. 14, 1864 was commissioned a 1st Lieut. in the 3rd Co., 17th Militia Dist.[2] and assisted with the protection of the town and with Gen. Wheeler's harassment of Sherman's Army.

Loyalty was one of Mr. S.A.'s leading traits. During the dire depression of the 1870's the records show that he used his strong financial position to protect the family of a bankrupt friend. At a sheriff's sale in June, 1874 he bid in the 197 acre homestead of his friend, and in Feb., 1876 deeded the homestead back to the friend's family.[3]

---

[1] In the early part of the 20th Century the former Thomas residence was the Emma Gray Walters home.

[2] Military Commissions, 1861-66, Ga. Dept. of Archives and History.

[3] Deed Book G., Folio 17 & 18, Jun. 12, 1874 for sale; and Folio 609 for deed, Feb. 25, 1876.

In the Waynesboro business directory, published in the first edition of The True Citizen, Apr. 28, 1882, S.A. Gray still held first place among the mercantile establishments. By this date ten merchants were listed. The same year the tax list shows that he was the second largest taxpayer in Burke.[4] In 1883 a new building (brick) for Gray's "department or New York" store was completed.[5] The building was two-storied, plus a basement with an outside entrance, and the building extended through to the next street. The post office and a barber shop with Henry Jones as barber were also in this building.[6] The top floor was for dry goods, clothing and shoes, and a dressmaker's shop under the supervision of Mary Ramsdale, whom Mr. Gray had for the ladies and clothing for boys and men, using material purchased for the store, and fulfilling a community need. Until her death in 1887 she lived in the family.[7] In 1885, Mr. S. A. replaced his wooden grocery store with a new brick building, 30 x 70 feet. This adjoined the larger building which had been erected two years earlier.[8] He also built Gray's Hall, which was located on the corner of Liberty and Whitaker (now 7th) Streets. Here was operated a ten-pin alley. At times it was also used as a skating rink and an exhibition hall. Lillian Powell in her book (p. 57) reports that a "Bicycle Fair" was held in Gray's Hall in Feb., 1897. The True Citizen (in 1885) carried descriptions of the interiors of three leading stores in the little city: S.A. Gray's, W.A. Wilkins & Co., and MacKenzie & Neely.[9]

In the 1880's The True Citizen reflected the rivalry which grew up among several of the "merchant princes". If one made an improvement, it was soon matched by one or more of the others. The initiative was usually with S.A. Gray or W. A. Wilkins. "Maj. Wilkins is putting nice plant sidewalks on all sides of his business buildings not paved." The same month the Citizen reported: "Mr. S. A. Gray has had a plant sidewalk placed beside his store (sic dry goods), grocery, and the full length of the short street between his store and the public squre. It is quite an improvement."[10] After one merchant placed a lamppost in front of his store,[11] the others followed. One innovation by Gray was an overhead cash conveyor system. The True Citizen marveled: "One of the greatest inventions of the age can be seen at S.A. Gray's store - a car on wheels that runs from the cashier's desk to different parts of the store on wires, taking the place of cash boys."[12] In 1885 Mr. S. A. erected a telephone line which ran from the railroad depot to his store,[13] and in 1886 added a drug department under the charge of a young physician. "He will attend to all prescriptions at all hours promptly. I propose to keep a full line of pure drugs that I will sell at bottom prices. - S.A. Gray"[14] The newspaper also noted in one edition that "Mr. Gray's dray mules are rigged up with bells and they 'make music wherever they go'."[15]

---

[4]T.C., Aug. 4, 1882.
[5]T.C., Mar. 23, 1883.
[6]T.C., Jan. 26 & Mar. 23, 1883.
[7]T.C., Oct. 7, 1970. She is buried in the Old Cemetery near the Gray family plot.
[8]T.C., July 10, 1885.
[9]Ibid., June 19, 1885.
[10]Ibid., Jan. 5 & 26, 1883.
[11]Ibid., Sept. 12, 1884.
[12]Ibid., Aug. 31, 1883.
[13]Ibid., Nov. 6, 1885.
[14]Ibid., Oct. 1, 1886.
[15]Ibid., Sept. 17, 1886.

Mr. Gray was not only progressive, but also public spirited. About 1858 he, together with Henry J. Blount, established the first newspaper ever published in Burke, The Waynesboro News.[16] Subsequently W. Rice took the place of Blount, and later Gray and Rice sold their interests to Walter A. Thompson, who was the editor and publisher until he entered the Confed. Army. Maj. W. A. Wilkins was the initiator and main supporter of the program for an artesian well in Waynesboro, but Mr. S. A. donated a lot for the second attempt at boring and contributed generously for continuation of the venture.[17] He served the community in a number of capacities. He was an elected member of the Board of Town Commissioners[18], served as Town Treasurer,[19] and as a director of the Burke County Fair Assn.[20] He was also selected as one of the delegates to a convention in Atlanta to support the nomination of Col. John J. Jones as the candidate for Governor;[21] and in 1891 and 1892 was elected Mayor of Waynesboro.[22]

Mr. Gray was active in the Methodist Church and the United Daughters of the Confederacy. The latter was founded by a group which met at her home.[23] Family vacations were often planned to coincide with Mr. Gray's buying trips in New York City. The famous springs at Saratoga, N.Y. were a favorite spot for their vacations.

Mrs. Gray d. May 9, 1897 and Mr. Gray on July 9, 1899. Both are interred in the Old Cemetery (now the Waynesboro Confderate Memorial). Some of their descendants are mentioned in a True Citizen article, "Burke Family Celebrates Five Golden Anniversaries", Oct. 7, 1970.

16
Kenneth W. Rawlings, "Statistics and Cross Sections of the Georgia Press to 1870", Ga. Hist. Quar., Vol. 23 (1939), 177-187.

17
Citizen, Jan. 19, 1883.

18
Ibid., Jan. 12, 1883

19
Ibid., Oct. 5, 1883

20
Ibid., June 16, 1882.

21
Ibid., Apr. 6, 1883.

22
From records in the City Administrator's office.

23
Citizen, June 7, 1924.

JOHN GREEN was an early settler in St. George's Parish, and an active Patriot during the Revolutionary Period. A headright grant was made to "Jns. Greene" in 1754.[1] His name appears among the 114 signatories in Sept., 1774, who protested the Resolutions of Aug. 10, 1774,[2] but he was selected as a

---

1
George G. Smith (2nd ed.) p. 560.

2
White, Historical Collections of Georgia, p. 283.

delegate to the eventful Patriots' meeting in Savannah, July 4, 1775.[3] And in early 1776, when the new Provisional Gov't. organized a battalion of State troops under Col. Lacklan McIntosh, Capt. John Green of Burke headed the 6th Co.[4] In June 1776 John Green and William Christie, both planters of St. George's Parish, attempted to protect the estate of the late William McDaniel against depredations by a Savannah merchant.[5] The next month the Council of Safety stepped in and appointed Thomas Burton as the executor.

After the Revolution ended, John Green represented Burke in the Assembly, 1784 and 1786[6] and his colleagues both times elevated him to the Executive Council.[7]

The last reference in this period found on John Green appeared in a Grand Jury presentment, Oct. term, 1786 of the Burke Superior Court:

> We present as a very great nuisance, that the Commissioners of the district of the river road, from Brier Creek to McBean, have turned the said road from where it crossed McDaniel's Creek (in a good place, and the road very direct, and on good high land) and have carried it by John Greene, Esq., through an arm of his mill pond where, when it hath a tolerable head of water, the water will run over the back of a horse, fourteen hands high, for many yards, and likewise crosses the creek below the mill, where it is affected by every small fresh, by which the bridge is often torn up, and the road thereby impassable.[8]

John Green was to have many prominent descendants in Burke County in the decades to come, including Jesse P. Green, Moses P. Green, Walter G. Green, and others. And a new community and railroad station, Green's Cut, was to be established on the original family land.

---

[3] C. C. Jones, Jr., Vol. II, p. 184

[4] George G. Smith (2nd ed.) p. 83; Jones, Vol. II, pp. 208-209, 217(?)

[5] Collections of the Georgia Historical Society, Vol. V, Part 1, pp. 64-65.

[6] O.R. 1961/62, pp. 1219 and 1220.

[7] O.R. 1961/62, pp. 1007 and 1008.

[8] The Georgia State Gazette or Independent Register, Nov. 25, 1786.

WILLIAM GREEN, prominent soon after the Rev. War, was probably a s/o John Green, the planter patriot in St. George's Parish.[1] He represented Burke County in the Assembly, 1785 and 1787,[2] and in the latter term was elevated to membership in the Executive Council. He died Apr. 18, 1787 in Augusta while serving in the Council. The "Capt. William Green's Militia District"

---

[1] A citation by Rev. George White, Knight, Vol. I, p. 342.

[2] The Georgia State Gazette or Independent Register, Apr. 21, 1787.

was still listed in 1790.[3]

C. C. Jones, Jr. mentioned a Capt. William Green, who distinguished himself under Gen. James Jackson's command, but was later slain.[4] He may have been a relative of Capt. William Green.

---

[3] *The Augusta Chronicle and Gazette of the State*, Nov. 6, 1790.

[4] C. C. Jones, Jr., Vol.II, p. 502.

HENRY D. GREENWOOD was b. Mar. 20, 1822. He was a man of large, muscular build and a practical joker of no mean distinction, and a planter in Burke County.

On Dec. 6, 1843 he md. Harried Eliz., d/o Jane H. McCullers and Elisha Anderson, Jr. The Greenwood's had a Brothersville summer place, but after the Civil War was over the summer house passed into other hands. Henry D. had a brother, Edmund, a sister who md. Ruddell, and another sister who md. a McCall.

Henry D. and Harriet had a son, John A. Greenwood, their only child b. Sept. 16, 1844. John never md.; d. on June 20, 1881 at age 37 years. Henry D. d. May 7, 1876.

Walter A. Clark in *A Lost Arcadia* remembered a July 4th celebration at Brothersville in 1860. While Henry's wife was preparing her share of the food, Henry D. gathered a supply of green persimmons and instructed his good wife to convert them into a pie without the aid of a single grain of sugar, or a single drop of flavoring of any kind whatsoever. To such as may be unfamiliar with the personal habits of the festive persimmon, that never loses its acrid, astringent flavor until sweetened by the alchemy of the Winter frosts, the following event may be educational.

And so amid the tempting dishes that graced the menu on that long gone July day there lay the Greenwood persimmon pie wearing upon its flaky crust no sign to indicate the sorrow that lay beneath. I do not now recall how many of the guests were taken in by its outward and seeming innocence, but I know that Judge John W. Carswell was among them. Frequent allusions to it during the after dinner hours fretted the Judge's nerves a little and when a boy attempted to twit him he said, "I ate the pie but I do not care for every whipper snapper on the ground to joke me about it," and this unsavory triumph of the culinary art became only a chastened memory.

ROSS ULLMAN HARDEN was b. in Rockford, Ala., Apr. 20, 1909, s/o Carrie Eunice (Ward) Harden and Dr. James Elzie Harden. Grad. Norman Institute H.S. 1925; Mercer Univ., A.B. 1929 and L.L.B. 1931.

On Dec. 14, 1938 he md. in Hall County, Ga. Annie Mandell Bates b. Aug. 7, 1917 in Burke County, d/o Annie (Bell) Bates and Sidney B. Bates, Sr.

(For some years his wife has run the Ann B. Harden Realty Co. in Waynesboro.)

Harden served as Law Clerk, Supreme Court of Ga. (1936-1943); Asst. Attorney General (1943-1947), except for the time in active military service, 1st Lieut., USMCR - WW-II,(May 1944-Oct. 1945).

Priv. law practice at Waynesboro, Ga., Jan. 1947 to date. Attorney for the Bank of Waynesboro, Ga. (1950 to date). He was the Burke Co. Attorney for about ten years until appointed as Solicitor of the City Court of Waynesboro (now State Court of Burke County). Jan. 11, 1965 to Jan. 1, 1979.

Public services: Burke County Dem. Exec. Com. (1950-76); (Chairman: 1962-1976).

Waynesboro Rotary Club; Waynesboro Amer. Legion Post 120 (Commander - 1962-63). Member of the First Baptist Church of Waynesboro, Ga.

Children:
1. Sydney (Harden) Rangeley, b. DeKalb Co., Ga., Apr. 25, 1941; now living in Birmingham, Ala.
2. Annette (Harden) Daniel, b. Fulton County, Ga., Nov. 24, 1942; now living in Savannah, Ga.

ROY BELMONT HARGROVE, JR. (M.D.), s/o Roy Belmont Hargrove and Pearl Folsom Hargrove, b. Dec. 7, 1924, Augusta, Ga.

He was educated in the Waynesboro, Ga. public schools; The Citadel, Charleston, S.C., B.S. (pre-med); and the Univ. of Ga. Sch. of Med.; Augusta, Ga., M.D. degree, 1947. Member Theta Kappa Psi (med. frat.) and Alpha Omega Alpha (honor med. society). His internship was in the Hospital Div. of the Med. College of Va., Richmond, Va., 1947-48. During WW-II he served as PFC, 1943-46, in the U.S. Army.

Began his medical practice as a resident in surgery, Univ. Hospital, Augusta, 1949-53. In 1953 he moved to Farmville, Va. and began private practice as a surgeon. Serves also on visiting medical staff, general surgery, of the Farmville Southside Comm. Hospital; surgeon Southern Railway System; company surgeon, Norfolk & Western Railway Co., and medical examiner of Prince Edward and Cumberland counties.

Married Margaret Ann Heaton, Augusta, Ga. They have three children:
1. Katherine Ann Hargrove, 1972 grad. of Randolph-Macon Woman's College, Lynchburg.
2. Margaret Eliz. Hargrove, student at Westhampton College, Richmond.
3. Roy Belmont Hargrove, III, student, Prince Edward Academy, Farmville.

Dr. Hargrove is very active in his community and state: deacon Farmville Baptist Church; director, First National Bank of Farmville; president, Prince Edward School Foundation; past president Farmville Lions Club; past president Farmville Jaycees; past president Longwood Golf Club; past president of the Country Club; member Farmville Area Development Corp.; member Virginia Wildlife Fed.; Assoc. member Natl. Wildlife Fed., and member Virginia Golf Assn.

His medical affiliations include: Va. Med. Society; Va. Surgical Society, Amer. Med. Assn.; Southern Med. Assn.; Tri-State Med. Assn.; Amer. Assn. of Physicians and Surgeons; Amer. Soc. of Abdominal Surgeons; Natl. Rehabilitation Assn.; Fellow Southeastern Surgical Congress; Fellow American College of Surgeons; Founders' Group of Amer. Board of Abdominal Surgery; and Diplomate Amer. Board of Surgery.

CAPT. JOHN A. HARLOW, M.D. was the s/o Rebecca Walker and Dr. Southworth Harlow, b. in 1823. He was not married; died at age 40. It was written of him that: "He was of the most modest and unpretending of men, but carried the heart of a lion in his bosom".

In March, 1862 the 8th Burke Co. was formed and known initially as the Burke Volunteers. John A. Harlow was elected Capt. The company was ordered to a training camp at Guyton on the C.R.R. near Savannah. When the 48th Regt. of Ga. Vols. was formed the Burke Volunteers became Co. D 48th Ga. Regt. Inf. The company was moved next to Grahamsville, S.C. for further training and there was a brief stay in Charleston, S.C. Then the company was shipped to Richmond, Va. and arrived there June 2, 1862, the day after the Battle of Seven Pines (also known as Fair Oaks). That was also the date when Gen. Robert E. Lee took command of the Army of Northern Virginia (ANV).

Capt. Harlow, with his company, was in several battles from June 1862 to July 1863. On July 2 Harlow fell at Gettysburg leading his company. Francis M. Allen, 1st Lieut. and Uriah Skinner, 2nd Lieut., also died in this battle. Harlow's earlier 1st Lieut. John R. Cox, had been wounded at Malvern Hill; had recovered but was again wounded in June, 1863 at Fredericksburg. Others in Harlow's company who died at Gettysburg were: Henry Utley and John O'Banion. Jefferson Prescott was the only one listed as wounded. Four privates were captured at Gettysburg: James H. Cardell, Starling Low, George F. Daniel and John M. Monk.[1]

---

[1] The Southern World, May 1, 1884.

SOUTHWORTH HARLOW, M.D. was b. Jan. 26, 1781 in one of the New England states. He began practicing medicine in Waynesborough about 1805, and became the best known of the early physicians in Burke County.

Throughout his life he was a civic leader. When the community was incorporated as a Town, he was elected as one of the five commissioners. The election took place Jan. 11, 1813.[1] He served also as a Commissioner of Burke Academy,[2] and represented Burke County for five terms (1828 through 1832), as a State Senator.[3] Within the medical profession he was very active. He

---

[1] The True Citizen, Jan. 18, 1884. From an old record in the possession of Judge M. Berrien which was reproduced at the time Waynesboro was incorporated as a city.

[2] At least in 1829 and 1830.

[3] Georgia Official and Statistical Register, 1961-62, p. 1044.

was one of the 20 members of the Central Medical Society of Ga. which lasted 1826-1836 [4]. And when the State Board of Physicians was created by legislative act in 1825, Dr. Harlow was one of the first appointees to license physicians.[5]

He md. in 1811, Rebecca Walker (1790), the d/o Bethiah Whitehead and Isaac Walker. She was a first cousin of John Whitehead (1783-1857). Ten children were born; seven died in infancy, and three reached maturity: John A. Harlow, Sarah Harlow (Green) and Ruth Harlow. The seven infant children were buried in the cemetery in the order of their death. Sarah Harlow (Green) d. Dec. 26, 1829, and Dr. Southworth Harlow, Feb. 23, 1832; Rebecca Walker (Harlow) in 1865, and Ruth Harlow on Mar. 14, 1877. It is said to contemplate that this was the end of the Harlow line.

---

[4] Cecilia C. Mettler, "The Central Medical Society of Georgia", G. H. Q., Vol. 24, (1940), p. 146.

[5] Jones & Dutcher, Memorial History of Augusta, (1890), p. 253.

HERBERT CLIFFORD HATCHER was born at Augusta, Ga. on May 19, 1889, the s/o Mary Augusta (Huntington) and Lonnie B. Hatcher. His mother d. in 1912. His father, a railroad man, d. in 1926. Clifford was educated in the public Augusta schools and at the Univ. of Ga. where he prepared for the profession of law. Graduated with the Bach. of Laws in 1910.

He played football one year at Emory but he switched to Ga. because of a better football program. He and Bob McWhorter were teammates. Bob could throw the ball and Cliff would catch it and was a fast runner. For years he went to Athens or Atlanta to see the Univ. of Ga. play.

Following his admission to the Bar, he entered practice at Waynesboro where his abilities won him recognition. In 1914 he joined a partnership with Judge E. L. Brinson and the firm became Brinson & Hatcher. In the same year he md. Miss Martha Chase Denning of Augusta. The wedding was in St. Pauls Church. The maid of honor was Miss Gretchen Brandenburg and the best man, Bertram Burdell Dales. The bride was attended by her father, Samuel True Denning.

He gave freely of his time in the field of public service during the course of his career. In 1925 he was the Boy Scouts master. During six years (1921-26) he was a representative in the Ga. Legislature where he played an important part through his term of office. In 1930 he was elected Mayor of Waynesboro, serving until Jan., 1936. He was also a member of the State Dept. of Public Welfare at that time.

During the WW-I he was commissioned and served for the duration. He later was a Maj. on the staff of the Judge Advocate-General of the General Natl. Guard. He was a member of the American Legion, and was prominent in the Exchange Clubs of Ga. In 1931 the Exchange Clubs of Ga. were the guests of the City of Waynesboro. He was elected to head the State Exchange Clubs, and Chas. A. Evans of Waynesboro was elected Sec. & Treasurer of the Ga. Affiliated Exchange Clubs. In 1939 he was made president of the Augusta Circuit Bar Assn.

He was a steward and trustee of the local Methodist Church and treasurer of the latter board. He was a prominent Mason, being in this order of all higher bodies of the Ancient Accepted Scottish Rite, including the 32nd degree of the Consistory, and a member of Alee Temple, Ancient Arabic Order Nobles of the Mystic Shrine at Savannah. He was also affiliated with the Knights of Pythias.

When WW-II began he was put in charge of the Judge Advocate-General office in Atlanta. He spent his time until 1960 and was promoted Brig.-Gen.

After his first wife died, he md. Audray Mitchell. They travelled some. He owned a cottage on the coast in McIntosh County. There they enjoyed the coastal beauty and collected driftwood. He credited his long life to "Behaving myself". A non-drinker he smoked once. A cigar following graduation in 1910. "It was the sickest day of my life". His philosophy of life? "Enjoy it."

In 1972 he was made President of the Burke County Historical Assn. He d. on May 3, 1978 and was interred _____.

LINWOOD CLINTON HAYNE, president of the Planters' Loan and Savings bank, and of the National Bank of Augusta, Ga., was b. in the fine old county of Burke, Ga., Apr. 23, 1858. He attended the schools of his native county for a number of years, and then, in 1881, took a commercial course of study in Atlanta. Returning to Augusta, he entered one of the great dry goods houses of that city, remaining therewith many years, and being successively promoted from subordinate clerk to the responsible position of credit man. In 1888, Mr. Hayne was elected president of the Planters' Loan and Savings Bank, and in 1894 President of the National Bank of Augusta. His career in the great world of business affords a striking illustration of what may be accomplished by strict attention to business and fair dealing; an object lesson well worthy of the attention of the youth of Ga. Beginning 13 years ago as a clerk, he has achieved wealth and reputation as a business man, and now occupies a most desirable place among the successful citizens of his section of the state. Mr. Hayne is an honored member of the Knights Templar, is past master of Webb Lodge No. 166, F. and A.M., and past commander of Ga. commandry No. 1, K.T. He is a member of St. John's Methodist Episcopal Church, South, Augusta. He has never embraced the matrimonial tie.[1]

---
[1]
Memoirs of Georgia, Vol. II (1895), p. 790.

LOVICK PIERCE HERRINGTON, M.D. was b. at what was known as Girth, on May 27, 1858, the s/o Frances L. and Berry Herrington. He was too young for service in the Civil War. His mother served on the District Committee (64th) of the Burke County Ladies, Volunteer Committee during the War.

Lovick Pierce taught school in Newton and Burke counties until 1882 when he entered the Medical Dept. of the Univ. of Ga. at Augusta and graduated in the class of 1884, received the degree of Doctor of Medicine. He returned to Girth, some 14 miles from Waynesboro, where he practiced his profession for some time and then attended Vanderbilt Univ., Nashville, Tenn., where he received the finishing touches of his medical education.

He md. Annie Laurie Davie, a fine pianist. Subsequently he removed to Waynesboro and in time built up a large practice and one of distinctly representative character. He joined the Ogeechee Med. Assn.; served as president of the Burke County Farmers Alliance. He also with his father gave the site for the Union Academy.

Dr. Herrington was the originator and sole proprietor of a remedy known as "Herrington's Liver Pills for Georgia People". He is the owner of the old homestead plantation, having purchased the interests of the other heirs, and devotes some of his time to his plantation interests. In 1902 he graduated at the "Institute of Science" of New York, the course being taken by mail and express. He was a Master Mason, a Phi Delta Theta, and the old time Democrat of Scotch-Irish descent.

In Sept., 1884, at age 17, his wife, Annie Laurie Davie came directly after graduation from Peabody Normal and from Ward-Belmont in music to teach music and other subjects at the Union Academy. She md. in 1886 and continued to teach at the Academy until 1893 when Dr. Herrington moved his practice to Waynesboro. As teacher of music at the Academy and organist for the Habersham Methodist Church and the Greenfork Baptist Church, she managed through music to enliven the social life of these adjoining country communities. The combined chorus of the academy and the two churches on several occasions completed with a chorus of the Waynesboro Methodist Church whose organist was Mrs. Annie R. Munnerlyn. Over the years the two organists became fast friends.

Dr. Herrington died Nov. 8, 1920 and is buried in the Waynesboro Magnolia Cemetery. His wife lived until Oct. 28, 1940.

Children:
1. Quida Mae Herrington (Morris), b. Nov. 8, 1896
2. Lovie Pierce Herrington, b. July 22, 1906

LOVIC P. HERRINGTON, JR., was one of the most distinguished native sons of Burke, (b. July 22, 1906). His brilliant career as a physiologist and creative research scientist is a matter of pride to his fellow townsmen, especially those who knew him in his boyhood days. His rise in the scientific world was meteoric. Graduating from the Waynesboro H.S. in 1923, he completed the A.B., M.A., and Ph.D. degrees at Stanford Univ. in seven years, concentrating in psychology and physiology. There he was a protege of Prof. Lewis M. Terman, noted for his creation of the I.Q. concept and the Army Alpha in WW-I, the first successful group intelligence test. From 1930-32 Herrington pursued a post-doctoral research fellowship in physiology at the Univ. of Berlin Med. Center and Charite Hospital; and from that time on his work was almost exclusively in physiology. In 1932, he was invited by the distinguished Yale bacteriologist, Dr. C.-E. A. Winslow, to join the staff of the John B. Pierce Foundation Lab. in New Haven, Conn. Within a ten-year period Dr. Herrington rose first to the position of Techn. Director, then to that of Director of Research, moving concurrently into the upper stratum of scholars in his field. From 1932 to 1962 he also held appointments in the Yale Univ. Dept. of Epidemiology, Public Health and Bacteriology. In due course he attained full professional rank in the field of public health, more specifically in physiological ecology and biometry.

About 1942 a new laboratory closely affiliated with the Univ., was constructed in the Yale Med. Center. The Pierce Lab. by that time had become world-famous for its studies on the relation of climate and socio-economic factors to mortality; for the development of new methods of human calorimetry; for the analysis of both indoor and outdoor climatic stress due to thermal factors; for the construction of stress measurement devices in the above fields; and for animal and human studies, particularly in relation to vascular and endocrine development. During these years Dr. Herrington, with great mental endowment and energy, and with adequate financial support for research, steadily widened his investigations. Their range is reflected by the journals which published his results: the American Journal of Physiology; American Journal of Hygiene; Yale Journal of Biology and Medicine; American Heart Journal; Journal of Industrial Hygiene; Journal of Aeronautical Science; Analytical Chemistry; Yale Scientific Magazine; A.I.A. Journal (architectural); Mechanical Engineering; and American School and University. He also published in such volumes as Proceedings of the National Academy of Science; Annals of the New York Academy of Science; Meteorological Monographs; Annual Review of Physiology; Proceedings of the President's Conference on Industrial Safety, Proceedings of the U. S. Technical Conference on Air Pollution, Methods in Medical Research, and reports of the National Research Council.

Dr. Herrington and his colleagues made a highly important contribution during WW-II. They developed a successful method of preventing pilot blackout from acceleration effects in aircraft capable of rapid turn or dive and pull-out at speeds from 300 to 700 m.p.h. To quote from the Yale Scientific Magazine:

> During WW-II he studied methods of using radiation insulation in high altitude flight; and with H. Lamport and E.C. Hoff, developed the capstan principle of acceleration and decompression protection now in general use by aviation personnel.[1]

---

[1] "Temperature and Human Action", Yale Scientific Magazine, Vol. XXXI, Nov., 1956.

As the "Responsible Investigator" of the project, the title used by the Committee on Medical Research of the Nat'l Academy of Science, Dr. Herrington represented the research team in signing over the Government in the immediate post-war period all patent rights to the air compression system and an intricately designed aviation suit which he and his associates had developed. The equipment is today in wide use, having been copied abroad, even including military and civilian agencies of Russia and China. No major changes have been made in this aviation equipment since WW-II. Also, the basic principle has become one of the elements in space exploration suits.

Other research teams, of which Dr. Herrington was a member, did scientific work for the Navy and the Office of the Quartermaster General. One of his monographis with Admiral J. D. Hardy deals with the environmental stress in undersea warfare. Of necessity, he and his colleagues developed over the years many new technical methods and machines in furtherance of their research.

As author and co-author, Dr. Herrington has published more than 100 articles, papers, and monographs. They fall into two well-planned series: one of the biophysics of human reactions to climate, vascular and endocrine development at different habitat temperatures; the other, studies of the interrelation of specific American mortality rates with climatic and socio-economic indices. An early book with Dr. Winslow, Temperature and Human Life, Princeton Univ. Press (1949), 276 pp, was an important pioneering study. An impressive research and publication record constitute the chief life work of this dedicated, disciplined and distinguished scientist.

Many well-deserved honors have come to Dr. Herrington: the chairmanship of the Army Quartermaster Command's committee on stress physiology; membership on committees of the Army Surgeon-General; the National Safety Council; the American Society of Mechanical Engineers; the President's Conf. on Industrial Safety; the Arden House Conf. on Tropical Development; and the physiology and human engineering committees of the Research and Development Board. He has also participated in many scientific conferences and symposia. He was invited to visit and lecture at the prestigous Mary Planck Institute at Bonn, Germany. In 1960 he shared the lecture platform with Dr. Harold C. Urey, a Nobel prize winner, during an afternoon program on "The Air We Breathe" at the Univ. of Cal. Med. Center. Many of his research contributions have over time been embodied in Starling's Human Physiology, which in 59 years of successive editions remains the oldest and most authoritative work on medical physiology.

Tragically, after 30 years of highly creative activity, Dr. Herrington's professional career was cut short at age 55 by a serious automobile accident from which he has never completely recovered. In retirement he holds the title of Director Emeritus of the John B. Pierce Foundation.

He and his late wife, the former Ruth Hembroff (1903-1972) lived at Hamden, Conn., New Haven for 40 years. Her field was English Literature and a graduate of Victoria College (Canada) and at Stanford Univ.

Apparently they have founded an academic line of succession. Their son, Lee, is Prof. of Biometeorology and Coordinator of research at the School of Forestry in the New York State College of Environmental Science and Forestry, Syracuse, N.Y. He and his wife, the former Nancy Tripp, have four children - Wayne, Bradford, Susan and Matthew. Their daughter, Brenda, is the wife of Dr. Walter Whitfield Isle, Prof. of American Lit and Dir. of Summer School at Rice Univ. They have two children, Ray and Timothy and reside at Houston, Tx.

Biographical sketches of Dr. Herrington appear, among other volumes, in the Yale Scient. Mag., Nov., 1956; Who's Who in the East (various editions), and American Men of Science.

ALBERT MILLER HILLHOUSE, s/o Cornelia ("Nell") Miller Thomas and William Chambers Hillhouse, II, b. Dec. 8, 1902 at Waynesboro, Ga. Educ: A.B. (1924) Davidson Col.; J.D. (1930) New York Univ. Law Sch.; M.A. (1931) Economics, Univ. of N.C.; Ph.D. (1937) (Economics) Northwestern Univ. (Evanston, Ill.). Member Omicron Delta Kappa, Phi Beta Kappa, Phi Delta Phi (Legal), Pi Kappa Alpha. Pres. Davidson student gov't.

On Feb. 15, 1937 md. Eliz. Mitchell Cheek (b. May 28, 1912), d/o Sadie Taylor and Dr. Frances Powell Cheek, Danville, Ky. Wife's educ: A.B., 1933 Centre Col.; grad. study Univ. of Chicago and Cornell Univ. Prior to marriage was an instructor at Centre. Wife's occ: English teacher, Ithaca (N.Y.) H.S. (12 years); homemaker, pianist.

Mil. Serv. WW-II; grad. School of Mil. Gov't. (1944) Univ. of Va.; Capt. overseas in Mil. Gov't; later as civilian, Chief of Public Finance Branch (Mil) Govt. Austria; transferred to Germany (Berlin & Frankfurt); chairman 9-man Tripartite Committee which drafted Occupation Costs Agreement between the three powers upon establishment of German Western Republic; participated in Currency Reform and in Ruhr Coal Task Force; Under U.S. High Commission, Germany (1949-51), Chief of Public Finance Branch.

Occupation: Economist, public administrator and author. Research staff, Municipal Finance Officers' Assn. of the U. S. and Canada (5 yrs). Taught Economics at Armour Inst. of Tech.; Davidson Col.; Univ. of Cincinnati and Grad. Sch. of Business and Public Admin., Cornell Univ. (18 years). Elected to Cornell Faculty Council (17 members); recipient of citation, Organization of Cornell Planners, Budget Officer, National Housing Agency in early part of war (1942-44). Consultant's panel, Gov'tal Affairs (Wash., D.C.); consultant to the N.Y. State Comptroller(Albany, 2 yrs.); contributing editor to The Federal Accountant; on Advisory Bd., The Administrative Science Quarterly. Sole author of 11 books; with one co-author, 11 books, and with several co-authors, five books. Contributor of articles. Member of professional assn's. Hon.Doctor of Law degree (1974) Davidson Col. Elder in First Pres. Ch., Ithaca, New York.

Biographical sketches in American Young Men (Vol. III); Davidson Col. Alumni Bul. (May 1940); Directory of American Scholars (1942 and 1951); Who's Who In the East (8th and 12th eds.); American Men of Science, Vol. III; Directory of International Biography (1971); Retired, Prof. Emeritus, Cornell Univ. Family lives now in Danville, Ky. after 24 years in Ithaca, N.Y.
Children:
1. Helen Tilford Hillhouse, b. Aug. 9, 1940
2. Margaret Logan Hillhouse, b. April 16, 1944.

WILLIAM CHAMBERS HILLHOUSE, II, s/o Martha Ann Steele and Capt. Wm. Chambers Hillhouse, C.S.A., b. Dec. 12, 1867 in Pickens Co., S.C. Most of his boyhood was spent in Greenville, S.C. where he was educated at Morton's Mil. Academy. Because of family finances in the post-Reconstruction days, he went to work as a boy of about 16 as a railroad operator, in Laurens, S.C. He rose rapidly, was made general agent for the Central of Ga. R.R. in Waynesboro, Ga. at the age of 21, and general freight agent for all the railroads in Augusta at 28. Later returned to Waynesboro, Ga. which became his permanent home.

On June 9, 1897, he md. Cornelia ("Nell") Miller Thomas (b. Jan. 10, 1879), d/o Ruth McHenry Miller and Charles H. Thomas. After one year, as again general railway agent at Waynesboro, he became general manager of the newly organized Waynesboro Grocery Co. (Wholesale). From 1898 to 1911 he directed his company and built up a prosperous business. Later he went into business for himself: drayage, farming, dairying and as a Standard Oil represnetative. Later, for almost four years, was the major stockholder in the Hillhouse-Haynie Creamery (ice cream mgrs.) in Augusta.

His main interests, however, over the years were dairying, farming and stockbreeding. When he died his dairy of over 100 head had been a going concern for about 46 years. He prided himself in his fine purebred Jerseys; was one of the earliest members in Ga. of the Amer. Jersey Cattle Club. His fine sires (St. Lamberts and others) greatly improved the quality of the milk cattle in Burke County. In 1928 the State College of Agric. conferred on him the title "Master Farmer".[1]

When first md. he rented a house on West Whitaker St.; later purchased from George Gordon the Winter Place (east of Waynesboro), and remodeled the house. After the original residence burned, he built a new home, completed in 1926. By purchase from P. L. Corker, Sr., he enlarged the place (Rosemont Farm) to approximate 600 acres. This was his main dairy and stock farm, although he rented other places at various times (a Rowland place, the Malabas farm, and the Thomas Rocky Creek place).

During WW-I he was a member of the directing committee responsible for the War Bond dues in Burke County. For 15 years he served as one of the Grand Jury Commissioners, a director of the Bank of Waynesboro; a founder-member of the Waynesboro Rotary Club, and the Waynesboro Country Club. He was also for years in the First Presbyterian Church as a Deacon and later an Elder; also for many years as the Sec. Treasurer of the Sunday School.

He died Oct. 7, 1944 after a year's illness. A good likeness of him was done in 1950 by the portrait painter, Georg Poppe, from a photograph, and hangs in the home of the author of this book. His wife lived until March 29, 1967. Both are buried in the Waynesboro Magnolia Cemetery.

Children:
1. Martha Ruth Hillhouse, b. May 19, 1898
2. William Charles Hillhouse, b. Nov. 13, 1899
3. Albert Miller Hillhouse, b. Dec. 8, 1902
4. Nell Hillhouse, b. June 23, 1906
5. Katherine Hillhouse, b. Aug. 2, 1911

JOSIAH HOLLAND, Attorney in Millen, Ga. and known as Col. Josiah Holland. He was admitted to the Bar before the Supreme Court in 1883. He may have been a Railroad Lawyer because he had passes on the following railroads, many of which are now extinct: Sandersville Railroad; Sylvania Railroad; Oconee & Western; Stillmore Air Line Railway; Louisville & Wadley; Millen & Southwestern; and Dover and Gladston Railroad. Most of these passes were dated in 1899 and 1901.

Prior to 1906 when Jenkins County was established, Col. Holland was often before the Superior Court in Waynesboro.

After Jenkins County was created (1906) members of the Jenkins County Bar formed a local Bar association. Holland was President, James P. Brinson, and James A. Dixon, Sec. & Treas. Col. Holland passed away in 1908.[1]

---

[1] The Millen News

WM. WYCLIFFE HILLIS, M.D., s/o Frances Whitehead and Henry Clayton Hillis, was b. Oct. 8, 1884. On June 23, 1921 he md. Mildred Kent of Alamo. She had taught school in Sardis for two years prior to her marriage. Young Hillis attended Cleveland Academy (also known as Mobley Pond School). Finally with the help of a family friend, W. J. Herrington, young Hillis in 1904 was able to begin medical school, and a career he had worked toward and dreamed of since he could remember. He graduated in the Class of 1909 at the Univ. of Ga. Medical College.

He began his practice at home in Girard but moved in 1910 to Sardis where he lived and worked the remainder of his life. In 1912 he built his present home and moved his office there. Initially he treated his patients in their homes, going to them in mud or dust in his buggy, pulled by his big horse, "Charlie Red". In 1916 he bought his first car, a Model I Ford, and in 1919 he moved his office to the Mallard building.

In 1927-28 Dr. Hillis built the present drug store building and he and Dr. Cook shared this building with separate offices. Dr. Cook died in 1933 and his death left the mammoth task of meeting the ills of the community. A vision impairment at this time made it necessary for Mrs. Hillis to drive the doctor to the homes of his patients at night.

Then Dr. Hillis built the Sardis Medical Clinic which was opened on his 45th anniversary in the practice of medicine. His son, in medical practice in Millen, assisted him in the clinic for a short time. Dr. Willis Hatcher then joined him in the clinic.

Dr. Hillis is a member of the Sardis Baptist Church, a Master Mason, a member of the local school board, a charter member of the Civitan Club. He has lived a rich, rewarding life and is beloved of the residents of his community. He died Oct. 19, 1968 and rests in the Sardis Cemetery.

Children:
1. Mildred Senie Hillis, b. in 1923 (now Mrs. Alan Sherrill)
2. William Wycliffe Hillis, Jr., b. in 1926.

There were six grandchildren while "Dr. Wych" was still alive.[1]

MARY LOUISE OLIVER HERRINGTON was b. in Burke County (Girard, Ga.), June 13, 1919, the d/o Belle McCullough and Maner C. Oliver (now deceased). She has two children: Franklin L. and Timothy L.

She was elected in 1964 and was the first woman in Burke County's history to fill the office of Judge of Court of Ordinary. In 1974 the Office was changed from the Judge Court of Ordinary to Judge of Probate Court, by a Constitutional amendment.

She is a member of the Ga. County Officer's Assn.; active member of the Waynesboro United Methodist Church. She has been re-elected without opposition for four consecutive terms. Her office is in the Burke County Court House. Her home is at 502 Woodbine Road, Waynesboro, Ga.

She has been honored in three important volumes: Who's Who of American Women; Who's Who in South and Southeast; and Personalities of the South.

W. J. HERRINGTON. The Herrington family furnished many a prominent figure in the state's history, and many good citizens to Burke County. About 1790 Richard Herrington, a native of N.C., moved to Ga. and took up a farm in Screven Co. He was of Scotch-Irish descent, of thrifty and industrious habits, and became very wealthy. He was a son of Martin, who received the bulk of his estate on the father's death, and with the same wise management increased the wealth to $500,000. He was b. in Screven Co., but moved to Burke Co., where he died. He md. Nancy Miller, and a son, Archibald M., was b. to them. He too was a large slaveowner and extensive planter of Burke Co. He was md. to Martha, d/o Seaborn and Eliza Ann (Lane) Johnston, natives of Emanuel Co., and the father was a wealthy planter. To Archibald Herrington and wife were born, among other children, W. J. Herrington, a farmer living near Hillis.

W. J. Herrington was just 16 years old in 1861, when he left the farm and country school to enlist in the war. He joined Co. D, 5th Ga. Regiment, under Capt. Joseph Shewmake and later Frank Godbee. He fought in a number of sharp engagements and severe battles. He was in the front of Sherman's army on the road to Savannah, at Rivers Bridge, Ablesboro and Bentonville, and remained in the army until the close of the war.

In 1890, Mr. Herrington was elected to the Legislature and served one term, being placed on the railroad, general agriculture, special judiciary, and banking committees. Like thousands of others, Mr. Herrington found himself obliged to begin life's struggle over again after the War, but he has succeeded in recovering himself and owns 1,800 acres of good land near Hillis, besides other property and stock.[1]

---

[1] Article from Civil War Centennial Edition, True Citizen, April 20, 1961. Article appeared in Memoirs of Georgia, 1895.

JAMES KOLLOCK HINES was b. Nov. 18, 1852, in Burke County, Ga. His father, Joseph Henry Hines, was a prominent planter of Burke and Washington counties, and represented Burke County in the Ga. Legislature of 1857-8. His mother, Susan Eliz. (Harrison) Hines, was a d/o William S. Harrison, a planter, of Chatham County.

During his early childhood, Judge Hines' parents moved to Washington Co., where he resided during his boyhood and young manhood. After attending the primary schools, he attended Oldfield and Barton Academies and Emory Col., from which he graduated with first honor in 1872, taking a post-graduate course at Harvard Law School. He was admitted to the Bar and began the practice of law at Savannah in 1873. There he practiced for a few years, and then returned to Washington County. He served with distinction as Solicitor-Gen. of the Middle Circuit from 1877 to 1881. In 1884 he was elected to the Leg., where he served during the years 1884 and 1885; and in recognition of his outstanding ability as a lawyer, he was elevated to the position of Judge of the Superior Courts of the Middle Circuit in 1886, where he continued until 1891. That year he returned to Atlanta, which was his home for the rest of his life. In 1894 he was a candidate for Governor upon the Populist ticket and established himself as a commanding figure in the politics of the State by his splendid race. At the time of its reorganization in 1907, he was appointed by Gov. Hoke Smith as Special Attorney for the Public Service Commission, and his splendid ability carried that body successfully through the early years of its existence and established the fundamental rights of the Commission before the courts.

He continued his service in this capacity until 1922, when, on Jan. 2, he was appointed by Gov. Thomas W. Hardwick as Assoc. Justice of the Supereme Court, where he served the people of the State until his death on May 19, 1932.

On Jan. 9, 1879, he was md. to Miss Belle Evans, of Sandersville, Ga., and after her death, he was on Dec. 28, 1885, md. to Miss Cora Lawson McBride, of Sandersville, who survives him. There were born to him of his first marriage two daughters, Lucy (Hines) Livingood and Susan Hines, and of the second marriage Elizabeth (Hines) Jones, Mary (Hines) Daniel and Lawson (Hines) Carter, all of whom survive him.

Few men, if any, have ever served their fellow-men as did Justice Hines. From the day of his graduation until the day of his death, his life was one devoted to the service of his State and the people whom he loved. He always espoused the cause of the common people. He was never bound by traditions or conventions and exercised always the privilege of determining for himself his honest convictions as to right and wrong, without restraint or fear of party or social conventions.

Fearless to a degree unknown to most men, both in personal and political matters, he was always prepared to lead the fight in behalf of the thing to which he had committed himself in his own heart as being right. He was a foe of intolerance in any form. Probably the most courageous act of his life, and one which exemplified the character of the man, was his attack, on the eve of his race for re-election upon the then politically powerful Ku-Klux Klan.

In the early days of June, 1926, standing before the Bar Assn. of the State of Ga., knowing that his re-election came before the people of the State at the election to be held during the fall of that year, with the caution of his friends sounding in his ears, and realizing that the Klan at that time had made and unmade Governors of the State and was considered all-powerful, but with the profound belief in his heart that the practices of that organization were deadly to the civilization in which he believed and to the principles upon which the commonwealth of Ga. was founded - in an address startling for its clarity and remarkable in its truth and logic, he attacked the doctrines upon which the Klan was founded, its spirit of intolerance and its threat to the very foundations of our government, and he called upon the Bar of the State to stamp out this danger. His overwhelming re-election in the fall of 1926 destroyed the power of the organization which he attacked, and to him is due the honor of destroying this menace to sound government. Such was the courage of the man and such his unfailing devotion to duty, which endeared him to the hearts of his fellow citizens and entitled him to the rank which he occupied as one of the greatist Jurists ever produced by the State of Ga.

His crowning glory lies in his record upon the bench of our Supreme Court, where his splendid intellect was given opportunity to reveal the real greatness of the man.

Within eight days after Justice Hines took his seat, the Supreme Court began to hand down decisions in cases wherein he had prepared the opinions. - See 152 Ga. 469.

Among his many opinions, which have attracted the attention of the profession, are:

Featherstone V. Norman, 170 Ga. 370, where it was held that the income tax was constitutional;

Howell v. The State, 164 Ga. 204, holding the electrocution law consitutional.

Curtis v. Ashworth, 165 Ga. 782, holding that a husband, under Civil Code, Sec. 4413, and existing statutes enlarging the rights and functions of married women, is not liable for an independent tort committed by the wife;

Bird v. Dyke, 158 Ga. 81, holding that the wife of an intestate, under our statute of distributions, occupies the same degree with children or those representing deceased children; and is entitled, <u>without election</u>, to a child's part in the <u>personalty</u> of the deceased husband;

His dissenting opinion in the case of Wilkerson v. City of Rome, 152 Ga. 784, which exemplified the depth of his hatred of intolerance, his fine conception of religious freedom and his courage in defending the principles in which he believed; and

Boykin v. Hopkins, decided Feb. 25, 1932, 174 Ga. 511, holding that courts cannot grant charters authorizing corporations to practice law, whether within or outside courts, and that the practice of law is not confined to practice in the courts of this State. No decision has ever been rendered by the Supreme Court of Ga. which is likely to do as much to maintain the dignity of the Bar and protect the profession as the decision in this case.

It would be impossible to decide whether he was better qualified by endowments or by acquirements for the duties of a Supreme Court judge. Certainly no one was ever better fitted for the office than he was at the time he was selected for the place. By nature, by education, by experience and by temperament he was a judge par excellence. He was quiet and gentle, but not to reticence. He was retiring and unobtrusive, till the time came when duty called for action. He had the judicial mind, that is, his conceptions were emphatically juridic and his reasoning powers inclined him to weigh and to consider. No judge ever sat upon our Supreme Court who more fully justified and fortified by authority the conclusions of his opinions. He was both a reasoning and a reasonable judge. The amplitude of his knowledge made him a tower of strength to the court. A large proportion of his opinions relate to consitutional questions. Indeed, he was to the Supreme Court of Ga. what Samuel F. Miller was to the Supreme Court of the U. S.

Counsel were delighted to argue their cases before him, for he always gave an attentive eye, an attentive ear, and an open mind; and when he propounded questions, it was to elucidate the issue or some particular phase of the case, but never to embarrass counsel.

His style was less ornate than that of Chief Justice Joseph Henry Lumpkin, less witty and unique than that of Chief Justice Logan Edwin Bleckley, less succinct and laconic than that of Chief Justice Thomas J. Simmons; but he had the erudition of Lumpkin, the sense of Justice Bleckley and the common sense of Simmons.

He was tolerant without being compromising, firm without being harsh, and dignified without being austere.

He was a full life, well spent in the service of his fellow-men, and it has left its imprint upon the State he loved.

In his passing, the Bar has lost one of its leaders and the Bench has added another name to that illustrious list of Nisbet, Bleckley, Lumpkin, Lamar, Simmons and others too numerous to mention, in which illustrious roll, by right of intellect, of courage, of honesty of thought, of the beauty of his logic and of an unwavering devotion to duty, his name must be inscribed to rank with those illustrious jurists who have preceded him.[1]

---

[1] 49th Annual Report, Ga. Bar Association (1932) pp. 219-223.

WILLIAM R. HOLMES, M.D. was b. sometime in 1821, s/o Jane B. Blount and Joseph B. Holmes of Charleston, S. C. (His parents md. May 10, 1820). Wm. R. was a physician and a perfect gentleman.

In anticipating the outbreak of the Civil War, he organized a new company, the Burke Sharpshooters and he was elected Capt. The first 39 in number were ready and was the first company to leave Waynesboro in April, 1861. After more recruits and more training the company was sent to Va. and his company was placed in the Second Ga. Vol. Regt.

At Malvern Hill, Holmes was promoted to Lt. Col. in charge of the Second Regt. and Walter A. Thompson became Capt. Holmes fought in Malvern Hill, Thoroughfare Gap, Manassas and the Battle of Sharpsburg, the beginning of the Maryland Campaign.

In the Thoroughfare Gap engagement Holmes' skill repeatedly attacted Col. Henry L. Benning (7th Ga. Inf., Comdg. Toombs' Brigade). In the Battle of Sharpsburg, Lt. Col. Holmes and his Second Ga. Regt. and Col. William T. Millican with the 15th Regt. together, with all their might tried to prevent the Union forces from using the bridge over the Antietam River because the bulk of the Confed. troops had not yet reached that point. Holmes had only 400 infantry, and Confed. artillery had been withdrawn to another position. Both colonels were killed and then regiments were enfiladed.

The first of the <u>Official Correspondence Reports</u> was from Maj.-Gen. David R. Jones: "Sept. 17th - In this day's battle fell Lt.-Colonel Holmes, Second Georgia and Colonel Millican, Fifteenth Georgia, dying as brave men should die." (p. 887).

The Report of the Brig.-Gen. Robert Toombs, CS Army, Commanding Div. (temporary) of the Battle of Sharpsburg was not made until he was back at Washington, Ga., Oct. 25, 1862 (p. 892).

"Lieut.-Colonel Holmes who commanded the Second Georgia Volunteer Regiment, fell near the close of his historic defense of the passage of the Antietam, and it is due to have to say that, in my judgment, he has not left in the armies of the republic a truer or braver soldier, and I have never known a cooler, more efficient, or more skillful field officer."

Holmes' body was not recovered. It is believed that at some earlier day a marker had been placed in the Neyland section of the Waynesboro Confederate Memorial. He was one of the Burke's most distinguished Confederate officers.

ALLISON T. ("POOLEY") HUBERT, SR.[1], d. Feb. 26, 1978 in an Augusta hospital. In his retirement he was living with his wife on Route 1, Waynesboro.

Mr. Hubert was a native of Meridian, Miss. He was a former All-American football player for the Univ. of Ala. Rose Bowl team of 1925. After retiring from college coaching, he led Waynesboro H.S. to its first state football championship in 1957. He was inducted to the Nat'l Football Hall of Fame in 1964 and the Ala. Hall of Fame in 1972. He was a member of Sacred Heart Catholic Church.

The funeral was held at 3 p.m. Wed., March 1 at the Waynesboro First United Methodist Church with the Rev. Dominic Duggins officiating. Burial was in the Burke Memorial Gardens.

Survivors included his wife, Mrs. Mary Belle F. Hubert; one son, Allison T. Hubert Jr., Atlanta; one daughter, Mrs. Patricial H. Mackey, Virginia Beach, Va.; one brother, Scott Hubert Meridian; one sister Mrs. Evangeline Eidt, Dallas, Texas; and six grandchildren.

Pallbearers will be Dr. C. G. Green, Dan Shuman, Bob Edmond, Porter Cohen, George Cane and Bobby Neely.

Honorary Pallbearers will be Hammond Blanchard, Aulus Sartin, Otranto Barracks No. 1049 (WW-I Veterans), Russ Cohen, Joe Reynolds, W. R. Fout, John Bolton, Dave Williams, Cliff Hatcher, Walter Green, Bill Walters, S. A. Gray, Bill Gathings, Tom Rackley, E. L. Jackson, Linwood Green, L. L. Lewis, Warren Lively, O.J. Cliett and Edgar Baggett.

---

[1] T.C. March 1, 1978.

C. W. HURST, sheriff of Burke County, was b. in the county he now so efficiently serves in 1851. He descended from a N. C. family, represented by John Hurst, a native of that state, who when a young man md. Eliz. Blitch and came to Ga. He located in Burke County and was a prosperous farmer. His son, George W., md. Margaret, a d/o Charles and Mary (Bell) Couttan. He was a s/o Peter J. Couttan and came to America with his parents direct from Amsterdam, where he was born. His father lived to the age of 95 years and was very wealthy. They settled in Burke County, where Charles md. his wife and became a well-to-do farmer and tavern-keeper. George W. Hurst was a successful farmer and now resides in Burke County, a sincere member of the Baptist Church and a highly respected gentleman. Mr. C. W. Hurst spent his boyhood days on the farm and was educated in the local schools. In 1875 he md. Martha S., s/o William and Jane (Darlington)Chandler. He was b. in Burke County, was a well-to-do farmer, a soldier in the late war, and is now living in Waynesboro. To the union have been born four living children: Lessie, Roger W., Sallie J. and Margaret. Husband and wife are members of the Baptist denomination and he is a member of the Masonic Order. Mr. Hurst was elected sheriff in 1889 and has held the office ever since, his administration of the office proving highly satisfactory to the people. Mr. Hurst commenced life as a farmer, but later moved to Waynesboro and began clerking for Broadis & Crocker, and later for S. A. Grey & Son. In 1883 he established a livery business and in 1892 opened a general merchandise store. He is a man of excellent business discernment and in his various enterprises has always been successful.[1]

---
[1] Memoirs of Georgia, Vol. II, p. 367.

JARED IRWIN, Gov. of Ga., was b. in Lunenburg County, Va., in 1751, the s/o Thomas Irwin, a native of Ireland, who came to Va. some years before. The family moved to Mecklenburg when he was only seven years old they came to Ga. and settled in the Parish of St. George, now Burke County. He was a man of some education and an ardent patriot. He entered the Revolution as captain, rose to the rank of colonel, and was active in the Ga. and Carolina campaign. After the war he was a member of the Legislature and removed in 1787 to Washington County, then almost without inhabitants. He was active in conventions, President of the Senate and served two terms as Gov. During his first term he signed the act which rescinded the act passed the year before for the sale of the Uazoo land and the act he signed wiped the Yazoo fraud from the public record. He was md. and had four children: Jared, John, Isabel and Jane. Jared and John were in the first class that graduated from the Univ. of Ga. Gov. Irwin was a Congregationalist, but gave a church and several acres of land near his home for the use of all denominations and it was called Union Church in honor of Union Hill, the Governor's home place. Some years afterward that church passed to the possession of a Baptist congregation and since then it was called Ohoopee. It is near Sandersville and Gov. Irwin was buried in this church yard. A shaft in his memory was placed by the State in front of the Courthouse at Sandersville. Gov. Irwin died at his residence, Union Hill, in Washington County, on March 1, 1818, in his 68th year. He was a member of the convention at Augusta in 1788 which ratified the Constitution of the U. S., was a member of the Convention of 1789 which made a Constitution for Ga. and was president of the Convention of 1789 which revised that Constitution.

He was Gov. of Ga. from Jan., 1796 to Jan., 1798, and again from Sept., 1806, to Nov., 1809. Irwin County was named for him.[1]

---
[1] The Story of Georgia, pp. 693-694.

ALFRED IVERSON, SR. the s/o Robert Iverson was b. in Burke County, Dec. 3, 1798. He attended private schools in Burke and Putnam counties, and graduated from Princeton College in 1820. He studied law, was admitted to the Bar in 1822, and began practice in Clinton (Jones County), Ga.; later moved to Columbus, Ga.

He was elected to the lower house of the legislature of Ga. three times and to the upper house once. He was the Superior Court Judge of the Chattahoochee Circuit, 1835-37 and 1849-54, and was elected twice to the U. S. Congress as a

Representative (1847-49) and as a United States Senator (1855-61).

After withdrawing from the Senate when Ga. seceded, (with his colleague, Robert Toombs), Iverson resumed the practice of law at Columbus from 1868 until his death, Mar. 4, 1873. He was also engaged in agricultural pursuits. Interment was at Columbus.

Sen. Iverson md. Julie, d/o Governor and U. S. Senator John Forsyth and his wife, who was a d/o Josiah Meigs, President of Franklin College (Univ. of Ga.). They had a son, Alfred Iverson, Jr., who served as Brig.-Gen. in the Conf. Army.

ABRAHAM JACKSON, was b. in 1766, too young for the Rev. War, and younger of his brother, Maj.-Gen. James Jackson (Rev. War) who was also later Governor of Ga. and U. S. Senator.

Abraham was a lawyer and Brig.-Gen. of the State Troops. He was one of a few lawyers who had practiced in Burke County at the same time with James Jones, and probably Alexander M. Allen. Alexander Wylly, from Savannah, had before the Revolution handled matters for St. George's Parish, and may have known James Jones.

Abraham Jackson served as Clerk of the Superior Court for Burke County. Later Jackson for 13 terms, between 1796 and 1809, represented Burke in the State House of Representatives[1], and for five terms he was the Speaker of the House.[2]

A letter from Abraham Jackson to John Milledge (Gov., 1802-06) dated Aug. 31, 1801, shows that Abraham lived in Burke County at the Buckhead settlement. From the letter one surmises that John and Mrs. Milledge were godparents of the Jackson's nine-year old, "Betsy".[3]

At a later time William Schley (1786-1858), lawyer in Augusta, Judge, Congressman and Governor of Ga. (1835-37) married Elizabeth ("Betsy"), the d/o the Jacksons of Burke.[4]

Abraham Jackson died at age 44 years in Burke County in January, 1810.[5]

---

[1]
Official Register, 1961/62, p. 1220

[2]
Ibid, p. 1195

[3]
Correspondence of John Milledge, Governor of Georgia, 1802-1806, edited by Harriet Milledge Sally, Columbia, S.C. (1949), p. 73.

[4]
From the Georgia Historical Commission Plaque in the Burke Courthouse Square, erected 1956.

[5]
Date of death appears in Mary Bondurant Warren, Marriages and Deaths, 1763 to 1820, p. 56.

REV. GEORGE L. JACKSON was for many years a prominent Baptist in Burke County. He was a pastor of the Big Buckhead Baptist Church after 1866, and also served many other churches in the County. He was b. in Screven County on Feb. 6, 1811, the s/o Sarah Whitfield and John Jackson.

Rev. Jackson md. Dr. Edward Alonzo Perkins to his daughter, Julia E. Jackson, on Sept. 9, 1870. Julia's mother had died; her mother was Elizabeth Zettrouer. Rev. Jackson's second marriage was to Ann Everline Thorn, widow of Middleton Thorn (b. Mar. 14, 1798, d. Dec. 15, 1858.) She and Middleton are both buried in the Big Buckhead Baptist Cemetery.

The old Jackson place at Perkins was originally the Thorn plantation and became known as the Jackson place after the marriage of Rev. Jackson and widow Thorn. The house on the Jackson place burned about 15 years ago and was considered a landmark. On one of the chimneys was the date 1840.[1]

---

[1] Donald E. Perkins, History of the Perkins' Family of Perkins, Ga., (1979), p. 93.

C. PRESTON JOHNSON, M.D. the first colored physician who has located in Waynesboro. He offers his services to the colored people of Waynesboro and surrounding areas. He was a graduate of Boston University and the Chicago Independent Medical College. He is a physician and a surgeon. His specialty is the treating of diseases of women and children.[1]

---

[1] T.C., January 26, 1901.

HERSCHEL VESPASIAN JOHNSON, the 23rd Gov. of Ga., U. S. Senator, Confed. States Senator, and Democratic Candidate for Vice-President of the U. S. was a commanding figure in Ga. He was b. in Burke County, Ga., Sept. 18, 1812, and after going through a preparatory school entered the State Univ. of Athens and graduated in 1834. He studied law at Augusta and was admitted to the Bar in 1835. He md. Mrs. Anna (Polk) Walker.

In 1839 Gov. Johnson moved to Jefferson County, bought a large plantation and divided his time between planting and the practice of law. In 1840 he declined a nomination for Congress but took the stump for the nominee for his party. He was a powerful orator, won a great reputation in his first campaign, and was an ardent Democrat.

He was a candidate for Gov. in 1845 and 1847 but withdrew his name and Gov. Towns appointed him U. S. Senator to fill the unexpired term of Walter T. Colquitt. In 1852 he was a delegate to the Nat'l Democratic Convention which nominated Pierce and in 1853 was nominated and elected Governor over Charles J. Jenkins and in 1855 was reelected.

Gov. Johnson was profoundly concerned with the development of trouble between the North and the South. He did not wish to see State Rights disregarded but did wish to preserve the Union if possible. For that reason he supported Stephen A. Douglas for President in 1860 as the one man he thought able to command the vote of both sections and work out a peaceful settlement between the North and the South. Unfortunately the Democratic party split that year, the extreme element nominating Breckenridge and Lane and the Union Democrats nominating Stephen A. Douglas for President and Gov. Herschel V. Johnson of Ga. for V.P. That split in the Democratic party resulted in Lincoln's election.

In the Secession Convention Gov. Johnson made a powerful appeal for the preservation of the Union and a peaceful settlement by further conference between the North and the South.

The convention voted for Secession and Ga. was soon in the war, which cost the State and lives of many thousands of its best men and immense destruction of property and institutions.

After the way Gov. Johnson presided over the Constitutional Convention in Oct., 1865, and the next year he and Alexander H. Stephens were elected U. S. Senators, but they were not allowed to take their seats.

In 1872 Gov. Johnson was elected Judge of the Middle Circuit and served until his death, in Jefferson County, on Aug. 16, 1880. Johnson County, created in 1958, was named for him.[1]

---

[1] The Story of Georgia, pp. 641-642. See also Herschel V. Johnson - Sketch by Hon. James K. Hines, Associate Justice of the Supreme Court of Georgia, pp. 179-230, in the Ga. Bar Ass'n Report.

L. D. JOHNSON, physician and farmer, Oatts, Burke Co., Ga., was b. in Green County, Ga., in 1836, and is the s/o W. B. and Eliz. (Boswell) Johnson. W. B. Johnson, a planter and life resident of Green County, was the s/o Gilbert Johnson, of N. C. Dr. Johnson was reared on a farm and given a good country schooling, and in 1862 enlisted in the War, joining Co. F., Cobb's Legion, under Capt. Malcolm B. Jones. He was in active service from the first to the last, and was in many hard-fought battles, including the seven days' fight about Richmond. In 1861 he md. B. J., a d/o John and Mary A. (McBride) Rollins. Mr. Rollins was b. and reared in Burke County, and one of its leading planters. He was the s/o William Rollins, a native of N. C., and grandson of Raleigh Rollins, of Scotch-Irish parentage. Raleigh Rollins came to America with Sir Walter Raleigh when a boy and settled near where Raleigh, N.C., now stands. Thomas A. McBride, the grandfather of Mrs. Johnson, was a native of Scotland and moved to America and settled in Ga. Mrs. Johnson's great maternal grandfather, William Pugh, was in the Rev. Army and was Capt. of Scouts, and was descended from a very old family in Wales. One child, Martin, has been born to Mr. & Mrs. Johnson. Both husband and wife are members of the Presbyterian Church. In 1857 Mr. Johnson began to read medicine under Dr. W. L. M. Harris, and then attended lectures at the Augusta Medical College, where he was graduated in 1859. He located in Burke County, and has sustained a very large practice. He ranks high in his profession, and his skill and great learning are recognized by his fellow physicians as well as the public. Dr. Johnson lives on a fine farm of 3,000 acres located near Oatts.[1]

---

[1] Memoirs of Georgia, Vol. II, p. 368.

PHILIP PELATIAH JOHNSTON, s/o Mariah H. Whitehurst and George Clark Smart Johnston, was b. Sept. 19, 1854, in a beautiful old colonial home, a few miles from Tallahassee in Leon County, Fla.

Philip was educated at home and at Fletcherville Institute of Thomasville, Ga., and in a school conducted by Capt. M. C. Edwards at Springvale in Ga. He left school in his 16th year and passed the following two years in Southern Florida. At the age of 18 in 1873 he took up residence in Waynesboro and lived with his elder brother, Rev. George S. Johnson, the pastor of the Methodist Church in Waynesboro, and his brother's wife. In Waynesboro he studied law in the office of Judge Heman H. Perry. He was admitted to the Bar at age 19 in Nov., 1873.

Though but 19 years of age at the time, he forthwith entered upon the active practice of his profession, in which he has attained marked prestige and met with unequivocal success, being known as one of the leading lawyers of the area and participated in important litigation in the courts.

He was a stanch supporter of the principles of the Democratic party, but invariably declined to become a candidate for office of purely political nature, but was induced to accept the judgeship of the City Court in view of the fact that the judge of this court is permitted to practice in all courts, except his own, and he is, therefore, still engaged in the active practice of his profession.

He was a Trustee and Steward in the Waynesboro Methodist Episcopal Church South. He was Chairman of the Board of Education, Past Master of the Waynesboro Masonic Lodge and a member of the Lester Chapter, Royal-Arch Masons. In the 1904 Report of the 21st Annual Session of the Ga. Bar Assn., he is listed as an honorary member of the Assn..

For some years one of his sisters, Clara ("Callie") F. Johnston, lived and taught school and was remembered with very real affection. One of his brothers, Charles W. Johnston, Lieut., was killed in the Battle of Gettysburg. Several of his older brothers also saw service in the Confed. Army.

On Dec. 11, 1883, Philip md. Lena Penelope Shewmake in Augusta, Ga. Lena P. was the d/o Eliz. Penelope Jones and Henry Philip Jones, the former owner of the Budsville plantation, and her father was John Troup Shewmake, b. in Burke County, s/o Joseph and Anna (Lassiter) Shewmake of Alexander, Ga. Lena's father was educated at home, at Judge Gould's Law School in Augusta and at Princeton Univ. He was Attorney-General of the State of Ga., 1851-1855; State Senator before and after the War; and a member of the Confed. Congress (Second Congress) in Richmond, Va.

Philip and Lena Shewmake Johnston had five children:
1. John, the eldest was educated at Emory Univ., Oxford, Ga. He was a graduate of Lebanon Law School, Lebanon, Tenn. WW-I Veteran - died unmarried.
2. Nona Johnston md. Emmet Burdell Gresham, s/o Annie Lassiter and Job Anderson Gresham.
3. Lena Johnston md. Thaddeus Cornelius Parker, Jr. Lena d. in Baltimore, Md., in 1925, where her husband was president of the Coca-Cola Bottling Works.

4. Adele ("Tin") Johnston md. Henson Estes Bussey. Lived in Atlanta, Ga. He was an electrical engineer with General Electric Co.
5. Philip Johnston was b. Mar. 27, 1892 but d. in infancy.

ALLEN W. JONES, Midville, a leading farmer and a public-spirited citizen of Burke County, was b. in Burke County in 1861 and was the s/o Malcom D. Jones and Virginia L. (Inman) Jones. Malcom D. Jones was an eminent lawyer of eastern Ga. He was a native of Burke County and was a graduate of Mercer Univ. He began the practice of law at Waynesboro and continued there with success until he died in 1869. He served several terms in the legislature, a member of the Baptist Church, and upon his demise left an estate of $200,000 to his heirs. The grandfather of Mr. Allen Jones was Matthew Jones, a native of Burke County, and a farmer by avocation; and his mother was the d/o Allen Inman, b. in N. C. and for many years a resident of Ga. He was a soldier in the War of 1812, as had his father, a native of England, served with the colonies in the War of Freedom. Mr. Allen W. Jones received his early educational training in the Hephzibah Bapt.H. S. and completed it at the state university. In 1886 he md. Hattie Crosland, d/o J. E. and Haseltine (Bush) Crosland. The father is a native of S. C., where he still lives, and was a major in the late war, serving with distinction and bravery. Mrs. Jones was b. in 1863, at Aiken, S.C., and is the mother of four children: Malcom, Crosland, Virginia and Kate. Mr. & Mrs. Jones are members of the Baptist church and Mr. Jones is a Mason. Mr. Jones has been interested in the banking business at Reidsville, N. C., and the manufacture of tobacco, but is now devoting his attention to his large farming investments. He is a progressive young man of fine business ability, and lives with his interesting family on a fine farm near Midville.[1]

---
[1] Memoirs of Georgia, Vol. II, p. 370.

BATT JONES was the s/o Margaret T. Jones and Henry Seaborn Jones. He was b. Sept. 11, 1825 in Burke County. His education was received at the Brotherville Academy one mile from the place where the Hephzibah H. S. was afterwards located. As a youth he was sober and orderly as a man, and was prudent, discreet and quiet.

He married Miss Amanda Corker of the same community and lived with her happily until he was bereaved by her death. In 1857 he md. Mrs. Caroline E. Hines, relect of his cousin, Dr. Henry C. Hines. She brought more possession to their household.

He was baptized at Big Buckhead Church about 1851, and soon after was ordained to the Deaconship. He was never known to be apent from his seat in the House of God, only through a providential interpose. Mr. Jones was not by nature a leader but he was one upon a leader could always depend to follow.

Batt Jones was the first Chairman of the Board of Trustees of the Hephzibah H. S. and continued to fill the position until he was removed by death on Sept. 18, 1862. He, together with John Franklin Carswell, Simeon Wallace, and Rev. W. L. Kilpatrick constituted the delegation from the Big Buckhead Church, which came before the Assn. in 1860.

JOHN JAMES "JENKS" JONES, lawyer, Waynesboro, was b. in Burke Co., Sept. 13, 1824, the s/o Margaret Jones and Seaborn H. Jones. Seaborn H. was a native and life-long resident of Burke Co. and died in Nov., 1859. He was a successful farmer but not a lawyer. He served however, several times in the legislature. Col. Jones was also known as "Jenks" Jones.

In 1819 Seaborn Henry Jones md Margaret (Walker) Jones and over time had four children: Mary and Sarah M. (never married), Eliza J. (md. Wm. E. Barnes) and John James Jones.

John James Jones was given the advantage of a good education and was graduated from Emory College in 1845. He read law two years and was admitted to practice in 1847 in the old State House in Louisville, Ga. In 1856 he md. Evelina Toombs, d/o Laurence C. and Mary (Flournoy) Toombs. Mr. Toombs was b. in Wilkes County and was a large farmer and brother of Gen. Robert Toombs.

In 1859 Mr. Jones was elected to Congress, and served one term, returning home, as Ga. seceded from the Union. He served a short time as Capt. of Jones' Hussars, mounted infantry. Howell Cobb was the Maj.-Gen., and Henry R. Jackson was Brig.-Gen. He was also made Col. of Gov. Brown's staff, and was on the staff at the close of the War. Mr. Jones was one of the leading lawyers of Eastern Ga. and enjoyed a large practice in Burke and adjoining counties. He was also interested in farming, owning a fine estate of 3,000 acres. Of all the Ga. members of Congress who were in Congress with Mr. Jones, he became the lone survivor.

After the close of the great conflict between the states he became a member of the State Legislature and took a conspicuous part in forming the laws of the commonwealth under the existing exigencies of the new regime. At the time of his death, Oct. 19, 1898, he was commissioner of roads and revenues of Burke County, having a large landed interests in the county. His wife, who d. in 1900, was a niece of Hon. Robert Toombs, whose name is writ large in the annals of Ga., which he represented in the U. S. Senate and was specially prominent in connection with military and governmental affairs of the Confederacy during the Civil War.[1]

[1]Cyc. of Georgia, Vol. II, p. 393 with additions.

JOHN J. JONES.- Professional and public life have provided John J. Jones of Waynesboro ample opportunity for service to his contemporaries.

He was b. Oct. 8, 1904 at Waynesboro, Ga., s/o Helen (Gresham) Jones and Seaborn Henry Jones. Graduated at the Waynesboro H. S. (1921); B.A. degree from Emory Univ (1925) and LL.B., the Emory Law School (1928). At Emory he was a member of Phi Delta Theta and Phi Delta Phi (legal fraternity).

He began practicing law in Waynesboro the same year. He was elected Representative to the State Legislature, serving in that body 1929 to 1934 continuously. In 1935 he became State Senator, serving during the 1935-36 session. He has long been a member of the Burke County Bar Assn., the Ga. Bar Assn., and the American Bar Assn. He took an active part in Democratic politics. Twice he was a delegate to the National Democratic Convention (1932) and again in 1936. But when Senator Goldwater ran for President, Jones was able to get the Burke County Democratic Committee to endorse Goldwater, a Republican. The County that year voted 80 per cent for Goldwater.

During his college days he earned a 2nd. Lieut. Reserve position and by correspondence and summer camps, he was promoted to Capt. J.A.G. Dept. Reserve. When WW-II began, because of bronchial asthma, he was declared not eligible for overseas duty. He spent during WW-II time at the 4th Service Command or 4th Corps Area in Atlanta. He was promoted to Major, Lt.-Col. and Colonel. For about one year he served as Staff Judge Advocate.

When Attorney Frank Burney resigned about 1957 from the position of Judge of Probate (formerly "Ordinary"), Jones served for some seven years in his place.

John Jones has been a President of the local Rotary Club and of the Burke County Farm Bureau. He has been a Ruling Elder in the Waynesboro Presbyterian Church for neary 30 years and was Clerk of the Session for some 19 years.

On Apr. 24, 1937 John md. Sara Eliz. Moore of Bishopville, S.C., d/o L.M. and Bertha (Thompson) Moore. She has been a leader in the building the Burke County Library and long served on the Board. She is also a loyal worker in the Presbyterian Church and very much interested in the local schools.
Children:
1. W. Seaborn Jones, b. Sept. 19, 1942. Graduate of Davidson College and at the Univ. of Ga. Law School. Served as a reserve officer in Vietnam. Partner of the Atlanta firm of Hurt, Richardson, Garner, Todd and Cadenhead, with about 50 lawyers.
2. Cynthia Gresham Jones, b. Jul. 22, 1945 is an assistant editor of a letter issued by Payment Systems of Atlanta, a subsidiary banking corporation of American Express.
3. Elizabeth Kirkland Jones, b. Sept. 24, 1949. She is one of several editors of Carrollton Press in Arlington, Va. As Federal classified documents are declassified and released, the editors summarize the interesting materials for writers and libraries.

MARGARET A. JONES was b. July 7, 1800 in Burke County, Ga., within about ten miles of Waynesboro on what is now known as the Moss Walker place. In 1819 she md. Seaborn Henry Jones and lived at the Canaan plantation near Waynesboro. She was the mother of Col. Jenks Jones, U. S. Congressman and a brilliant lawyer. The family was Methodist. The Rev. Bascom Anthony referred to her as "another of the Lord's annointed". She lived to be 93 years of age and maintained her mind undimmed as long as she lived. Cheerful and active, she visited the sick and was in her place in the church through the four years four years she was there. She said to me one day: "I have been a grown woman for 75 years and have tried to study life and the world through all that time to find out what is worthwhile and what is not. I have seen people live for everything that is under heaven. I have seen many fail in their undertakings. I have seen many succeed. I have seen lots of those lose what they have gained, and many others hold it to the end. After watching it all these years, I have reached this conclusion that there are only two things in life worth bothering about, and they are 'good health and a good existence! Keep these, my son, and the other things needful will add themselves to you.'"

"She was very industrious. She told me that when her son, Col. Jones, started to college she make all his clothes and molded all the candles by which he studied at night. And for four years during the Civil War, she wove every yard of cloth worn by the negroes in the plantation and with her own hands she cut and made their garments and that, too, before the days of sewing

EIGHTH GENERATION

Ronald Ingram Archer, s/o Shirley Ruth Ingram and Ernest Archer, was born Feb 14 1952 at Millington, Tenn. Education: Graduate High School while in Air Force service. On Mar 10 1973 married Teresa Eddalene Holbrook (b Nov 12 1956), d/o Marjorie Smith and Willis Edward Holbrook. Occupation: Ronald is self-employed, Phillips 66 Service Station in Memphis. Family lives in Memphis, Tenn.
Children:
    1. Brandon Ronald Archer   b Aug 14 1977

Tedford Charles Archer, s/o Shirley Ruth Ingram and Earnest Archer, was born Sept 28 1956 at Memphis, Tenn. Education: Graduate Overton High School; B.S. degree in Business, Memphis State University (May 1978). Occupation: At present, Management Trainee with the McLean Trucking Company. Not married.

Douglas Paul Embrey, s/o Ann Ingram and Robert Barry Embrey, was born Jul 11 1958 at Memphis, Tenn. Education: a Junior at Mississippi State University. Occupation: Full time student.

Michael Emanuel McComas, s/o Elizabeth Blanche Houston and Jesse Emanuel McComas, was born Feb 24 1953 at Barstow, CA. Education: High School graduate (1971). On May 6, 1972, married Melody Ann Gironda (b Nov 2 19__), d/o Marilyn Louise Gawne and Francis David Gironda. Michael's occupation: Oceanside, CA. city employee. Family lives at Vista, CA.
Children:
    1. Christopher Michael McComas   b Dec 23 1972
    2. Nichole Louise McComas   b May 5 1975

Timothy Patrick McComas, s/o Elizabeth Blanche Houston and Jesse Emanuel McComas, was born Jul 16 1954 at Corona, CA. Education: Graduate, San Marcos High (1973). On June 6 1972 married Deborah Kay O'Dell (b June 14 19__), d/o Joyce Essex and Robert O'Dell. Divorced in November 1975. Timothy's occupation: Employee of Camper Land, San Marcos. Family lives at San Marcos, CA.
Children:
    1. Anthony William McComas   b Nov 16 1972

Dianne Maureen McComas, d/o Elizabeth Blanche Houston and Jesse Emanuel McComas, was born Aug 29 1959 at Yuma, Ariz. Education: Grad (1978) San Marcos (Calif.) High School. Lives in Vista, California.

Donald Lee Wilcox, Jr., s/o Janette Louise Houston and Donald Lee Wilcox, Sr., was born Apr 25 1951 at Upland, Calif. Education: Grad (1970) Sprayberry High School, Marietta, Ga. He was an honor roll student. On June 10 1972, married Pamela Jean Hogsed of Murphy, N. C., d/o Wanda Moss (of Hiawassee, Ga.) and Farrel Hogsed (of Hayesville, N.C.). Occupation: Employed by Fruehof Mfg. Co., Atlanta. Donald is an ordained Deacon in the Baptist Church. Family lives in Marietta, Ga. Their two children were born in Marietta.
Children:
    1. Andrew Lee Wilcox   b Jan 10 1974
    2. Jonathan Bradley Wilcox   b June 26 1978

machines. Thursday, Jan. 26, 1893 at 8:00 A.M. this pure soul of Margaret A. Jones passed from earth to glory!" Interred in the Canaan Plantation family cemetery close by her home.[1]

---

[1] Bascom Anthony *Fifty Years in the Ministry*, J. W. Burke Co., Macon, Ga. (1937) 280 pp and *The True Citizen*, Feb. 18, 1893.

PHILIP JONES was b. in 1759, the s/o Frank Jones, and with his three elder brothers - Frank, John and James were soldiers in the American Army, fighting the War of Independence. Philip owned land in Burke County. Even in that early time, Burke, with its agricultural resources, was a county of some agricultural wealth. The British were then in possession of Savannah and adjacent sections, spanned squads of raiding parties that plundered counties above Savannah. They went up as far as Burke which became the meeting-point and battleground, where these raiders were met by the "Liberty" men as they were called, or rebels, from the counties and sections above, who, hastily organizing, would drive the raiders back. On one of such occasions Philip Jones was on a scout with one of his slaves, named Caesar, near his mill when suddenly he was surprised by three British soldiers and captured. The soldiers disarmed him and bound his arms, giving his rifle and their own to Caesar to carry, and, with their prisoners began their march along the mill-dam which yet stands. Two soldiers in advance, Caesar following, and his master next, and the third soldier in the rear as guard. Faithful Caesar was quick to see the opportunity to release his master and himself, and as quickly aiming with his rifle at the back seam of the coat of the soldier ahead of him, shot him through, and wheeling instantly, with his knife cut the cords from his master's arms, and give him his rifle. Thus suddenly was changed the fortunes of war, and Philip Jones and his slave became the captors, and promptly began their march with their prisoners to the headquarters of the American forces at Augusta. For this daring, successful feat, Caesar was granted his freedom by his master, and for the remainder of his life was honored with the title of "Rebel Caesar."[1]

---

[1] *Memoirs of Georgia*, Vol. II, pp. 368-369.

INEZ FLORIDA WILKINS (JONES) was b. Aug. 4, 1862 at Brothersville, Ga., the eldest d/o Moselle Carswell and Maj. Wm. Archibald Wilkins. Her parents left Louisville, Ga. and moved to Waynesboro in 1871. Her education began under private tutors and later she went to Mary Baldwin Seminary at Staunton, Va.

On Sept. 14, 1880, at age 18, she md. Wm. Everett Jones, s/o Sidney Ann Eliz. Sapp and Dr. William Beaman Jones, M.D. William Everett was b. Oct. 12, 1856 and had reached age 24. He had studied in Germany and had a taste for the military.

They had seven children:
1. William Wilkins Jones   b. June 23, 1881   d. Oct. 3, 1908
2. Moselle Jones (infant)   nd   nd
3. Sydney Carswell Jones   b. July 2, 1883   d. Oct. 3, 1947
4. Nina Treutlan Jones   b. Oct. 3, 1884   d. Nov. 5, 1959
5. Henry Phillips Jones   b.   d.
6. Lillian Everett Jones (Greely) b.   d.
7. Inez Wilkins Jones (Wright)   b. Nov. 15, 1890   d. Jan. 25, 1969

Mrs. Jones was a devoted daughter, wife and mother, a faithful friend, and her beautiful Treutlan Hall was known as a center of gracious hospitality. After the death of Col. Jones in 1904, she assumed and supported the numerous charities which he loved. And during all her life she never flagged in her efforts to obtain the greatest possible advantages for the younger generation, including her own children and others whom she loved.

She was a woman of striking personal charm, and this combination with her mental ability, her unusual force of character, and strength of decision, made it possible for her to carry out many projects beneficial for Waynesboro, Burke County and a wider circle.

She retained her great interest in the Ladies Memorial Association for the soldiers in Gray. She had held the presidency in 1908 and realized that services for the aging veterans were still very important. Noted for her unfailing generosity and sympathetic interest in those in trouble or distress, she served as advisor and helper to those in need.

She was a Chairman Emeritus of the Burke County Chapter of the American Red Cross, which she organized. She was also founder and past president of the Waynesboro Woman's Club. The Club came into doing when there was no other organization in town to do certain civic work. She also worked unceasingly to lay out, beautify and maintain the Magnolia Cemetery.

During WW-I she took up patriotic enterprises, serving as a Chairman of the four Liberty Loan Drives, and in a similar capacity for the Council of Defense as well as the Red Cross.

Mrs. Jones maintained her membership in the Presbyterian Church, and gave willingtly of her support. She also served as a Trustee of the Tallulah Falls School and always supported their motives and achievements.

Death called her from home peacefully at six o'clock Sunday morning, Dec. 27, 1931. She was laid aside for her loved ones in the Magnolia Cemetery, but her untiring spirit of generosity, helpfulness and uplift will go on for "They are not dead who live in the hearts of those they loved."

HENRY A. JONES, M.D. was b. in Herndon, Ga., (Burke County) on Aug. 27, 1868, the s/o Martha (Ackens) Jones and Henry W. Jones. The paternal grandparents of Dr. Jones were Sarah (Vickers) Jones and Henry Philips Jones of Burke County where the respective families were early founded. Henry A. secured his literary education in Emory College at Oxford, Ga. and then entered the medical dept. of the Univ. of N.Y. He graduated in the Class of 1892, with the M.D. degree. He began his practice at Herndon, but after four years he moved to Millen. He rapidly built up a fine practice. He was a close student of his profession and kept abreast with the profession's advances. He was a member of the Medical Association of Georgia, and was the local surgeon of the Millen and Southwestern R. R.

On November 28, 1897, he md. Miss Sarah Daniel, d/o Elias Daniel of Millen, and they had one daughter, Miriam Daniel Jones, b. May 4, 1899.

He and his wife were members of the Methodist Episcopal Church South, in which he was a Trustee. He was also affiliated with the lodge, chapter and commandery of the Masonic fraternity, with its adjuncts organizations, the Ancient Arabic Order of the Nobles of the Mystic Shrine, and also with the Independent Order of Odd Fellows and the Knights of Pythias. He was for several years a member of the Burke Troop of Cavalry, a part of the First Ga. Regiment, and he served for a time as regimental surgeon.

SEABORN H. JONES, of Waynesboro, was one of the leading members of the Burke County Bar, and a representative of the old and honored families of Ga. He was b. in Waynesboro, Dec. 20, 1863, s/o Evaline (Toombs) and Hon. John J. Jones, a member of the U. S. Congress at the time when Ga. seceded from the Union.

Seaborn H. Jones was graduated in Emory College, his father's alma mater, at Oxford, Ga., when 21 years of age. He then took up the study of law under the preceptor-ship of his father, one of the most prominent members of the Bar of eastern Ga., and was admitted to practice in 1887. He forthwith entered into a professional partnership with his father, and this alliance continued until the death of the latter, the firm having a large and important practice, which the son still controls, the original firm title having been John J. Jones & Son. In his political proclivities Mr. Jones is a stalwart supporter of the principles and policies of the Democracy, in whose cause he has been an active worker. He served three terms as solicitor of the Burke Co. Court, and in 1898-9 he represented his county in the State Legislature. In 1901 Gov. Allen D. Candler appointed him Judge of the City Court of Waynesboro, and he remained incumbent of his office until 1902, when the court was temporarily abolished. Judge Jones is chairman of the Burke Co. Democratic Exec. Committee. He has extensive plantation interests in the county, owning a portion of the old Jones homestead, known as "Canaan", adjoining the City of Waynesboro, and property having been in the possession of the family for many generations. His only sister, Mary T., wife of Judge George F. Cox, of Waynesboro, owns a portion of the old homestead, the estate having been divided after the death of their mother. On Nov. 19, 1902, Judge Jones was united in marriage to Miss Helen Gresham, d/o John J. Gresham, of Waynesboro. They have one child, John James Jones, who was b. Oct. 8, 1904, and who was named in honor of his paternal grandfather.[1]

---
[1] Cyc. of Georgia, Vol. II, p. 393.

WARREN W. JONES. Born in Burke Co., near Green's Cut. Education: Grad. of Boggs Academy; B.S. Johnson C. Smith Univ. (Charlotte, N.C.) 1928; M.S. Cornell Univ. Also has completed his years of graduate study at Univ. of Mich. (Ann Arbor), and one-and-a-half years study at the Grad. Institute of Math. and Rational Mechanics at Indiana Univ.

Chairman of the Dept. of Physics and Mathematics, Ky. St. Univ (Frankfort, Ky.) and Chaplain at the college. He has rendered distinguished service and holds memberships in scientific, honorary and professional organizations.[1]

---
[1] Taken from a program at the Celebration of the 50th Anniversary of Boggs Academy (May 27-29, 1956).

WILLIAM EVERETT JONES, was b. Oct. 16, 1856, the s/o Sidney Ann Sapp and Dr. Wm. Beaman Jones of Birdsville, Burke Co. He graduated at the Va. Military Institute and finished his literary course at the Univ. of Heidelberg, Germany.

He md. Miss Inez Florida Wilkins, the eldest d/o Moselle Carswell and Maj. Wm. Archibald Wilkins. From his military training at V.M.I. and his studying in Germany, he was interested in the local comapny and became Capt., and later was made Col. of the 6th Ga. Reg't.

He was a partner of the large mercantile co. of Wilkins, Jones and Neely. Subsequently Mr. R. C. Neely left the firm and the firm became Wilkins & Jones. This two-fold partnership was one of the largest business firms managed by Maj. Wilkins and his son-in-law, Col. Wm. E. Jones. The firm was a large cotton buyer and merchandiser. Col. Jones owned a large farm and was a peach grower. The Col. was a member of the Waynesboro Lodge No. 96 of the Knights of Pythias.

Col. Wm. E. Jones d. suddenly on July 27, 1904. He had attended a baseball game and drove back to Waynesboro, talked with some of his friends until about 7:30 p.m. when he reached his home on Baduly Street. He partook of a hearty supper and left the dining room and went into the hallway where he took a seat on the large hat rack. He was found by one of the servants. His head was bowed and he was already dead. Maj. Wilkins came and summoned Dr. McMaster. Apoplexy was cause of the sudden demise. He was only 48 years at the time of death.

Survived were his wife and six children: Wilkins W; Sidney and Harry; and three daughters, the Misses Nina, Inez and Lillian.

CAPT. WILLIAM WILKINS JONES, was b. June 23, 1881, the eldest s/o Col. W. E. and Mrs. Inez W. Jones, in Waynesboro , Ga. As a boy he was much interested in the military because his father was a trained military officer. After college at the Univ. of Ga., he joined Co. E and became first a private; then a 3rd Lieut. on June 3, 1905. He was again promoted, this time to 1st Lieut. on Apr. 20, 1906, and after the retirement of Capt. Wilkins, he was elected Capt., Nov. 16, 1907. He was one of the best commanders in the First Regiment and his company one of the best in the National Guards.

He d. on Oct. 3, 1908 at Graymont, Ga. and at the home of Mr. W. M. Durden. He had not yet married. Lieut. E. B. Gresham met the train at Millen and an escort of Co. E. attended the funeral on Sunday. He was buried with military honors in the Waynesboro Magnolia Cemetery.

ANDREW ZADOCK KELSEY. Principal. b. Dec. 25, 1871, Millen, Ga. Son of Margaret and Rev. Robert Kelsey. Md. Marie H. Jones on Feb. 20, 1906. Two children: Andrew Z. b. Dec. 28, 1909 and George D., b. July 24, 1911.

Education: A.B. Morehouse College (1903); Tuskegee Inst. (1904). Principal: Calvin Creek H.S., Griffin, Ga. Superintendent: Baptist Reformatory, Macon, Ga.

Membership: Nat'l Ass'n of Colored Teachers in Public Schools; Ga. State Teacher's Ass'n; Ex-Sec, YMCA, Columbus, Ga.; Interracial Committee; Masons; Republican; Religion - Baptist, Address: Griffin, Ga.[1]

---

[1] Who's Who in Colored America (Fifth Ed., 1938-40), p. 387. Ibid, (2nd Ed., 1928-29), p. 223.

REV. JAMES HALL TANNER KILPATRICK was one of those who aided greatly in elevating our denomination in Ga. to its present high standard in a missionary point of view. He was b. in Iredell Co., N.C., June 24, 1793. In his younger years he had excellent educational facilities, received an exceptionally classical education, and prior to his permanent settlement in Ga. he taught school in several places in Louisiana. While in that State he md. his first wife, and also took an active part in the campaign of 1814 and 1815, participating in the Battle of New Orleans, Jan. 8, 1815. He was converted in 1817, and joined the Baptist Church at Cheneyville, La., June 22. In 1820, after the death of his wife, he returned to the East, was prevailed upon to remain and preach at Robertvill, S.C., from whence he removed to Burke Co., Ga., where he md. Miss Harriet Eliza Jones, June 23, 1822. Afterwards he removed to Richmond Co., and at once identified himself with the most prominent Baptists in the State, taking a high position among them. His field of labor lay within the Hephzibah Ass'n, which, when he first became connected with it, was violently anti-missionary. With great zeal and prudence he promulgated missionary sentiments, and after the lapse of 13 years had the pleasure of seeing it entirely revolutionized on the subject of missions. A tract written by him in 1827 or 1828, entitled "A Plain Dialogue on Missions," which was afterwards published in the "Baptist Manual" in connection with denominational articles by Pengilly, Booth, and Andrew Fuller, was prepared specially for the Hephzibah Ass'n, and had a most salutary influence. Mr. Kilpatrick was, through the force of circumstances, a great champion of baptism and temperance in his Ass'n, and to him those two causes owe much able and eloquent support by both pen and voice. He aided, too, greatly in promoting the Baptist educational interests of Ga. The land upon which Hephzibah H.S. is situated was donated by him, and at the State Convention of 1829, at Milledgeville, he, Sherwood Sanders, and Mercur promptly raised the $2500 necessary to secure the Penfield legacy, - an action which proved to be the inception of Mercer University. His life was prolonged until Jan 9, 1869, and was one of remarkable usefulness.

The following is a part of a sketch of Mr. Kilpatrick, written by Gen. G. W. Evans, of Augusta, which appeared in the minutes of the Hephzibah Association for 1869:

"As a citizen, he was quiet, retiring, and unobtrusive; as a man, open, honest, and unsuspecting; as a friend, true but undemonstrative; as a pastor, laborious and constant, always punctual to his appointments; as a preacher, he was logical and profound, and when aroused oftentimes sublimely eloquent;

as a writer and controversialist, he was true, accurate, and resistless; as a Christian, uniform and faithful; and in his expiring moments, as if to seal the holy record of his life with his dying testimony, his last words were 'Precious Jesus!'

Such, brethren, is the brief and imperfect record of the man now gone to his reward, who, before many of us were born, became, by the power of his intellect, we might also say the father of this Association, and who, by pen and voice, aided by the late Rev. Joshua Key, was the main instrument of building up the missionary interest among us, and who for years was the triumphant defender of our peculiar views and the eloquent vindicator of our denominational honor. Gifted with a massive intellect and an iron constitution, he literally wore out in the service of his Master. We deem it no injustice to the living or the dead to express our honest conviction that in his death is extinguished the brightest intellectual light which it has ever been our prize to honor." [1]

---
[1] William Cathcard (ed.), The Baptist Encyclopaedia, Louis H. Everts, Philadelphia, 1881, pp. 655-656.

REV. JAMES HINES KILPATRICK, youngest son of Rev. J. H. T. Kilpatrick and Miss Harriet E. Jones, was b. in Burke Co., Ga., Oct. 18, 1833. He entered Mercer Univ. in 1849 and graduated in 1853, sharing the highest honors of his class. While at Mercer he made a public profession of religion and united with the church, and was called to ordination by the White Plains Church, Greene Co., in 1854. He began his labors as pastor of that church in 1855, succeeding Rev. V.R. Thornton. Since that time his energies have been concentrated upon the White Plains Church, of which he has been the pastor ever since, though he has had charge of other churches, and he has succeeded in so developing its capabilities that it has become one of the most spiritual, efficient, liberal, and enlightened churches in the State. For years it has been regarded as a model church, and Mr. Kilpatrick as the model pastor of the State. In his preaching he makes no effort at display, his aim being to present gospel truth in such a manner that all may understand and few fail to appreciate it; and perhaps no minister in the State is uniformly heard with more interest and profit.

In public life he is very quiet and unobtrusive, but is ever ready to maintain his opinions with ability. He has always taken a prominent part in the affairs of the Ga. Assn., and since his majority has invariably occupied a seat in the Ga. Baptist and Southern Baptist Conventions.

In private life he is simple in his habits, affable in manners, and pleasant in social intercourse. He is fond of books and study. He has published several valuable sermons and a series of articles in the Christian Index on the subject of "Baptism" which were masterly in character and exhaustive in execution. He exerts a strong influence in the denomination within his own State, and might deservedly occupy a much more prominent position were it not for his modesty. He is a strong, terse, sensible writer, a forcible speaker, and a man of great power every way.[1]

---
[1] William Cathcard (ed.) The Baptist Encyclopaedia, Louis H. Everts, Phila., 1881, pp. 655-656.

REV. WASHINGTON LAFAYETTE KILPATRICK, eldest son of Rev. J. H. T. Kilpatrick, was b. in Burke Co., Ga., Oct. 18, 1829. He was graduated from Mercer Univ., with the first honors of his class, in 1850; was ordained in 1852, entered upon the duties of a country pastor, and to the present time, with persistent and untiring energy and faithfulness, has labored in the ministry, serving different churches within the bounds of the Hephzibah Assn. So eminent have been his abilities, so exalted his character, so uniform his courtesy and kindness and so efficient have been his labors and so Christian his deportment, that he wields an influence possessed by no other in his Assn. He is commanding in person, with a fine open countenance, great benignity of expression, and a pleasing address that secures the confidence of strangers. Having a tender heart and liberal impulses, the suffering have ever found him a ready friend and the poor a generous almoner. As a preacher; he speaks extemporaneously, is always practical, pointed, and clear. Too deeply concerned in presenting sound and wholesome instruction, which he does in a solemn and impressive manner, to seek for mere ornamentation in speech, he makes no special effort to embellish his sermons. By his preaching he has attained the most gratifying results, and has secured for himself an enviable reputation; for, while an unflinching Baptist, and ardently devoted to the spread of Baptist sentiments, he seeks for success more by the firm maintenance of truth than by directly combating error.

But other labors pertaining to the welfare of our Baptist Zion, besides those of a pastor, have engaged his attention. For 22 consecutive years he managed the mission and colporteur work of the Hephzibah Assn. Chiefly through his instrumentality in the Hephzibah H. S. was established in 1861, and that school he taught, as president, with eminent success, from 1866 to 1876. In 1868 he organized the Walker Colored Assn., and since its formation he has been the chief and trusted counselor of its iministers and churches. Prior to emancipation the members of those churches belonged to the Hephzibah Assn. Since 1869 he has faithfully discharged the duties of a trustee of Mercer Univ.; and in 1878 he succeeded in securing the organization of the Ga. Baptist Historical Society, of which he is the efficient corresponding sec.

Mr. Kilpatrick has sought to make his attainments more and more available for wide-spread usefulness; and, whatever his influence may be as a public man, - and unquestionably it is very great, - it is but the natural and logical sequence of an unblemished private record and consecrated talents.[1]

---
[1] William Cathcard (ed.), The Baptist Encyclopaedia, Louis H. Everts, Philadelphia, 1881, p. 656.

THOMAS JACKSON LANCE - As pres. of Young Harris College, Thomas Jackson Lance heads one of the State's well-known institutions of higher education. He has devoted his entire career to educational work and has occupied his present office since 1930.

Pres. Lance was b. in Choestoe, Union Co., Ga., on Jan. 31, 1886, s/o James Washington and Verissa Jane (Henson) Lance. He was educated at Young Harris College, from which he was graduated in 1908 with the degree of B.A., and in 1910-11 carried on grad. work at Emory College. In 1913 he took the degree of B.A. at the Univ. of Ga. and in 1917 received the degree of M.A., from the same institution. Meanwhile, his professional career was well under way. From 1908 to 1910, he served as principal of the H.S. at Hopewell, Ga. In 1911, he was appointed teacher of languages at Young Harris College, continuing for one year, and from 1914-16, was head of the English Dept. of the college. In 1916-17, he was head of the English Dept. of Richmond Academy, Augusta, and at the end of that time went to Waynesboro as superintendent of public schools, an office which he filled successfully for 13 years. In 1930, he was called to the presidency of Young Harris College, returning to head an institution in whose progress he had naturally been interested for many years. His administration has been both enlightened and effective, reflecting his thorough qualifications for the position of educational leadership which he fills.

President Lance is a member of the National Education Association and of the Ga. Education Assn., in which latter organization he was president of the Dept. of Superintendence in 1928. In 1935 he was pres. of the Assn. of Ga. Jr. Colleges and is also former sec. of the assn. He has contributed to the "H.S. Quarterly", the "Educational Journal" and other professional publications, writing on subjects of general interest to educators. Pres. Lance is a Democrat in politics, and a member of the Methodist Episcopal Church, So. In 1934 he was lay delegate to the Gen. Conf. of the Southern Methodist Ch. held at Jackson, Miss.; he was elected to the Gen. Conf. of this church as lay delegate for the 1938 meeting to be held at Brimingtham, Ala., in Apr., 1938. He was appointed by Gov. E. D. Rivers in Apr., 1937, to membership on the Board of Regents of the Univ. of Ga. to serve until 1942. He was also appointed in 1938 by the Gov. as Chairman of the Advisory Com. on Personnel for the Bureau of Unemployment Comp. for the State of Ga. Mr. Lance was elected to Phi Beta Kappa, Univ. of Ga. Chapter Alumnus membership, in June, 1938. He was a member of the Rotary Club in Waynesboro. He also was awarded an honorary degree from Oglethorpe Univ.

On May 3, 1914, Thomas Jackson Lance md. Annie Rose Erwin of Blairsville, Ga. They became the parents of four children: Jack, Jr., deceased; Robert Park; Alice Rose; and Thomas Bertram.

He retired in Calhoun, Ga. for several years and died there at age 94, on Jan. 27, 1980. He is interred in the Fain Cemetery.

JOSEPH LAW was b. near Herndon in Burke Co., Ga., on Aug. 4, 1886, and d., after a brief illness, at his residence in Waynesboro, Ga. on Nov. 22, 1940. He was a s/o Robert Law, an extensive and successful planter of Burke Co., a native of Thomas Co., and Clara E. Jones, a native of Burke Co.

Joseph Law received his elementary education in the public schools of Burke Co., graduated from Young Harris College in 1905, and was graduated from the Law School of the Univ. of Ga. in 1907. He began the practice of his profession at Millen in Jenkins Co., in 1907 and moved to Waynesboro, in 1910, where he practiced until his death.

In 1909 he was md. to Carrie Lane of Americus, Ga., and was survived by his wife, and one daughter, Miss Emma Law of Charlottesville, Va.

Joseph Law was naturally endowed with those qualities that made him a successful practitioner. As a result of his skill and industry he had developed a splendid practice and was regarded as one of the best jury and trial lawyers in his section of the State. He was particularly skilled in the realm of criminal law, but uniformly devoted his services to the defense.

Mr. Law was a Rep. in the Gen. Assembly from Burke Co. from 1917 to 1920 and in 1920 was elected Ordinary of his county which position he held continuously to the time of his death. He had been re-elected without opposition for another four-year term. For several years he was County Attorney as well as City Attorney for the City of Waynesboro. He was a member and Vice-Chairman of the Burke County Democratic Exec. Committee and was also a member of the State Democratic Executive Committee. He devoted himself unceasingly to the interest of his county and particularly to the improvement of the public roads of the county. It was due largely to his untiring efforts that so many roads of Burke County have been paved.

He was a member of the Waynesboro Methodist Church in which he took an active interest and for more than ten years prior to his death had been a teacher in the Men's Bible Class. He was a member of Waynesboro Lodge No. 274 F. and A.M. of which he was a Past Master.

This man led an extremely active life; the burden of monotony was never his experience. He was a most hospitable host in his home, a most agreeable companion in field or on stream, and a practitioner with whom it was a pleasure to come in contact. He held positions of prominence in his community and state, but his influence was never exercised to promote his own interests. He loved his county and its people with an intense devotion; his chief concern was how he might best serve his community and the interests of his county. He was thoroughly unselfish, had an abiding faith in humanity, and was a most loyal and sincere friend. The Bar of the Augusta Circuit and this Assn. has lost a member whose ideals and methods embodied the highest conception of a Lawyer.[1]

---

[1] 58 Annual Report (194), Ga. Bar Ass'n pp. 112-113, by Preston B. Lewis.

ALEXANDER J. LAWSON, b. in Liberty Co., was ten years old when his father, John Lawson, moved with his family to Burke in 1796. John Lawson, b. in Liberty Co., 1734, was a Capt. in the Rev. War, was captured at Georgetown, S.C. and taken to a British prison in Cuba.[1]

Alexander grew up on his father's farm; md. Barbara Tuttle, d/o Francis Tuttle, a native of N.J. who became a successful merchant in Burke. Alexander, known as Judge Lawson, was a large farmer and prominent politician; served 10 terms in the State Senate between 1825 and 1857.[2] In 1840 he was the Democratic candidate against Robert Toombs for Congress, and in 1860 was an elector upon the Douglas and Johnson electoral ticket for the State at large. Judge Lawson

[1] Civil War Centennial Edition, The True Citizen, Apr. 20, 1961, p. 6B
[2] Official Register, 1961/62, pp. 1044-45.

opposed the Secession movement in 1861, but did not live to see the dire results of Secession. He d. in 1862. During his prime he was a leading member of the Methodist Church, and for a number of years presided over the Burke Co. Inferior Court.[3] His son, Edward F. Lawson, b. in 1836, became a leading lawyer of Burke, Ordinary of the County for 13 years, and achieved both professional and pecuniary success at the Bar. Judge Edward F. Lawson md. Leora Martin, d/o John and Eliza (Walker) Martin.[4]

NOTE: See slaveholdings of Alexander J. Lawson 1850 Census and 1860 Census - pp. 47 and 48 B & H. I do not believe that he was a lawyer.

QUERY: Did he have a son, John Lawson?

---

[3] Civil War Centennial Edition, supra.

[4] Ibid. (Check Memoirs of Ga., 1895)

NOTE: For his father, John Lawson, (or brothers), see Hugh Lawson biographical sketch notes.

EDWARD F. LAWSON, a leading lawyer of Burke Co., was b. in 1836, and is the s/o Alexander J. and Barbara (Tuttle) Lawson. Judge Alexander J. Lawson was b. in Liberty Co., and was ten years old when his parents moved to Burke Co. He was a large farmer and a prominent politician, serving in the State Senate from 1825 to 1840. In the latter year he was the democratic candidate against Mr. Toombs for Congress. He was an elector upon the Douglas and Johnson electoral ticket for the State at large in 1860, and opposed the Secession movement in 1861. He was a leading member of the Methodist Church and Chairman of the Board of Justices of the Inferior Court for a number of years. He was a s/o John Lawson, who was b. in Liberty Co. in 1734, moved to Burke Co. in 1796, and purchased a farm, which Mr. Edward F. Lawson now owns. He served as Capt. in the Rev. War, and was captured at Georgetown, S.C., and taken to the British prison in Cuba. The Lawson family came to America in 1712, the progenitor of the Ga. branch settling in Liberty Co., a few years later. Mrs. Alexander Lawson was a d/o Francis Tuttle, a native of N.J., and for years a successful merchant in Burke Co. Mr. Edward F. Lawson was graduated from the Ga. Military Institute in 1857. He then went to Savannah and began the study of law in the office of Ward, Owen & Jones. He practiced one year after he was admitted to the Bar, and then enlisted in the Civil War. He served as Capt., and was afterward made Major. On account of sickness he was obliged to leave the service after about 18 months, and returned home and took the active management of his father's farm, the parent having died in 1862. In 1861 he md. Leora Martin, d/o John and Eliza (Walker) Martin. Mr. Martin was a native of N.C. and a wealthy broker, who moved to Macon, where he d. in 1842. Mrs. Lawson was b. in Macon in 1842. Mr. and Mrs. Lawson are members of the Methodist Church. He has always been prominent in state and county politics and served as member of the constitutional convention of 1866. He was Ordinary of Burke Co. for 13 years, and has been a frequent delegate to conventions. He has practiced law with great professional and pecuniary success, and operates a fine and improved farm of 1,500 acres. At the close of the war his property was stripped of everything but the land value of a small farm, and his present circumstances are the result of his own industry and energy.[1]

---

[1] Memoirs of Georgia, Vol. II, pp. 370-371.

HUGH LAWSON was one of Ga.'s foremost citizens during the generation which followed Yorktown. He was first a citizen of Burke Co., primarily during the post-Revolutionary period, but later a citizen of Jefferson Co., when it was created. Hugh Lawson was a kinsman of Roger Lawson and Alexander J. Lawson, and most probably a s/o Capt. John Lawson, who moved from Liberty Co. to Burke and later to Jefferson Co.[1]

He was an able man and served faithfully in the Rev. War and won a Captain's commission. The citizenry in Burke believed in him and he spent most of his time in representing his constituents. Burke citizens sent him to the State General Assembly in 1781, 1782, 1787, 1788, and 1789.[2]

In 1783 he was one of three Commissioners to administer the acts having to do with sale of confiscated lands, the creation of a sinking fund to liquidate the State debt, and to adjust the jurisdiction of the courts in reference to the sales.[3] On Sept. 1, 1786 he was the Senior presideng Justice of the Land Court.[4]

In 1786 the presentments of the Grand Jury of the Burke Superior Court, Oct. term, show that he sat on the Superior Court bench, together with Col. John Jones, as an Assistant Justice in aid of Wm. Stith, the Chief Justice.[5]

During Edward Telfairs governorship, Nathan Brownson, Wm. Fern and Hugh Lawson were commissioned to select a place for a state capitol, to provide for the erection of a state building and for the establishment of a state univ. The place for the capitol was selected and the town of Louisville laid out.[6] An advertisement in The Augusta Chronicle and Gazetteer of the State read: "We do hereby inform the public that we will sell lots in Louisville by private sale. Signed, H. Lawson, J. Shelman, Comm'rs. Date, April 27, 1789." Louisville was made the State Capitol in 1795 and continued such for some ten years until the capitol was moved to Milledgeville.

Hugh Lawson was elected by an Act of Jan. 27, 1785 to the Univ. "Board of Trustees" for the regulation of the literature of the State. The Board of Trustees appointed a committee of five (including John Twiggs and Hugh Lawson) to select a site in Jackson Co. (then including Clark and Jackson), and to contract for the erection of college buildings to accommodate 100 students.[7] The Board of Visitors and the Board of Trustees were to constitute "The Senatus Academicus". This Senate was to "consult and advise, not only upon the ifficers of the Univ., but also to remedy the defects and advance the interests of literature throughout the State in general."

Hugh Lawson was elected to the Supereme Exec. Council in 1782 (Jan. 2), 1788 and 1789. In 1789 he was elected Pres. of the Executive Council.[8]

Upon the creation of Jefferson Co. in 1796 from portions of Burke and Warren counties, Lawson became a citizen of Louisville and Jefferson.

---

[1] The True Citizen, Apr. 20, 1961 (6B).

[2] Official Register (1961/62) pp. 1219, 1220.

[3] William Baron Stevens, History of Georgia, II, p. 347.

[4] The Georgia State Gazette or Independent Register, Nov. 25, 1786.

[5] Ibid.

[6] George G. Smith, The Story of Georgia and The Georgia People (2nd ed.) p. 118.

[7] Stevens, op. cit., p. 363.

[8] Official Register, pp. 1006, 1010 and 1011.

ISAM SAMUEL LEE, M.D. was b. in Due West, S.C., Nov. 26, 1891, the third s/o five sons b. to Harry and Evelyn Lee. He came of stock that had resided there since the early settlements. His grandfather was a slave who escaped for his freedom to S.C.

He was inspired at a very early age to become a country doctor, as a result of observing doctor's visits in his home and other rural homes.

As a boy he worked in the fields with his father and brothers during the planting and harvesting seasons. Many times he would walk to school in all types of weather, a distance of four miles one way, and cannot ever remember arriving late at school. He finished his jr. work in Due West, S.C. and then enrolled at the Allen Univ., Columbia, S.C. to be able to enroll at the univ., his father took out a loan to start his son's college career. However, the next five summers Isam worked and saved enough to pay his tuition and board. He earned the B.S. degree from the Univ. He was an exceptional athlete and could play all positions on the baseball team and in other school sports.

He enrolled in Meharry Med. Col. with money he had earned and saved while at college. He was granted a Degree in Medicine in 1919. His internship was done under Dr. A. B. Johnson of Aiken, S.C. who operated a hospital there. Upon completion of his work, he returned to Due West, S.C. and was md. to his childhood and college sweetheart, Lula Bell Hawthorne.

He passed the State Board Exam. to practice medicine in Ga. He came to Augusta, Ga. where friends in the profession persuaded him to come to Burke Co. for it was a large co. and needed a black physician. He came to Waynesboro and saw the need for his services to humanity and to a community, regardless of race or religion.

He brought along his wife who was a Christian lady of the same faith, and two sons were b. to this union. Fourteen years after beginning his medical practice, he lost his wife and for five years he was mother and father to his two sons and a country doctor to this large community. One of the main factors causing his decision to remarry was to have a mother for his two sons: Hawthorne Isam Lee and Sammi J. Lee.

He never refused to make a call whether it was to be paid or not. Some patients paid him with chickens, watermelons, vegetables, hams, and other items raised on the farms. He was a practising doctor in Burke Co. for 42 yrs.

RUFUS EZEKIEL LESTER was b. in Burke Co., Ga., Dec. 12, 1837, and was the only s/o Ezekiel Lester who d. in 1840, leaving a child of three years. His mother made it possible that he could get a good education at Mercer Univ. where he displayed abilities of a high order. He graduated with first honor of his class in 1857. After the Bar he joined the law firm of Norwood, Wilson and Lester.

On Nov. 9, 1859, he md. Miss Laura Hines, d/o James J. and Georgia (Bird) Hines of Burke Co. To this union a daughter, Laura, was b. who md. Thomas J. Randolph.

In August, 1861, he enlisted as a Lieut. in the 25th Ga. Vol. infantry, commanded by Col. C. C. Wilson, and was made adjuted of the regiment. He served with distinction until the surrender. He participated in the campaign of Gen. Johnston's Army in Miss., and subsequently in the ever memorable operation of the Army of Tenn., receiving two wounds at the Battle of Chicamauga.

When the War was over he returned to Savannah and resumed his professional duties. In 1868 he was elected to the State Senate; was re-elected in 1871, 1877 and 1878 and during the last two terms was Pres. of the Senate. From 1883 to 1889 he served with distinction as Mayor of Savannah and his administration was among the best the city had ever enjoyed.

While in the Congress he was for the greater part of his service a member of the river and harbors committee. In his political affiliations he was an unswerving Democrat and was one of the admitted leaders of that party in his native state. He was an active member of the Masonic fraternity, the Independent Order of Odd Fellows, the Knights of Pythias and the United Confederate Veterans.

In 1888 he was elected representative in Congress from the First Dist. of Ga. and by successive re-elections he remained a member of that body until his death on June 16, 1906. He fell through a skylight in Washington, D.C., about 30 feet causing internal injuries and both of his legs were broken.[1]

---

[1] A. St. Clair - Abrams, Manual and Biographical Register - State of Ga., For 1871-2, Atlanta (1872), p. 8; <u>Cyc of Georgia</u>, Vol. II, pp. 463-464.

CLIFFORD LEWIS (the following story appeared in the Georgia Vs. Cincinnati football program of Oct. 30, 1976).

Clifford Lewis, first woman member of the University's Athletic Board was described recently by a friend as a "very comprehensive person."

A very astute observation for this smiling and enthusiastic professor, who is so busy with campus committee assignments and personal projects that, as she puts it, "Might make you think I don't have time to work."

She is a full-time teacher on the undergraduate and graduate level. In the past two decades she has either held offices and/or served on no less than 47 national and regional committees. Local offices held, or committes served on, number 30.

An avid follower of many sports teams at Ga., she is, in addition to her support of the women's teams, a season ticket holder for Ga. varsity football and basketball events.

A golfer and a very good tennis performer, she sails on Lake Burton; canoes down South Ala. rivers and the Okefenokee swamp; hikes in the North Ga. mountains; collects art and is a regular at the Atlanta Symphony.

A native of Waynesboro, she says enthusiastically, "I come from a sporting family."

"My father, Preston, was captain of the LSU basketball team and my uncle, Ralph, held many track records at La. State. They were born in S.C., but the family then moved to La. which is why they went to LSU. My mother, grandmother and all my aunts were graduates of Lucy Cobb Institute and there never was any doubt about where I was going to school."

At Ga., she was Pres. of ADPi, served in Student Gov't and was selected for Mortar Board.

She then obtained a Masters from Columbia and her PhD from Ohio State to know the controversial Woody Hayes, whom she describes "as colorful off the field as he is on the field."

In July of 1975, she was asked to become a member of the Athletic Board by Pres. Fred C. Davison. "I was very pleased with the decision to include a woman on the board. It has been a rewarding and interesting experience. I find myself enjoying the association because of the respect I've gained for the way our athletic program is conducted."

"Last year, as a member of the board, I was invited to travel with the team to Jacksonville for the Fla. game. That was a very rewarding experience because I got to see first hand how the team conducts itself for a road game. Everything was so well organized and efficiently operated. The players were very well mannered and well disciplined. I was really impressed."

"I've been a strong supporter of the Ga. football program for many years, but that trip really was the highlight of my football association at Ga."

The women's athletic program at Ga. is improving rapidly, she notes. "I think there should be an opportunity for women's sports to exist and the Ga. Athletic Dept. has taken the interest and is providing that opportunity. We are now getting girls with excellent athletic skills for our teams. In the past, women with high skills didn't go to college because there was no opportunity."

She predicts that in the 21st century there will be as much interest in national women's championships such as basketball as there is in men's championships today.

As the Ga. Alumni Record noted in its spotlighting of Dr. Lewis several issues back, she has had problems with her name.

"When she applied to the Univ., housing officials", says editor Bill Simpson, "assigned her to Joe Brown Hall, a men's dorm.

"Alpha Tau Omega, Phi Delta Theta, and Sigma Chi fraternities all sent representatives to Waynesboro to rush this incoming freshman.

"After enrollment figures were in, Dean William Tate called the phys. ed. major into his office to find out why the student was cutting ROTC."

"To Clifford all this was very strange. Both her mother and grandmother were named Clifford, and the folks in the east Ga. town had accepted the name as properly feminine."

"It took only one look at the attractive coed for the univ. and frat. officials to realize that Joe Brown was not a suitable dorm for this Clifford, who was naturally exempt from cadet life and would never be a food fraternity brother no matter how hard she tried."

"The mix-up, she found, was not confined to Ga. When Miss Lewis applied in writing at Columbia Univ. to room with close friend Martha Latimer, she received a curt reply explaining that that sort of thing was not done at the New York school. Even today she often has a hard time convincing callers that Clifford is indeed a woman."

Those who know anything about her and her work know that she has made many valuable contributions to the Univ. She, indeed, is a very "comprehensive" person

JONATHAN LEWIS was from Cates, Jr's great-great-grandfather. Mrs. Sue Cates found a record in the DAR Archives at Atlanta. The record of Jonathan Lewis stated a Lieut. 5th Co., 2nd Battalion, 2nd Regt., Burke Co. Militia, Dec. 15, 1796.

An old Negro on the Cates' place told "Miss Sue" that "He died while makin' the Law." Jonathan was a member of the State Legislature. After a careful research his grave was located in Milledgeville, formerly the State Capitol.

The State marked his grave with a flat marble slab on which was written:
"Sacred to the memory of the Hon. Jonathan Lewis, Senator of the County of Burke who department this life at Milledgeville in the discharge of the duties of his Station."
After this quite a tribute closing as following:
"A wit's a feather and a chief's a rod,
An honest man's the noblest work of God."

Jonathan Lewis owned and lived on what we now call the Cates Place. My husband was born there and the land is very dear to us.

THE REV. JOSIAH LEWIS was the first minister of the Presbyterian Church in St. George Parish. He was a licentiate from New Castle Presbytery in Pa. who had visited the church in 1766 on a missionary tour. He preached at Brier Creek in 1768. A formal call was made to Mr. Lewis to pastor both the Walnut Branch Church and one at Queensborough.

Josiah Lewis was a chaplain in the Rev. War. A following land grant indicates he may have been killed in the conflict:

"The Rev. Josiah Lewis, Chaplain(deceased), is entitled to a bounty of 750 acres as a refugee from N.C. and 250 as a citizen, after his return to this state. John Twiggs (Brig.-Gen.), on Apr. 10, 1784, petitioner for Savannah widow of Josiah Lewis for self, Jonathan Reese Lewis ten years old, Benjamin Thomas Lewis eight years old, Susannah Lewis, three years old and Josiah Lewis, Jr., one year old, praying that from separate bounties in Washington Co. be granted to Banjamin Lewis, brother of Josiah Lewis deceased, in trust for the four minors."

The Rev. Lewis had started the church in a long and interesting career. Leading members were John Whitehead and Gidion Dowse who migrated to Burke from Liberty Co. in Colonial times. In 1819 Mr. Whitehead founded a scholarship at Princeton Theological Seminary, one of the first scholarships at this old school.

THOMAS LEWIS, SR. was a Rev. soldier and a prominent citizen of Burke from about 1776 to his death in 1800.

On July 12, 1776 he was approved by the Council of Safety as a Magistrate in the District of Queensborough, the same date as First Lieut. of a co. of militia in the lower dist. of St. George's Parish.[1] In 1781 and 1782 he was elected to the Gen. Assembly and in 1782 was chosen by his colleagues to serve on the Executive Council. After a brief period, however, he resigned from the Council.[2] His son, Thomas Lewis, Jr., was in the Assembly with him in 1782.[3] Both father and son were appointed in 1783 to a commission of five to oversee the first sale of lots for the newly laid-out town of Waynesboroug

By 1788 he was Col. of the Burke Militia. Gov. Samuel Elbert wrote him the following letter:

"In Council, 16th Sept., 1785.
Sir: - I have just had the honor to receive a letter dated the 14th Inst. from General Pickens, one of the Commissioners appointed by Congress to treat with the Cherokees and all other Indians southward of them, in which he writes as follows, nz: 'The Treaty with the Creeks is to begin the 24th October next at Galphintown on Ogeechee, and with the other tribes the 15th Nov. at or near Seneca. The Guard which the Comm'rs mentioned to your Excellency in June last, I make no doubt they will be under obligation to you for at the time now appointed, and would wish twenty of them mounted, with a careful officer.'

You are therefore hereby ordered to govern yourself accordingly, and in place of the third Monday in this month have the detachment ready on the spot on the 24th of next October, and twenty of them mounted, with a careful Officer, when and where they are to act agreeable to my former order.

I have the honor to be, etc.
S.E.
To Colonel Lewis, or Officer Commanding the Burke Militia."[5]

Colonel Lewis was returned to the Assembly each year from 1785 to 1789 inclusive, and again in 1791-92 and from 1796 to 1799 incl.[6] In 1786, he was once more a member of the Executive Council.[7] He also, together with David Emanuel, represented Burke in the State Constitutional Convention of 1789,[8] and was listed in 1790 as one of the Justices in Burke.[9] He died on Nov. 4, 1800.[10]

---

[1] Proceedings of the Council of Safety, July 2, 1776 in Collections of the Georgia Historical Society, Vol. V, Part 1, pp. 69-70. It is possible that one of these appointments was for his son, Thomas, Jr.

[2] Official Register, 1961/62, pp. 1219 and 1006.

[3] Ibid., p. 1219.

[4] Knight, Georgia's Landmarks, Memorials and Legends, Vol. I, p. 341; (p. 21 B&H).

[5] Letter Book of Governor Samuel Elbert from Jan. 1785 to Nov. 1785, Collections of the Georgia Historical Society, Vol. V, Part 2 (1902), p. 216.

[6] O.R. 1961/62, pp. 1219 and 1220; The Augusta Chronicle and Gazette of the State, Sept. 5, 1791

[7] O.R., 1961/62, p. 1008.

[8] The Georgia State Gazette or Independent Register, Jan. 24, 1789.

[9] The Augusta Chronicle and Gazette of the State, Feb. 20, 1790.

[10] William H. Dumont, Some Early Residents of Burke County, Ga., 1969, p. 8.

GEORGE LISLE, a former slave and pioneer Baptist minister, very early established a place for himself in Burke's Colonial history. Probably b. in St. George's Parish, he was owned by Maj. Henry Sharp who lived in the vicinity of "Dropping Ford" on Big Buckhead Creek.[1] The pastor, Matthew Moore, was the brother-in-law of the Maj. Moore had converted the slave and baptized him, and most probably he persuaded Maj. Sharp to free the new convert in order that he might be licensed to preach.

Soon after emancipation and licensed, he took the name of "George Lisle".[2] His first productive field as a minister was on George Galphin's plantation at Silver Buff, across the Savannah River. There Rev. "Elder" Wait Palmer of Conn. had begun to preach there, as a part of itinerary activities, to a large slave audience at Galphin's mill.[3] For a time Rev. Lisle preached there, supplementing when Elder Palmer was away.

Later he went to Savannah when the British had captured the city. Here he was under British protection and remained there, often preaching to large numbers of runaway slaves assembled on Tybee Island, and at Yamacraw and Brumpton Land. He also used his organizational talents effectively in his chosen work.

When the War was over and the British evacuated Savannah in 1782, Lisle left with them. He took his abode at Kingston, Jamaica in British West Indies. He had become an effective church organizer and an active minister of the Gospel. Just as he had used his talents in Savannah, he worked hard to relieve the lot of his people and to preach the Gospel.

The Silver Bluff Church suffered the viccissitudes of War after 1778, but its work was begun anew with the cessation of hostilities. It was more prosperous than ever in 1791 and found in Thomas Galphin a benefactor and protector as effective as his father.[4]

---

[1] Minutes of the Hephzibah Baptist Association, Oct. 14-16, 1881, pp. 21-22.

[2] Ibid.

[3] Brooks, op. cit., pp. 177-178.

[4] Brooks, op. cit., p. 178, 181, 182.

ALEXANDER LIVELY, farmer, near Sardis, was b. in Burke Co. in 1832, and came from a long-lived ancestry. He is the s/o Mathew and Eliz. (Odim) Lively. Mathew Lively was a Rev. soldier, and d. in 1834, aged 84 years. He was a big farmer and slave holder and a man prominent in the affairs of the Methodist Church. He was of Scotch descent, his father, Abram Lively, having been b. in Scotland and located in Ga. before 1750, when the Indians were numerous and settlers far apart in the marshy woodlands of Burke Co. Mr. Alexander Lively was brought up on the farm and educated in the old field schools. In 1852 he md. Valinda, the d/o Moses and Martha (Royal) Godbee. Mr. Godbee was b. in Burke Co. and was in the second war with Great Britain.

The mother was b. in 1836 and d. in 1861, leaving one child - Mark. In 1862 Mr. Lively md. Eliz. Kimbrell, d/o Wm. and Eliza (Sapp) Kimbrell. The father was a successful farmer and a worthy gentleman. Mrs. Lively was b. in Burke Co. in 1821. She is a Baptist in her religious faith and Mr. Lively a Methodist and a member of the Masonic order. For 24 years he was Justice of the Peace in his county and in 1884 he was elected to the Legislature, serving one term. He did some valuable work there on the agricultural and other committees. Mr. Lively owns a nice farm near Sardis, which he has developed into a fine state of cultivation, and he is a man highly esteemed for his honesty and uprightness.[1]

---
[1] Memoirs of Georgia, Vol. II, p. 371

WILLIAM LORD was among the first of the Rev. Patriots in St. George's Parish. Lord and Henry Jones were two of the 26 delegates from all the parishes who gathered at Tondee's Tavern in Savannah, Aug. 10, 1774, to seek redress of certain American grievances, to come to the aid of blockaded Boston with food supplies, and to protest recent Acts of the British Parliament including taxation of the American colonists without representation. To the strong resolutions adopted these two courageous men affixed their signatures.[1] Despite repudiation of their action by some 114 signatories in the Parish, Jones and Lord plus David Lewis attended the Provencial Congress at Savannah, Jan. 18, 1775 and were two of the eight delegates from St. George's to the Second Congress at Savannah, July 4, 1775.[2]

William Lord had come to Ga. from S.C. in the 1760's with a wife, four children and five Negroes.[3] In June, 1767 he was granted 350 acres in the fork of Rocky Creek, a branch of Brier Creek about three miles from the mouth and in May, 1770, 100 acres adjoining the original grant.[4] He (or a son by the same name) appears as an Ensign in the Militia, 2nd Co. (Capt. Gideon Thomas) of the 4th Regiment (Col. John Thomas), Feb. 23, 1774.[5] By the Council of Safety (the Revolutionary Government) Lord was named a Magistrate in the Lower Dist. of the Parish, July 2, 1776.[6]

During the War the records show that he was appointed Commissary of Hides and Tallow, Nov. 6, 1781; was chosen for membership in the House of Assembly from Burke, Jan. 2, 1782 and moved from the Assembly to the Governor's Executive Council the same date, but declined to take his seat in the Assembly.[8]

---
[1] See Charles C. Jones, The History of Georgia, Vol. II, pp. 152-153 for a text of the resolutions.
[2] Ibid., p. 184; also George G. Smith, The Story of Georgia and The Georgia People, 1732-1860 (2nd ed.), p. 77.
[3] Letter from David B. Lord, The True Citizen, June 9, 1965.
[4] Colonial Records of Georgia - Candler (1907) Vol. X, p. 194 and Vol. XI, p. 47.
[5] Letter from David B. Lord, op. cit.
[6] Proceedings of the Georgia Council of Safety, 1775 to 1777, July 2, 1776.
[7] Letter from David B. Lord, op. cit.
[8] Official Register 1961/62, pp. 1219 and 1006.

On at least two occasions, the Exec. Council issued "rations for Mrs. Lord, Mr. Lord to be responsible", which suggests that Lord spent more time fighting, or otherwise serving the American cause, than in growing crops.[9] After the War he was Clerk of the Superior Court, 1783-1787. As court clerk he signed on Oct. 21, 1783, the charges drawn up by the grand jury, and presented them to George Walton, Chief Justice, which listed the names of the traitors and others in Burke who had worked with the British during the War. Other positions held included Road Commissioner (River Road) for a Burke Militia Dist., 1783; Coroner, 1790 and 1792, and a Justice of the Burke Inferior Court, 1797. Some of his descendants now live in Screven Co.[10]

---

[9] Letter from David B. Lord, op. cit.

[10] Ibid.

JUDSON W. LYONS, although a native of Burke Co., was a resident of the city of Augusta for many years. He came to Augusta in his early manhood and graduated from the old Augusta Institute now located in Atlanta, and known as Morehouse College. After leaving college he taught school for several years and later entered the Harvard Univ. Law School where he received the degree of LL.B. from Harvard Univ. He returned to Augusta and was admitted to the Bar, of which he has been a member ever since.

As a figure in National politics, Judson W. Lyons ranked high, and honors above the average were conferred upon him. Pres. William McKinley appointed him Register of the U. S. Treasury Dept., a position he held during both terms of the McKinley administration from Apr. 7, 1898 to June 1, 1906. He was serving his country in this capacity at the outbreak of the Spanish-American War in 1898, and was also at that time Republican Committeeman from Ga. and a dominating force of the Republican part of the State.

As a token of appreciation the entire force of the Treasury Dept. presented him with a solid silver tea set on his retirement from office. The deceased was a 3rd degree Mason, a veteran member of Bennekes Lodge No.3, Augusta, and was the first colored man to be elected a member of the American Academy of Politics and Social Science. He was a devoted member of the Harmony Baptist Church.

He was survived by his wife, Jane Hope Syons, three daughters - Hope, Edith and Alice Lyons; one son, Judson W. Lyons, Jr., and four nephews and four nieces.

In the passing of Judson W. Lyons, the colored race lost one of her outstanding leaders. He was affable, unassuming and retiring to a faulty. He was never known to have spoken ill of anybody, not even of his enemies and was always loyal and true to his friends. That the deceased was a leading character and the colored race is an assured fact, and he was considered a natural character upon giving advice on matters pertaining to the political party of his choice.

He died at his home, 1329 Gwinnett Street, Augusta, after an illness of but three days. Death resulted from a heart attack. - The Augusta Chronicle.[1]

---

[1] Reprinted in the T.C., June 28, 1924.

HUGH ANGUS MACAULAY, M.D. was b. Sept. 4, 1885 in Chester, S.C., the s/o Sallie McMaster and David J. Macaulay. He grew up in Chester and completed his schooling there and entered the Ky. Med. College, now known as the Univ. of Louisville Med. College. Hugh A. was a nephew of Dr. McMaster. When Dr. McMaster began to lose his strength he associated Dr. Macaulay with his practice. Dr. McMaster d. on August 21, 1908.

On Sept. 21, 1916, Eliz. McMaster md. Dr. Hugh A. Macaulay with a beautiful wedding in the Waynesboro Methodist Church with Balk's orchestra and Mr. Robert Irvin of Augusta. Rosa McMaster was the maid of honor, and the best man, D. A. Macaulay. Dr. J. P. McFerrin most impressively performed the ceremony. The honeymoon spanned several weeks of New York, Boston, Washington, Baltimore and other places of interest.

Dr. Macaulay was a fine physician and built up a following. His sister, Eliz. Macaulay, had md. Arthur Forte Evans which brought these two families together. Dr. Macaulay was a good citizen and in 1928 was Pres. of the Rotary Club.

Elizabeth and Hugh had two children:
1. Hugh Angus Macaulay, Jr., b. Feb. 4, 1919.
2. Rosa Moore Macaulay, b. Feb. 10, 1924

Dr. Macaulay d. on Feb. 4, 1931 and was interred in the Waynesboro Magnolia Cemetery.

ANNIE REID MACKENZIE was b. Feb. 20, 1878 in Waynesboro, Ga., the d/o Angelina May Lawson and James Hope Campbell MacKenzie. She received her education with private tuitors at the Waynesboro Academy and graduated at the Ga. State College for Women, at Milledgeville, Ga.

Lucien Knight in his preface to the late Frederick Hays', History of Macon County stated that only a "child of the soil" can write its' country history. She spent 16 years collecting material, which includes all extant records of the land that is Burke Co.

Primarily during the 1940's and 1950's Mrs. Humphrey published in The True Citizen a series of carefully researched sketches of early Burke citizens and towns. To this series the author owes his initial interest in writing with his sister the first draft of a history on Burke Co. The Humphrey sketches were of Birdsville; Early Waynesborough; the Rev. Josiah Lewis; Capt. Patrick Carr; the Rev. Edmund Byne; Capt. W.S.E. Morris; Congressman Rufus E. Lester, and many others.

In 1929 she received a certificate award for meritorious research and in 1935 a Fellowship. She was a member of the Richmond County Historical Society and the Ga. Historical Society in Savannah, Ga. In background she had also done research in Canada, England, Wales, Scotland, Ireland and Belgium. She has worked in the Library of Congress, the DAR Library, the Ga. State Archives in Atlanta and the Library of Alexandria, Va.

During the period of six years, 1950 through 1955, The True Citizen published her Historical Notes on Burke Co. which ran to approximately 140 such notes.

She md. John Franklin Humphrey, b. Dec. 8, 1895, the d/o Alice Hardwick and David M. Humphrey. He d. Dec. 7, 1935. She d. Apr. 30, 1974. Both are interred in the Waynesboro Magnolia Cemetery. They had one daughter, Alice May Humphrey, who md. Hanford Meeker Edsall of St. Louis, Mo. The Edsall family lives in Alexandria, Va., and have three sons.

SIDNEY J. MCCATHERN was b. in 1888, s/o Sarah J. Chandler and Walker McCathern (CSA). His father showed himself as a fearless soldier in the Civil War. The son served in WW-I, Infantry TOTC.

He d. at his home "Charney". His condition was not considered serious, so his death was a great shock. Mrs. McCathern and the two children were away from home in the mountains of N.C.

Studied law and passed the Bar, but he did not long practice. He turned to farming and was successful. He possessed a wonderful voice and sang with church choirs and many occasions gave much pleasure to those who heard him sing. He was 41 years old; member of the Waynesboro Baptist Church and the American Legion. He was interred in the Waynesboro Magnolia Cemetery.

He was survived by his wife, Mrs. Charlotte Reynolds McCathern, two children, four brothers and a number of other relatives in the city and county. His death occurred Sept., 1928.

WALKER MCCATHERN was b. on the Hughes plantation, ten miles distant from Waynesboro, in Burke Co., Feb. 10, 1840, a s/o Anna Ingram and Daniel McCathern. His mother was b. in Richmond Co.; his father was b. in Scotland. When he was but seven years of age his father died, but his mother lived to attain the age of 75 years. He was reared on the plantation and received his education in the Richmond County schools.

In Apr., 1861 at the age of 21 years he enlisted as a private in Co. A, Third Ga. Volunteer Infantry (Burke Guards Co.). He was wounded at Malvern Hill, and twice wounded, receive two wounds almost simultaneously. Again at Belfield, N.C. he was wounded, captured and was imprisoned at Ft. Delaware. He and one companion, George C. Tanner of the Cobb Ga. Legion, made an escape. They were recaptured and returned to Point Lookout where they were confied for five months when they managed a second but successful escape.

Mr. McCathern after the War continued to live in Burke Co. where he acquired valuable plantation interests, and successfully engaged in the raising of cotton and other products; also conducted a general store on his plantation. Later in 1880 he moved into Waynesboro. He served as Mayor three terms. He was a Master Mason and a member of the Baptist Church.

On Feb. 23, 1868, Mr. McCathern md. Sarah J. Chandler, d/o William and Leslie (Darlington) Chandler of Burke Co. They had six children who lived: Wm. Walker; Porter F.; J. Jenks; Otis A.; G. Metz; and Sidney. Mr. McCathern d. Oct. 14, 1915. His wife lived until Feb. 23, 1924. Both are interred in the Waynesboro Confederate Memorial Cemetery.[1]

---

[1]*Cyc of Georgia*, Vol. II, pp. 657-658.

WILLIAM WALKER MCCATHERN, JR. s/o Katheryn Woodward and William Walker McCathern, was b. in Waynesboro, Ga. on Aug. 15, 1908.

He attended Waynesboro H.S. and is an alumnus of Ga. Tech. and the Stonier Graduate of Banking at Rutgers. He was a representative of Universal C.I.T. Corp. before joining the staff of Colonial American National Bank in Roanoke, Va.

In 1946 he was made a Vice-President, elected Senior Vice-President in 1961; a Director in 1962 and Executive Vice-President in 1963; and the President of the bank, Nov., 1970; Chairman of the Board.

On Oct. 12, 1934, he md. Florence Halbert Moss, d/o Florence Pugh Moss and George A. Moss.

Children:
1. William Walker McCather, III, b. Oct. 25, 1936. He md. Jessie Howbert of Roanoke, Va. They had four children: one girl and three boys and they live in Richmond, Va. He is an architect.
2. George Moss McCathern, b. Nov. 7, 1941. Md. Catherine Heslip of Roanoke, Va. and they have three children: two girls and one boy. They live in New York City, and he is a commercial artist.
3. Ann Halbert McCathern, b. Jan. 13, 1947. She md. Leslie W. Burnley, Jr. of Roanoke, Va. They now live in Roanoke and have two children: one boy and one girl.

Mr. McCathern is a past president of the Roanoke Merchants Association, Better Business Bureau, Roanoke Recreation Association, and Blue Ridge Game and Fish Association.

He has also served on the finance committee at Virginia Heights Baptist Church, and on the boards of Roanoke Youth Council; Jr. Achievement; Salvation Army Boys Club; Roanoke Booster Club; Lions Club; Sales Executive; Izaac Walton League; and the advisory council of distributive education and Victory Stadium Committee. Director of Shenandoah Life Insurance Company.

THE MCCLOUD FAMILY[1]

George Washington McCloud was b. Sept. 20, 1903 in Emanuel Co. On Jan. 23, 1927 he md. Miss Sophronia Lenora Folley of Jefferson Co., b. Apr. 5, 1904. They were md. at the home of the bride's parents, Mr. & Mrs. Willie Follie of Burke Co., Jan. 23, 1927. They have come a long way since their marriage in 1927.

The McClouds worked as sharecroppers for 32 years. Most of their share-cropping work was done on the Paul Dye Plantation. They raised six children. All were educated at Boggs Academy, near Keysville. They were unable to pay cost for their schooling so they were allowed to substitute with farm products. The children helped with the tuition fees through the work aid program at Boggs.

1. Since their graduation from Boggs, the oldest, Willie L. McCloud received his BS degree in Agriculture from Ft. Valley State College and his MA degree from South Carolina State in Orangeburg, S.C. He is presently a math instructor at Blakeney Jr. H.S.

2. George F. McCloud is a self-employed contractor. He received his training in masonry from Boggs and in Cincinnati, Ohio, and technical school in Augusta.

3. Elijah E. McCloud, carpenter and barber in Brooklyn, N.Y., received his masonry training from Boggs and while enlisted in the U. S. Air Force.

4. Mrs. Gordon (Viola) Quaye received her training as a registered nurse at an Augusta Nursing School. She is presently a nurse at Boggs.

5. Miss Lucy McCloud received her BS in elementary school education from Barber-Scotia College in Concord, N.C., and her MA degree in educ. from S.C. State. She is teaching at Hendy Elementary School in Elmira, NY.

6. Dr. J. Oscar McCloud, a doctor of humanities and Rev. graduated from Warren Wilson Jr. Col. and received his BS degree in Theology from Berea College in Berea, Ky, and his Masters theological degree from Union Theological Seminary in NY City, NY. He is director of the program agency of Presbyterian Churches USA in NY, NY and resides at Teaneck, NJ.

The McClouds have lived in Waynesboro for the past 17 years where Mr. McCloud was employed as a yardman and Mrs. McCloud settled back as a housewife.

They are now retired and residing at Apt. 47, Magnolia Acres.

In honor of their 50th Wedding Anniversary the McCloud children entertained with a banquet at the American Legion Home Post 562, Saturday evening, January 22, 1977.

1
T.C., Jan. 26, 1977

EVANS HOWELL MCELMURRAY, was b. Jan. 30, 1890 in Waynesboro, s/o Mary Chandler and Thomas Jefferson McElmurray. He studied at the Waynesboro public schools and the Univ. of Ga., where he was a member of the A.T.O. frat.

He was Capt. of Co. E., 1st Ga. Infantry on the Mexican border during 1916-17. Upon entrance of the U.S. in WW-I, Capt. McElmurray was transferred to Battery A, 118th Field Artillery of the 31st Div., AEF. He served in such capacity on American soil, and later commander of this outfit in France where his gallantry and bravery listed him among the outstanding American soldiers serving on foreign soil. He was a handsome young man and a good officer.

He never married. His business in Waynesboro was insurance and selling automobiles. He was a prominent Mason and Shriner. He served two terms as Master of the Waynesboro Lodge, No. 274, F. & AM., a charter member of the B.L.I. Post of the American Legion and was its first commander. He was a member of the Waynesboro First Baptist Church. He was twice elected Tax Collector of Burke Co., but resigned in 1917 to stay with his co. on the Mexican border.

He held his Captaincy until his health failed. He was Commander of Co. A, 105th Ammunition Train, until this outfit was merged with the Battery A., 118th Field Artillery. He died on Oct. 1, 1932 at age 42 years.

Survivors are three sisters: Mrs. N. B. F. Close in Savannah; Mrs. J. R. Cothran of Atlanta; Mrs. Frank Bninson; and one half-sister, Mrs. Charles A. Gray of Waynesboro. Two brothers, H.G. McElmurray and Joe H. McElmurray, and one half-brother, W. Leslie McElmurray in Waynesboro.

JOHN F. MCELMURRAY, member of the legislature and farmer, was b. in Burke Co., in 1842, and is the s/o Minis H. and Emily (Leslie) McElmurray. The father was b. in S.C. and moved to Ga. in 1834. He was the s/o Andrew and Mary (Hankinson) McElmurray. Mr. McElmurray's mother was a d/o William L. and Sarah (Hankinson) Leslie. Mr. J. F. McElmurray was educated at Mercer Univ. and in 1861 he enlisted in the late War with Co. K, 32nd Ga. Reg't. He served as Capt. in the Co. and fought at Ft. Sumter; John's Island; Rivers Bridge; Ocean Pond, Fla.; Averasboro and Bentonville, and served to the close of hostilities. In 1865 he md. Anna Shewmake, d/o Judge Joseph A. and Caroline (Hankinson) Shewmake. Judge Shewmake was a native of Burke Co. and occupied a seat on the bench of the Inferior Court, and was a member of the legislature from Burke Co. for years. He was a first Sgt. in the Indian War and in politics and as a citizen was one of the most prominent men ever b. in Burke Co. Mr. & Mrs. McElmurray have six living children: Leslie; Caroline; Lorraine; Thomas J.; John F., Jr.; Sarah. The mother was b. in 1842 and d. in 1881. She was a member of the Methodist Church, while her husband's faith is that of a Baptist. Mr. McElmurray was a Justice of the Peace for several years, and is a member of the county school board. In 1894 he was elected to the legislature and served on the committees on temperance, special, agriculture and manufactures, education and school for the deaf. Mr. McElmurray owns a nice farm of 2,000 acres near Alexander, and is a citizen highly esteemed not only for his public usefulness, but private character.[1]

---
[1]
Memoirs of Georgia, Vol. II, p. 372.

JUDSON SAPP MCELMURRAY was b. Aug. 17, 1866, the s/o Louisa E. Barron and Thomas Jefferson McElmurray. Judson was one of four children by his father's first wife: Leslie; Tommie; Judson S; and Minis Hunter McElmurray. He studied at the Waynesboro Academy and at the Univ. of Ga. (1883).

Judson was interested in politics and liked to have some part of it. At one time he was a Reading Clerk in the Ga. Senate in Atlanta. At another time he was the private Secretary of Charles G. Edwards, Congressman of the First Congressional District. He also worked in the Burke Co. Courthouse. He wrote with a flourish, then fashionable, but later readers who look up some documents find the flourishes difficult.

Judson had a talent for writing and produced a number of short stories and poems, over some quite a number of years. Once he wrote in The True Citizen:
> "For years I have tried to be an author. I have written quite a number of articles for various newspapers scattered over the U.S. and not a few short stories that I have sold to magazines. When the ex-Governor and Sen. Robert L. Taylor was publishing Taylor's Magazine in Nashville,

Tenn., I found no trouble in disposing of almost any story that I could write to that very excellent publication. Some of the poorest tales I have penned brought me greater rewards XX."

Over quite some years he assisted The True Citizen with finding items, or stirring up some discussions. In his "department" he signed himself as "The Roust-A-Bout", "Judson Mack", or sometimes "Mack Judson". He noticed that the poem, "Little Griffin of Tennessee" was credited to Mr. John Hay from Ohio, Private Secretary to President Abraham Lincoln, and Cabinet Member under Pres. Garfield. I beg to call attention to an article in a book written by Mr. L. L. Night of Atlanta, Ga., Georgia Landmarks, memoires legends, page 39. Mr. Knight tells how the famous ballard came to be written. Mr. McElmurray went on to show that the Southern side had the best proof. The Dr. Frank O. Trikner of Columbus, Ga. was the author and not John Hay of Ohio.

Two of his best short stories in The True Citizen were entitled, "King of the Big Black Mountains" (A Title of a Moonshiner), and "A Chesterfield Burglar", somewhat like an O'Henry story. Two original poems also appeared in The True Citizen: "A Girl I'll Ne'er Forget - A Fantasy", and another one, "Poem to Briar Creek".

He md. Haidee Routzahn, the d/o Florence Byne and L. H. Routzahn. They had a daughter, Florence McElmurray, b. July 4, 1893, who md. Peyton Wade Thompson, s/o Josephine Wade and Wall Tattnall Thompson. Peyton W. Thompson was a Capt. in A.E.F., WW-I.[1]

Judson d. on Nov. 25, 1930. He is interred in the Waynesboro Magnolia Cemetery.

---

[1] For Judson S. McElmurray's grandchildren, see the sketch of Peyton Wade Thompson.

MARY LOUISE MCELMURRAY (and Family) was b. Feb. 27, 1877 at Waynesboro, Burke Co., Ga., the eldest d/o Thomas Jefferson McElmurray and his second wife, Mary E. Chandler. Mary Louise studied in the Waynesboro Academy, and spent one year in _____ at Milledgeville, Ga.

On Dec., 1900 she md. Nathaniel Bedford Forrest Close, b. April 13, 1863, in Trion, Chattooga Co., Ga. He was the s/o Emily Georgia Morgan and Gideon Pinckney Close. Forrest Close was educated at Vanderbilt Univ. He moved to Waynesboro to take up a teaching position at Waynesboro Academy. Prof. Close was promoted and became Principal of the Waynesboro Academy. Subsequently he moved to Savannah and was first Principal of the Anderson Street School, and later Principal of the 37th St. School. He was a member of the Board of Stewards of the Wesley Monumental Church and past Master of Landrum Lodge No, 48 F & AM.

In appearance Mary Louise was 5'4", slender in youth, with black hair and flashing dark eyes and a ready smile. She was fond of social events; enjoyed playing bridge, and was active in church affairs.

At the time of her growing up, in the later part of the 19th century, her father was a prosperous cotton farmer and owner of large tracts of land near the Savannah River in Burke Co., Ga. The glorious age of Southern chivalry with its devotion to duty, gracious living and Victorian sense of propriety was her heritage. An age that was rapidly coming to an end. She exemplified the best of this society.

Children of Mary Louis McElmurray and N.B.F. Close:
1. Forrest Close, b. Jan., 1904, in Waynesboro, Ga.
2. Thomas McElmurray Close, b. Dec. 26, 1905, in Savannah, Ga.
3. Leslie Pinckney Close, b. Mar. 21, 1908, in Savannah, Ga.
4. Marie Wilkins Close, b. Nov. 7, 1910, in Savannah, Ga.

Prof. N.B.F. Close d. June 30, 1929 at Savannah. He was interred in the Bonaventure Cemetery at Savannah. He left his widow and a sister Miss Clyde Close. Mary Louis McElmurray Close taught school, mostly the 4th grade, about 30 years in Savannah. She had begun teaching before her husband died. She was a widow for 25 years. All of her four children were still living when their mother was living. At the time of her death there were ten grandchildren and a number of great-grandchildren came later.

SECOND AND THIRD GENERATION

1. FORREST CLOSE, was b. Jan., 1904 at Waynesboro, Ga. He received his commission in the U.S. Navy and a Class of 1924 at Annapolis. He had a distinguished career in the Navy, including many battle engagements in WW-II. He retired with the rank of Capt. in 1950. He d. in 1973; Madrid; was buried in Arlington Cemetery. His first wife was 1) Peggy Wood; they were divorced and he married 2) Katherine Phelps. He and his second wife, Kitty, then chose to live there and there she is still living.

Children of Forrest and Peggy (Wood) Close:
(1) William Close, b. Oct. 1931; living in NY where he is a stockbroker. Md. Anne Purvis, divorced; had two sons, Forrest, b. 1963 and George, b. 1967. Married (2) Carolyn Brook, had one son, William, b. 1970 and a daughter, Carolyn, b. 1973.

Bill earned a BA at Princeton and holds a Masters in Business Administration from Harvard.

Child of Forrest and Katherine Phelps Close:
(1) Jonathan Close, b. CA 1945. Not married.

2. THOMAS MCELMURRAY CLOSE was b. Dec. 29, 1905 at Savannah, Ga. He md. Eliz. Richmond of Savannah on June 8, 1935. Tom received a BA degree from the Univ. of Ga. at the age of 20. He taught at the Univ. for a few years and then chose a business career in Savannah, working for Savannah Electric Power Co. for 40 years.

Children:
(1) Thomas McElmurray Close, Jr., b. Oct. 15, 1939, graduated from Sch. of Business Adminis., Univ of Ga. Is engaged in business in Savannah. Md. Katherine Corish; divorced. They had two sons: Bryan Frances Close, b. Apr., 1968 and J.B. Close, b. 1970 living with their mother in Lynchburg, Va.

(2) <u>Margaret Close</u>, b. Oct. 10, 1942, graduated from Wellesley; md. Hugh O'Neill McDevitt, M.D. Divorced, living in Palo Alto, Calif. Has three children: Eliz. Richmond McDevitt, b. 1964, Katherine O'Neill McDevitt, b. 1965 and Thomas McElmurray McDevitt, b. 1968.

3. <u>LESLIE PICKNEY CLOSE</u> was b. Mar. 21, 1908 at Savannah, Ga. He md. Clarabelle Bradshaw of Bradenton, Fla. Leslie attended Annapolis for three years receiving an honorable discharge in 1931 as a result of an ear injury. He was the owner of Close Construction Co. in Savannah, Ga. He d. Sept. 15, 1955 and buried in Bonaventure Cemetery, Savannah, Ga.

<u>Children</u>:
(1) <u>Alva Ann Close</u>, b. June 9, 1934, Sarasota, Fla. She received a B.A. degree from Randolph-Macon College for Women in 1956. For many years she has been an Editor with Knopf Publishing Co. in New York City. She has not married.

(2) <u>Mary Louis McElmurray Close</u>, b. Dec. 26, 1939, Charleston, S.C. Md. 1969 Phillip Carl Wrangle at Lake Charles, La.; living at Houston, Tex. where he is legal counsel in an oil exploration co. She earned a BA degree from the Univ. of Ga. and a Masters in Social Work from Tulane. They have children: Anderson Phillip Wrangle, b. Aug. 28, 1970, Houston, Tex.; and John McElmurray Wrangle, b. Oct. 14, 1975, Birmingham, Ala.

4. <u>MARIE WILKINS CLOSE</u>, b. Nov. 7, 1910 Savannah, Ga. Married Robert Frank McDowell of Madison, Ga. She died April 12, 1977, Atlanta, Ga. Buried at Monticello, Ga.

<u>Children</u>:
(1) <u>Robert Frank McDowell, Jr.</u>, b. 1940, is md., has three children, lives in Madison, Ga.
(2) <u>Louise McDowell</u>, b. 1941; md. Maxwell Sadler, lives in Doraville, near Atlanta, Ga. Has twin boys.
(3) <u>Michael F. McDowell</u>, b. 1950. Has never married.

THOMAS J. MCELMURRAY was one of the influential and honored citizens of Burke County, which was his home through life, and he was possessed of large and valuable landed interests in the county, including the fine homestead plantation, "Sunnyside", six miles south of the city of Waynesboro. On the plantation of his father, in Burke County, Mr. McElmurray was b. Mar. 1, 1841, being a s/o Minis H. and Emily (Leslie) McElmurray, both native of the State of S.C. He was reared to maturity in his home county and educated at Mercer Univ. in the city of Macon.

At the inception of the Civil War he manifested his intrinsic loyalty to the cause of the Confederacy by tendering his services as a soldier, first enlisting in a regiment of Ga. infantry, later being in the artillery branch of the service, and during the latter part of the great conflict was a member of the militia commanded by Joseph Brown.

After the War he continued his identification with the vocation to which he had been reared, residing on his plantation of "Sunnyside" until 1881, when he completed the erection of a beautiful home in the city of Waynesboro, where he passed the remainder of his life, his widow still remaining in this residence. Besides the home plantation he owned several other farms in the county, retaining all in his possession until his death, which occurred April 9, 1898. He was a man of fine intellectual and moral attributes, loyal and public-spirited as a citizen and successful in his business affairs. He was a staunch adherent of the Democratic party and was an influential factor in its affairs in the county. He served as Judge of the Burke County Ordinary Court, and was a member of the State Senate one term. He was a consistent member of the Methodist Episcopal Church South, of which his widow also was a devoted member; was identified with the Masonic Fraternity, having served repeatedly as master of his lodge, and was also a member of the United Confederate Veterans.

Mr. McElmurray was twice married. On March 5, 1861, he wedded Miss Louisa E. Barron, who d. Sept. 24, 1873, leaving four children, namely: Leslie, b. Feb. 22, 1862; Tommie, b. Nov. 5, 1863, and became the wife of Charles Gray; Judson Sapp, b. Aug. 17, 1866; and Minis Hunter, b. Mar. 30, 1868. All are residents of Waynesboro except Minis H., who resides in Harlem, Columbia County. In Oct., 1875, Mr. McElmurray was united in marriage to Miss Mary Chandler, who was b. in Burke County, Feb. 22, 1855, being a d/o William and Jane (Darling) Chandler, representatives of old and prominent families of Ga. In conclusion, is entered brief record concerning the nine children of the second marriage: Mary Louise, b. Feb. 27, 1877, is the wife of Forrest Close; Genevieve, b. Jul. 7, 1879, d. Oct. 7, 1880; Emily Jane, b. Aug. 22, 1883, d. Oct. 31, 1884; Edmund Burke, b. Feb. 9, 1885, d. Nov. 3, 1886; Sarah Annie, b. Dec. 19, 1887; Henry Grady and Evan Howell, twins, b. Jan. 30, 1890; Joseph Hamilton, b. Dec. 6, 1891; and Ruth Whitehead, b. Apr. 3, 1894. The younger children remained with their widowed mother, and the family, prominent in the social life of the community.[1]

---

[1] Cyc. of Georgia, Vol. II, pp. 668-669.

WILLIAM LESLIE MCELMURRAY was b. Feb. 22, 1862. He md. Clifford Gray (b. Jan. 31, 1872; d. June 29, 1964). She was the d/o Simeon A. Gray. They had six children:

Children:
1. Louise, b. Sept. 13, 1894; d. Dec. 9, 1901
2. Elizabeth, b. Nov. 29, 1896. She md. in the Edward Fulcher family but had no children. She is not well.
3. Mary Lovell, b. Sept. 3, 1898. She md. Claud B. Barrett. They had Clifford Ann Barrett. She d. Feb. 4, 1969. She md. Dawson Orme George, III. They have three grandchildren: A. Dawson Orme George, Jr. B. Claudia George Singletary, and C. William B. George. Mary Lowell passed away Sept. 13, 1980.
4. Clifford was b. Aug. 11, 1900. She md. Preston B. Lewis, Attorney at Waynesboro. They have two children: Clifford and P.B. Lewis, Jr. Clifford d. Jan. 27, 1946. P.B. Lewis, Jr. has several children. Clifford is the coach at the Univ. of Ga. girls. She is not married.
5. Emily was b. Sept. 13, 1904. She md. William M. McNeill, adopted and has one daughter who married Anthony R. Dees, Director of the Ga. Historical Society.
6. Alice was b. Oct. 15, 1906. She has been a fine teacher wherever she has taught. She has never married.

Mr. "Bill" McElmurray served in both parts of the General Assembly and was over the years a fine citizen.

HUGH BUCHANAN MCMASTER, M.D. was b. Feb. 13, 1856 at Winnsboro, S.C., the s/o Eliz. Fleming and H. B. McMaster. He was educated in the public schools at Winnsboro, and graduated from the Ky. School of Medicine (Louisville, Ky.) in 1886 and moved to Waynesboro, Ga. He was a general practitioner.

Some after he came to Waynesboro, he became one of the leading citizens. His affable manner and pleasing personality evidenced him to all who met him. He became one of the most prominent physicians in the city, as well as in this section of Ga.

He was a member of the Railway Surgeons, a member of the City Council, the Board of Education, State Med. Assn., a member of the Lester Chapter, No. 76, Royal Arch Masons, and prominent in all affairs pertaining to the best interests of his town and people.

In 1893 he md. Miss Rosa Moore, d/o Eliz. Sanderford and John W. Shultz Moore. She was a graduate of the Wesleyan Female College. He had bought the home of Dr. Burdell and had the house and premises renovated for his bride.

He was a man of fine physique, loving outdoor sports, especially horses, dogs and shooting ducks. But he knew very little of the field trial game until the first Ga. Trials in 1901. He started one of his shooting dogs, an old pointer, "Grady", and succeeded in placing him third in the stake. The editor of the American Field recalls a remark made by Dr. McMaster in his library the night after this stake had been run: "I will never be satisfied or quit the game until I have won this stake and the National Championship." As to how well he kept his word the field trials world knows. Who have ever owned a greater "quailet" than Caesar, Dot's daughter, Mary Tucker and Champion Whitestone II.[1] His name was known to every lover of the sport and to each and all he always was the same: a perfect gentleman, an honest competitor, and an impartial judge whose word was his bond.[2]

---
[1] County Whitestone, II won the champion trophy at Grand Junction, Tenn., Jan. 1908. This is the highest honor a dog can win on the field trials in the USA.

[2] C.D. Jordan, editor of the American Field, Sept. 19, 1908.

The editor further added: "While a great admirer of the class field trial dog, I don't think that Dr. McMaster was ever so fond of any of his dogs as his first winner, old "Grady". He often referred to old Grady. If there be any truth in the Indian legend of the happy hunting ground, hunting of the Great Beyond, old Grady is his companion there."[3]

The McMasters had three children: Misses Elizabeth, Rosa and Rachael. Dr. McMaster was a loving husband, a fond father and a most useful citizen. His death, at about 52 years old was keenly felt by those who knew him. In the summer of 1908 he was trying to retire from business, and go in search for health. But he died on Aug. 21, 1908. He provided his family well. The McMaster Drug Store was bought by Mr. Sidney Cox. County Whitestone II was sold to Joseph F. Hindis of Baltimore.

The funeral took place at the Methodist Church at 8:30 P.M. Sunday evening. Rev. J. H. Scruggs conducted the services. The Burke Light Infantry (of which he was the second Capt.), acted as honorary escort under the command of Lieut. E. B. Gresham.

---

[3] Ibid.

BALDWIN BUCKNER MILLER, M.D. was b. Oct. 31, 1798, the s/o Frances Mann and Richard Miller of King & Queen Co., Va. He moved to Ga. in 1823 as a young man, after studying medicine at the Univ. of Pa.[1]

Dr. Miller's father, Richard Miller, was in his late teens and served in the 8th & 12th Va. Regt. under Col. James Wood and in the company under Capt. Benjamin Casey.

The doctor's new home was with Mr. Bryant Daniels in the upper part of Burke whose home was near Farmer's Bridge on Briar Creek. Here he boarded until his marriage. He travelled first by horseback. Whether he went to the "big house" or the slave quarters, he was always the attentive and careful physician. Later horseback riding and the saddlebags were exchanged for a gig. The two-wheeled vehicle possessed a top and in the cold and rain of winter permitted of more comfortable traveling.

He md. _first_, Rosa Anderson (widow of John Morrison), the d/o Mary Holzendorf(Glenn County) and Elisha Anderson, Sr. They had two children: Frances Miller who md. Henry J. Schley, and Baldwin B. Miller, Jr., who md. Vannah Chew of Augusta. But she divorced him and md. Henry Landrum of Augusta. Both Frances M. Schley and B.B. Miller, Jr. are interred in Wharton, Texas.

On Oct. 9, 1851 Dr. B. B. Miller md. _second_, Cornelia Ellet Polhill (b. Jan. 30, 1834), the d/o Julia Guion and Rev. Joseph Polhill. They had seven children:
1. Lavinia C. Miller   b. Nov. 20, 1852
2. Joseph B. Miller   b. Jan. 26, 1855
3. John P. Miller   b. July 29, 1857

---

[1] Most probably Dr. Miller came to Burke County because Bynes and Greshams had come to this part of Georgia.

4. Ruth McHenry Miller   b. Dec. 2, 1859
5. Louisa Maria Miller   b. Feb. 4, 1864
6. Benjamin F. Miller   b. Aug. 17, 1867
7. Robert Lee Miller   b. Sept. 28, 1870

Dr. Miller was in his 53rd year when he married Cornelia Ellet Polhill. The wedding occurred at "Rose Hill", the Burke County home of the Polhills near Dye's Hill.

Dr. B. B. Miller all his life in Ga. prospered and he bought two or three hundred acres until he owned about 2600 acres. Later other plantations were purchased: In 1833 he bought a summer home at Mt. Enon in Richmond near the Richmond Baths.

Venturing into large scale farming never brought neglect to his medicine. Each place was in the care of an overseer and the doctor's rounds to his place were made to fit with his visits to patients.

He attended first at the Old Rocky Creek Baptist Church but later when his winter home was moved to the Piney Woods plantation in upper Burke he transferred to the Hopeful Baptist Church.

Dr. Miller was 63 years old when the Civil War began. His son-in-law, Henry J. Schley, organized a company, The Miller Volunteers, and was made Capt. Dr. Miller supplied the company.

Dr. Baldwin Buckner Miller d. Feb. 24, 1873. His will included Col. Jenks Jones, Judge John W. Carswell and Col. Edmund Byne Gresham. Judge John W. Carswell greatly helped the widow, Cornelia Polhill Miller, with the plantations until there were sons-in-law to take over the various plantations.

JULIA CARTER (MILLER), was b. Jul. 28, 1855, the d/o Angelina M. Carpenter and Edward J. Carter, M.D. in Waynesboro, Ga. Her father was a fine physician and also a well educated and brilliant man.

Julia Carter graduated from a private school, Mrs. Kate Davis' School in Waynesboro, and studied later at Mary Baldwin Seminary at Staunton, Va. She was an honor student in music and received her literary degree during the latter days of the Reconstruction Period.

On June 23, 1875 she md. Joseph Baldwin Miller (b. Jan. 26, 1855), the eldest s/o Cornelia Ellet Polhill and Baldwin Buckner Miller, M.D. The wedded couple had known tragedy. Julia's only brother, Brig.-Gen. John C. Carter, died in the Battle of Franklin, Tenn., Nov. 30, 1864). Both had lost their fathers (Dr. Carter in 1869 and Dr. Miller in 1873). Their joy when a son was born, Jan. 29, 1878, who brought first great hope, but lived only until July, 1878. Already Joseph Miller had grieved about his younger brother, (b. July 29, 1851), John Polhill Miller, and his death on Aug. 2, 1877. These two deaths brought Joseph to a low ebb and he died Aug. 25, 1879.

Mrs. Julia Carter Miller had had four years of devoted companionship but was a strong Christian woman and devoted herself to her close kinsfold, friends and her church. For more than three generations of a century she was a leader in civic, social and religious life of the community. A greater part of her life was devoted to the philanthropic work of the First Presbyterian Church. A most hospitable woman, she combined the graciousness of the old period of the South with the customs of the present day and that influence will last long after she has trod down life's last hill and reached its golden sunset.

Mrs. Miller d. Nov. 19, 1932 at the age of 77. Her funeral service was held on Monday morning at 11:00 in the First Presbyterian Church, with Rev. John Benson Sloan officiating at the church and at the graveside. Active pallbearers were Clarence C. Rowland, John T. Palmer, M. K. Tucker, Peyton M. Thompson, William C. Hillhouse, Sr. and William Walters. Interment in the "Old Cemetery" (now the Waynesboro Confederate Memorial), where under a profusion of late colorful field blossoms she was borne by those whose life had been enhanced by an intimate contact of her beautiful companionship.

She was survived by the following grandnieces and grandnephews: Mrs. J. Frank Rackley with whom she made her home; Mrs. William Bailey of Nashville, Tenn.; Mrs. Sydney McCathern of Saluda, N.C.; Mr. Oliver Reynolds of North Augusta, S.C.; Mr. Heman Perry Reynolds of Savannah, and Mr. Joseph Jones Reynolds, Jr. of Waynesboro, Ga.

JOSEPH BALDWIN MILLER, b. Jan. 26, 1855, d. Aug. 25, 1879 in his home. He was the youngest member of the Waynesboro Bar, a member of the Knights of Honor and the Royal Arcanam.

TRIBUTE OF RESPECT. Resolutions adopted by Sturges Council, Royal Arcanam in reference to the death of Joseph B. Miller, Esq.

When the Spring foliage is blighted by an untimely frost, we have set before as an affecting picture of the death of the young; and if, when contemplating such a picture, we had only the analogies of nature to instruct us, we might well deplore the death of the young as premature, and have no more hope for them than for the blighted foliage. But the Holy Scriptures and the principles of our cherished ORDER teach us that there is no such thing as premature death. God has given us existance that we may accomplish His purpose and prepare ourselves for the spirit world. When this destiny is fulfilled our discipline here is ended and we are removed from our early spheres.

These thoughts are suggested by the death of Bro. Joseph B. Miller, one of our youngest members, who in the vigor of early manhood is suddenly removed from our Council. And though we are saddened by what may be a premature death, who of us will refuse to say that the Supreme Regent in Heaven doeth all things well and wisely? Therefore, be it resolved -
  1st. That while we deplore the death of Bro. J. B. Miller, one of the charter members of Sturges Council, Royal Arcanam, we recognize in such affliction the hand of a living and merciful Father.
  2nd. That we will ever cherish the memory of our departed brother for his many virtues and for his devotion to our Order.
  3rd. That the Secretary be instructed to set apart a page in our minutes, on which he shall inscribe, in a fair hand, the name and date of death of Brother Miller.
  4th. That the Secretary be instructed to prepare a copy of this preamble and these resolutions for the family of Bro. Miller, and that the same be published in the public prints of Waynesboro.

Committee:
R. C. Neely
P. O. Johnston
L. Cohen
J. H. Roberts

Mrs. Miller was absent from home at the time of his death and did not reach here until Tuesday at 3 A.M. When Dr. B. B. Miller died, a few years since, he left four living sons in Georgia, as fine healthy looking boys as were to be found anywhere, of this number, three lay buried in the cold, cold earth. The funeral was more largely attended, than any here for years, showing the esteem in which the deceased, and his family are held.

This is the sixth one of our citizens in three months, all in the full enjoyment of vigorous youth, who has been suddenly summoned from our midst. Let not these constant reminders of the uncertainty of Life pass us unheeded, you or I may be the next to pass away.

ROBERT LEE MILLER, M.D. was b. Sept. 26, 1870, the s/o Cornelia Polhill and Dr. Baldwin Buckner Miller, at Hephzibah, Ga. He was the youngest of seven children.

He graduated at the Hephzibah H.S., and then went to Mercer Univ., where he was a member of the Kappa Alpha Fraternity. He received his M.D. from the Univ. of Medicine at Augusta, Ga. Later he did post-graduate at the N.Y. Polyclinic. He was a general practitioner, but was mainly interested in pediatrics work. He began his practice in Tennille, Ga. There he met Eliz. Dean Joyner (b. June 21, 1875) at Sandersville and md. her on Nov. 22, 1893. She was the d/o Mary J. Graybill and Virgil S. Joyner of Oconee, Ga.

They moved first to Hephzibah and at Tennille, but later moved to Waynesboro. Burke County was notorious for its epidemics of malaria fever. The medical profession seemed unable to completely conquer it and Dr. Miller pioneered in passmothian, a drug to combat malaria. He spent 28 years in Burke County. He d. on Mar. 30, 1936, having served humanity for 44 years.

They had no children. Mrs. Miller was a leader of the W.C.T.U. in Burke County and into wider areas. She was a member of the First Baptist Church. She outlived her husband by 41 years. She remained in her home on Jones Avenue for most of those years, but in a very few years she lived in the Bibb County Hospital. She d. on July 21, 1977 at the age of 102 years. She was interred in the Magnolia Cemetery in Waynesboro and now sleeps beside her husband. She left behind a small book, A Hundred-Year Old Lady Tells Her Story, Memoirs of Mrs. R. L. Miller (1977) 12 pages.

ELLIS W. MILLS - Although only since July, 1936, a resident of Waynesboro, Ellis W. Mills has become a prominent and popular figure in its life. His purpose in moving to the city was to establish himself in the undertaking business and the Mills Funeral Parlor is one of the most beautiful and best equipped in all this section of Ga.

Mr. Mills was b. Sept. 23; 1913, at Wadley, Ga., s/o Grady W. and Sally Lou (Newsom) Mills, his father being a merchant of that town. After being graduated from local public schools, he entered the Univ. of Ga., finishing a Bachelor of Science in the pre-medical course with the class of 1933. After some experience as an assistant to the Pitts Mortuary, at Macon, Ga., Mr. Mills went to the Gupton Jones School of Embalming, at Nashville, Tenn., from which he was graduated in 1934. He then became a funeral director with the Henson Funeral Home at Waycross, removing to Waynesboro and his own establishment in July, 1936. Pleasant in personality and genuinely interested in civic and social affairs, Mr. Mills has many friends in the community and is recognized as being one of its most progressive citizens. He is a member of the Rotary Club, and attends the First Baptist Church.

On Nov. 11, 1935, Ellis W. Mills married Myrtle Jenkins, a native of Burke County, Ga.[1]

---

[1] The Story of Georgia, p. 554

CHARLES T. MILNER, M.D. was b. Dec. 31, 1867. He first came to Waynesboro in the 1880's and was engaged as a druggist by the late Dr. A. G. Whitehead. Later he left to finish his medical training and returned with an M.D.: He established himself as one of Burke County's leading physicians. For some years he also operated a drugstore and found patronage.

He md. Kate Thomas (Green), d/o Nancy Cates and Jethro Thomas. She md. first, George A. Green who d. in 1885, and his widow md. Dr. Milner. They had one daughter who md. Mr. Blair in Greenville, S.C. The Blairs had no chilren. Dr. Milner d. on July 14, 1916. Dr. McPhail of the Presbyterian Church officiated. Dr. Milner was interred in the Waynesboro Magnolia Cemetery.

JOHN MILTON of Burke County, Revolutionary soldier and Georgia's first Secretary of State, came into prominence in 1777 when the first state government was established. The Assembly chose him as Sec. of State. He was true to his trust during the British invasion and occupation of Ga. When he could no longer function in office, he removed the great seal and the records and archives of the state to Charleston. When this city was endangered, he took them to Newborn, N.C.; the seat of the N.C. State government. And when the British were on the point of over running that state, he again removed them, this time to Baltimore, Md. Subsequent to cessation of the War, they were returned to Ga.[1] John Milton was elected Sec. of State again in 1781 and 1783 and over the years served 20 years in that position.[2]

---

[1] E.M. Coulter, Georgia - A Short History, p. 171; National Cyclopedia of American Biography, Vol. IV, p. 305.

[2] William H. Dumont, Some Early Residents of Burke County, Ga. (1969), p. 8.

He was one of three delegates from Burke in the State Constitutional Convention of 1798.[3] Subsequently he became a citizen of Jefferson County. That was natural because some of his land holdings were in that part of Burke which became Jefferson in 1796, and, as Sec. of State, his office was in Louisville, the new State Capitol. He died Oct. 19, 1817 at age 61.[4]

Two of his sons preceded him to the grave. Julius Caesar Milton, the youngest son, d. May 14, 1801.[5] Fabine Maximus Milton, d. Dec. 27, 1813 at age 22.[6] Another son, Homer Virgil Milton, was elected to the State Senate from Burke, 1807-08. Later he was a State Senator from Jefferson County, 1818, 1818 and 1819.[7] A biography of a grandson, John Milton, who was Civil War Gov. of Fla., appears in the National Cyclopaedia of American Biography, Vol. XI.

---

[3] Albert B. Saye (ed.), "Journal of the Georgia Constitutional Convention of 1798", Georgia Historical Quarterly, Vol. 36 (1952), pp. 350-393.
[4] Dumont, supra.
[5] Dumont, op.cit., p. 9.
[6] Ibid., p. 8.
[7] O.R. 1961/62, pp. 1044 and 1112.

WILLIAM ST. CLAIR MORRIS was b. in Savannah in 1812. He md. Susan Walker (1810-1873), d/o Bethiah Whitehead and Isaac Walker. Both, in Richmond County, was their home. He was a planter and in 1861 was past mid-life (age 49 years). Nonetheless, at the outbreak of the Civil War, he organized the Poythress Volunteers, and was elected Capt.

He was a genial, jovial gentleman, immensely popular, espeically with the young. But he was entirely lacking of knowledge of military tactics and made no effort to comprehend drills and Hardee's Tactics. Other, however, in the company, did understand tactics, and despite the Captains' defects, the company became a well-drilled and efficient company.

Captain Morris took his saddle horse, his umbrella, bathrobe, beaver hat and his blowing horn, along with him to Va. and when encamped at Yorktown, actually sent his boy, Tom, home to Ga. to bring four of his fox hounds. He boarded at a private home and amused himself with his dogs and games of poker with Col. Winston of N.C. and Gen. Magruder. He was a picturesque figure, dressed in his fine uniform and beaver hat, and his embrella in hand and his horn suspended at his shoulder and dangling at his side, as he walked about the lines at Yorktown.

On retreat from Yorktown he rode his horse at the front of the regiment as the troops floundered through the mud. At this late time, his co. had become Co. E, Inftry Battln., Cobb's Legion, Ga. Vols. The co. had been a part of Gen. B. Magruder's army on the Peninsular. Capt. Morris drew his co. up and made them a speech:

"Boys", said he, "I am too old for a soldier and I am going home. I formed you into a co. and brought you this far. I don't want to hear of any of you backing, but fight well. When you go into winter quarters, I will come back and take command of you."

This was the last they saw of the good old captain, and there were many moist eyes and sad heart as they bid him goodbye, while the booming of the cannon and the rattle of the picket line told them that there was reason to fight well. Capt. Morris never came back to take over his last command. He long retained the esteem and affection of his old company.[1]

When the Union Gen. David Tillson took charge of the Freedman's Bureau in Ga., Sept., 1865, he saw that it would be necessary for the freedmen to work and support themselves. Tillson had secured permission to designate civilians as Bureau agents wherever competence and fitness could be found under the assurance that justice would be done without reference to condition or color. At this point ex-Capt. Morris became once more on the scene, and spent a year or more helping the Bureau to normalize the work force for the good of the planters and the freedmen who were farm hands.

Morris d. in 1871 and his wife in 1873. Both rest in the cemetery of the Bath Presbyterian Church.

---

[1] A part of this sketch was written as a Historical Sketch for The True Citizen, Sept. 22, 1955, by Mrs. Anne Mackensie Humphrey.

ROBERT MADISON MURPHREE, was b. Oct. 21, 1859, the s/o Eliz. T. Jordan and Augustus W. Murphree. He md. Lou Dudley Crosland, d/o Wm. Crosland of Bennetsville, S.C.

For 45 years he was connected with the Burke County government in several official capacities: as Chairman of the County Commissioners for a number of years, as Foreman of the Grand Juries, and as a member of the Board of Education. He built the first brick school building in the county, and was responsible for the construction of the first free bridge across the Ogeechee River.

He was a member of the Methodist Church in Midville for 38 years. He was Chairman of the Board of Stewards. He was also selected for delegate to the District Conference and to attend the Gen. Conf. of the Methodist Church.

Surviving him were his widow, his brother Charles Murphree, and a sister, Mrs. Susan Murphree Sheppard, both of Midville. Mr. W. L. McElmurray of Waynesboro was a staunch friend of Mr. Murphree.

ROBERT A. MURPHY. The subject of this sketch is descended from one of the oldest families of Ga. His grandfather, Edmund Murphy, settled in Augusta before the Revolution, and at one time had the position of Indian Agent under King George's Government, but on the outbreak of the War he embraced the patriot cause and with gallantry as an officer in the Continental Army. His grandson, Robert A. Murphy, was b. in Burke County in 1833, received a thorough education at private schools, after which he decided to apply agricultural pursuits, in which he has always been engaged.

He entered into political life as a Democrat but did not become prominent in party politics until after the War, although he supported the Secession movement with enthusiasm. In 1862 he volunteered in Cobb's Legion of Cavalry and served with it in Va., participating in all the campaigns of Stewart's Div. of Hampton's Corps to which his command belonged until the downfall of the Confederacy.

After the surrender Mr. Murphy resumed planting. He also took an active part in politics, and in 1870 was nominated by the Democracy of Burke County for the Legislature and was elected by a decisive majority. Since taking his seat, he has performed his legislative duties with ability and diligence and has made one of the most useful members of the Lower House.

In 1856 he was md. to Miss Jones, a member of a prominent family of Burke County of Revolution fame, and which, like his own, had always been prominent and influential in the country.[1]

---
[1] A St. Clair-Abrams, Manual and Biographical Register - State of Georgia for 1871-2, Atlanta, 1872, p. 73.

ALVIN WILKINS NEELY, SR. was b. Apr. 12, 1887 the s/o Lillian Wilkins and Robert C. Neely, Sr. of Waynesboro, Ga. He studied in the Waynesboro schools and entered the University of Ga. where he graduated. Member of the S.A.E. fraternity. He was a loyal and generous alumnus of the Univ. He loved football and usually saw the big games in Athens or Atlanta.

In WW-I he went overseas with the famous Second Division, A.E.F., France, as 1st Lieut., 5th Machine Gun Battalion. From Sept. 1917 he fought through the War with this outfit, taking part in every movement of the battalion. He received a Croix de Guerre medal and a citation for distinguished service, he having brought in a wounded soldier back to safety. Alvin received no wounds, a remarkable feat. On June 6,7,8 in 1920, he attended the reunion in Atlanta, and returned greatly enthused over meeting with so many of his old comrades in arms.

Alvin Neely was the first Legion Commander of the Burke Legion Chapter. In 1931 later Roy Hargrove succeeded Alvin. That year Alvin headed the Red Cross Roll Call.

In 1920 he was Wallis Carswell's best man in the marriage of Mary Lee Davis and W. Carswell. In 1928 two additional duties fell to him. He was made President of the Burke County Chamber of Commerce, and Vice-Commander of the Ga. Dept. of Legion.

After his father's death in 1923, he took manage over his position of the plantations. He rightly moved into tobacco and beef cattle. In 1931 he was made President of the Waynesboro Bonded Warehouse. The same year he was added to the Waynesboro Board of Trustees which guides the schools through the administrators and teachers. Like his father he was interested in building up the County and Waynesboro schools. Alvin W. Neely was a real gentleman, and always willing to work to make Waynesboro and Burke County a better place to live.

At the age of 38 years he married in Apr. 1925, Julia Abbott, the d/o Mr. & Mrs. Wm. Wright Abbott of Louisville, Ga. They had one son, Alivin W. Neely, Jr., b. _____.

LILLIAN WILKINS NEELY, d/o Moselle Carswell and Maj. Wm. A. Wilkins, was b. Oct. 16, 1863, the second daughter of the Wilkins. The family moved to Waynesboro in 1871. She was educated under private tutors and a governess, except for the time spent at Mary Baldwin College at Staunton, Va.

On Apr. 28, 1886, at the age of 23, she md. Robert Caldwell Neely. She was a member of the Waynesboro Methodist. For some years she was the State Pres. of the Methodist Missionary Society. She was also a charter member of the Colonial Dames, DARS and the UDC, and served as Pres. of the American Legion Auxiliary and at one time filled the presidency of the Woman's Club.

Mrs. Neely was gifted with a soft charm which in social contact won the love of all who knew her well. At one time she owned a home in Asheville, N.C. and again maintained a home for two or three years in Augusta, Ga. Mr. R. L. Neely demised in 1923.

She d. on Dec. 4, 1930, and after a service at the Methodist Church, she was interred in the Magnolia Cemetery. Her two sisters, Mrs. Inez W. Jones and Mrs. Nina Wilkins Scudder and a brother, William A. Wilkins survived her. She left two sons, Alvin W. Neely and Robert Caldwell Neely, Jr., one daughter, Mozelle (Mrs. John R. Palmer) and seven grandchildren: Marion Phinizy Neely, Lillian Wilkins Neely, Robert Caldwell Neely, III, John R. Palmer, Jr., Robert Neely Palmer, Lillian Neely Palmer, and Moselle Carswell Palmer.

HORACE P. ODOM. A student center and a plaque unveiled during an impressive ceremony in May, 1970, on the campus of the South Ga. Tech. and Voc. School in Americus, Ga., honoring the memory of the late Horace P. Odom.

Mr. Odom was b. in Girard, a graduate of Waynesboro H.S., the former Waynesboro Jr. Col. and the Univ. of Ga. He d. in 1968, leaving his widow, his two sons, a brother, and two aunts, Mrs. M. V. Stephens and Mrs. Naomi Scott of Waynesboro, Ga.

Mr. Odom had devoted his life to young people. He first taught math and science to jr. and sr. high school students at Rocky Ford H.S. At Monroe, Ga. he was the Principal and later as the system Superintendent. Later he served as Dean of Students at the Ga. Southwestern Col., before he was appointed Dir. of the technical and vocational school at Americus.

Dr. James S. Peters, Chairman of the State Board of Educ., Dr. Jack Nix, State School Superintendent, and George W. Mulling, State Director of Voc. Educ. participated in the ceremony. Dr. Jack Nix praised the late Mr. Odom as a prime example of what a good administrator should be. "He was genuine, sincere, honest, kind, efficient and he was dedicated."

In Americus Mr. Odom was Chairman of the Board of Stewards in the Methodist Church, President of the Americus Kiwanis Club, Lieut. Gov. of the Fifth Kiwanis Div., and recipient of the coveted Silver Beaver Award. His record is recorded in Who's Who in the South and Southeast and Who's Who in American Education.[1]

1
The True Citizen, May 27, 1970.

JOYCE PITTMAN ODOM was b. in Miami, Fla,, Feb. 8, 1927, the d/o Caro Ellis Pittman (now deceased) and Warren William Pittman. She studied at the Henry Grady School of Journalism at the Univ. of Ga.

On May 24, 1947 she md. James Collins Odom. Their marriage was divorced in 1975 after 28 years. Their children are:
1. Caro Joyce Odom, b. Nov. 27, 1950. She md. Thomas Ernest Roberts of Sylvania, Ga.
2. Jill Ann Odom, b. Oct. 28, 1954.
3. James Collins Odom, Jr., b. Jan. 9, 1957. Now is md. to the former Catherine Sharkey of Savannah. They have a six month old, Oliver Faith Odom.

Joyce Pittman Odom was with The True Citizen approximately 16 years. She was also assistant state editor of The Augusta Chronicle for one year; director of the Burke County Training for two-and-a-half years; and now is Editor, Publisher and one-third owner of The Goose Creek Gazette (S.C.) She moved to Goose Creek in Aug., 1979.

She served four years on the Governor's Council of Disabilities. Gov. Carter first appointed her and was re-appointed by Gov. George R. Busbee. She was also a member and two-term Chairman of the Burke County Library Bd.

Joyce Odom could always find interesting matters for her able pen. If she took a stand for the right, she would open the issue and weigh judicially the two sides. To Burke Countians this able journalist was a loss to those who followed The True Citizen.

JAMES OGLETHORPE, an able portrait painter and schoolmaster arrived in Burke County before the Civil War. He may have adopted this name, but he is remembered by none other. One surmises that he must have been a good teacher, otherwise his lack of sobriety, at times, would probably made it impossible for him to continue teaching, his main source of income.

Only two references to him have been found. The first was in a biographical sketch of J. H. Daniel, Sr., b. in Burke and founder of a leading family in Millen.[1] As a young boy he went to school at the Hutchins school house, under Oglethorpe, which was situated in the 73rd militia district, between Midville and Millen, not far from "8½ Station" on the Central of Ga., R.R. (Macon to Savannah). W.N.H. Hutchins after 1861 belonged to the Vigilance Committee for internal security.

The second reference to Oglethorpe appeared in A Lost Arcadia by Walter A. Clark. Most probably Oglethorpe had found a more acceptable post in upper Burke or in Richmond County. He painted some portraits reproduced in that book.[2]

Two fine portraits, one of Seaborn H. Jones and his wife, Margaret (Walker) Jones, are owned by John J. Jones, attorney, living in Waynesboro. Since Seaborn H.

---

[1] Daniel's biography appeared in The Millen News, Oct. 5, 1905, and reprinted in the same paper, Sept. 29, 1955.

[2] See page _____.

died in 1859, these portraits would have been painted before 1859.[3]

---
[3] A portrait expert might compare the two Jones' portraits with those in *A Lost Arcadia* and might reach the opinion that they were, or not, by Oglethorpe.

JAMES H. OLIVER, JR., s/o Florence Fulcher (Heath) and James H. Oliver, Sr. is a native of Waynesboro, b. _____. Received his B.S. degree from Ga. Southern College (1952); M.S. degree, Florida State Univ. (1954) and his Ph.D. from the Univ. of Kansas (1962). He conducted post-doctoral work at the Univ. of Melbourne, Australia (1970). He joined the Ga. Southern College faculty in 1969.

Dr. Oliver has become a widely-known scientist and holds the chair of the Fuller E. Callaway Professor of Biology at Southern College. He has also branched into entomology. In 1976 he was invited to open and participate in tick research at Rhodes University's Tick Research Unit in Grahamstown, South Africa. His travels were financed from a grant of the South African Meat Board, and upon the invitation of Prof. Greaeme Whitehead, director of the Tick Research Unit. He also shared with the South African Unit his research and results of the work which he has done at Southern with various aspects of tick biology and tick cytotaxonomy. On the way back from South Africa he spent sometime in South America observing tick research.[1]

He married _____.

---
[1] "Burke Native to Observe Tick Research", *T.C.*, Dec. 8, 1976.

C. L. PAGENHART, was a machinist and a dreamer who settled in Waynesboro for a few years. He had one patent accepted for a railroad engine, so he naturally attempted to build a steam automobile.

Unfortunately, others in the U.S. were trying to make a good car. He believed that he could produce a steam wagon. By the pneumatic tire (1902) was on the market. Pagenhart had little help, also suffered from some illness. In 1902 he asked six Waynesboro men to put up for him a Waynesboro Automotive Steam Wagon shop down near the railroad. The shareholders were: Col. Phil P. Johnston, Dr. L. R. Ford, Dr. C. H. Cox, Capt. F. L. Scales, Hon. W. H. Davis, and W. H. Walters.

He had not completed his one machine, but he was already referring its name, "The Blue Falcon". There was a car which belonged to Sydney Jones, known as the "Red Devil".

On Mar. 7, 1903 the first automobile accident happened. Last Tuesday evening as two of the Waynesboro steam automobiles were out for a run, and were retiring to their respective houses, Pagenhart, accompanied by his two little daughters, occupied one of the machines and when near Judge Lawson's residence a wheel hit a mud hole with a jerk, knocking the steering rod out of his hand, and crashed into Mr. Sidney Jones' machine, just a short space ahead. The machine was captized, but the steam was shut off and fire put out by little Alma Pagenhart who had the presence of mind to know that those under the machine might be severely scalded or burned. And the strange part of the story was that no one was hurt. The automobiles were fixed within a very few days.

Mr. Pagenhart did not stay more than two years when other automobiles began to be bought in Waynesboro. He found a position in one of the railroad mechanic shops in the Carolinas.

HOWARD E. W. PALMER of Atlanta, Ga. has lead an active life, which is now at the beginning of its prime, with the promise of increasing usefulness. His ancestors on both sides came to Ga. from Va. and the Carolinas. His paternal grandfather was Edmund Palmer, a planter of Burke County, Ga., and his grandmother was Jane Allen of Richmond County, in the same state. Prof. James E. Palmer, his father, was educated at Emory College, Oxford, Ga. and graduated with distinction. After his graduation he established a boarding school at his home in Burke County known as Grove Mount, and which some called "Rugby". After conducting this school awhile Prof. Palmer was elected to fill the chair of Latin in Emory College, in which he displayed the abilities of a true educator until Dec., 1861, when his highly useful life was cut short by death, when he was only about 33 years of age. The mother of Judge Palmer was Mary M. Weaver of Greensboro, a descendant, in the paternal line from the Weavers and Daniels of N.C. Her connections, by blood and marriage, extended among the Mounger, Wingfield, Eve and Grimes families of Ga., forming a very wide and influential relationship. His mother is still in life and graces the home of her son as a member of his family. Judge Palmer was b. in Burke County, Ga., Oct. 19, 1854; but on the election of his father to the professor- ship of Latin in Emory College, the young family moved to Oxford, where the father died; and after the bereavement, Judge Palmer's boyhood was spent in Greensboro and Burke County, Ga. At Greensboro, when but a lad he learned the printer's trade in the office of the Greensboro "Herald". His education was secured in Emory College where he was graduated in the class of 1872, and afterward he taught school for two years. This was followed by his entering the law office of Judge P. B. Robinson as a law student, and his admission to the Bar in the Superior Court at Greensboro during the Sept. term, 1874, Judge George T. Bartlett being then the presiding judge. His first office and practice as a lawyer was in Greensboro, where he was admitted, and in 1876 he moved to Waynesboro, Ga., and in 1877 was appointed when only about 22 years of age to the office of judge of the county court of Burke County by Gov. Colquitt. After discharging the duties of this honorable position nearly a year, he resigned in order to form a law partnership with his uncle, by marriage, Judge S. A. Corker, under the firm name of Corker & Palmer. His course of life was changed a few years later when, in 1883, he accepted the voluntary tender to him, by Gov. McDaniel, of the position of Sec. of the Exec. Dept. and moved to Atlanta, where he was remained to this date. This important position was held for nearly five years, and terminated by his resignation and appointment as Ass't U. S. Dist. Attorney for the northern district of Ga., during the first administration of Pres. Cleveland. This office, however, he resigned after holding it about a year, to accept a responsible and new position as the southern manager of the Thomson-Houston Electric Co., which he held for several years. The electric business was then somewhat of a novelty, but Judge Palmer entered with his natural, enterprising spirit into the work, and to him is due the credit of a pioneer in establishing the electric system, which is now in such successful operation in Atlanta. The Edison Co. and the

Thomson-Houston Electric Co. afterward combined and formed the General Electric Co., which Judge Palmer represents in Atlanta as attorney. Having resigned the place of gen. mgr. to resume his profession, the firm of Palmer & Read was formed, and does a successful general practice. Judge Palmer, since his removal to Atlanta has been influentially interested in many business enterprises besides those above mentioned. He was among the earliest and most earnest advocates of the Cotton States and International Exposition. Without any solicitation on his part, he was unanimously elected to the position of Director-Gen., when this important work was organized, but unfortunately and unexpectedly, he was stricken with a serious and protracted illness--typhoid fever--which caused him to resign. He has, however, done very efficient work on several committees. Judge Palmer has been an active friend of general education and, in appreciate of that interest, he was elected the alumni trustee of his alma mater, Emory College. The present successful movement to endow a chair of history and political economy in that college, through the voluntary donations of alumni, was inspired by him, and he is practically at the head of the enterprise. Recently he was elected president of the Atlanta branch of the Alumni Assn., and may be relied on for intelligent activity in promoting the general interests of educ. as well as the particular welfare and his college. In his church relations he has confided to him the positions of superintendent of the Sunday School of the First Methodist Church South, in Atlanta, and is also chairman of the Board of Stewards. He has a delightful home in the suburbs of Atlanta. Early in life he md. Miss Emma Stone, d/o Prof. G. W. Stone, who for nearly 25 years, and to the date of his death, was prof. of math in Emory Col. Mrs. Palmer is the granddaughter of the distinguished and lovable Bishop Wm. Capers, who, as is well known, devoted his great life with singular consecration and eminent ability to the Christian ministry. She is as earnest in church work as her husband, and is constantly found in association with others in active benevolence. Judge Palmer, now just past 40 years of age, enjoys a fine physique and has strong vital force, which he employs in a great deal of hard work. He speaks forcibly, often eloquently. Cordial in manners, earnest in whatever he undertakes, with his equipment of natural abilities and educational attainments, he is destined to large success in life. In politics he is a democrat and always active in support of his party, but has never aspired to office.[1]

---
[1] Memoirs of Georgia, Vol. I (1895), pp. 887-888.

JAMES P. PALMER, M.D. s/o Anna Rheney and James Price Palmer, was b. in 1900 at Waynesboro, Ga.

Dr. Palmer, a gynecologist, served on the staff of Buffalo (N.Y.) General Hospital and Cleveland Hill Clinic in New York. He was a former associate clinical professor of gynecology at the former Univ. of Buffalo School of Med. He joined Roswell Park in 1941 as an associate cancer gynecologist and became head of the dept. in 1953, the position he held until retirement. Before retiring in 1959, because of illness, Dr. Palmer had served as head of Roswell Park Memorial Institute's Department of Gynecology for six years.

During WW-II he served as a Maj. with the 136th Station Hospital in England

Dr. Palmer was a member of the Buffalo Obstetrical Gynecological Society, the Erie County and N.Y. Med. Society and the Amer. Med. Assn., and an Elder of the First Presbyterian Church in East Aurora, N.Y. He d. July 18, 1971. On July 20 his service took place in the First Presbyterian Church of East Aurora and the burial in Oakwood Cemetery.

His survivors included his wife; three sons, James P. Palmer, Jr., New Shrewsbury, N.J., Sydney W. Palmer, East Aurora, and Robert W. Palmer, Buffalo, and two grandclindren.

Included among his survivors was Mrs. C. E. Johnson, Sr. of Waynesboro. Other relatives, all deceased, were his parents; sisters: Mrs. Henry Blount, Waynesboro and Mrs. Ebben Smith, Wrens, Ga.; brothers, Paul Palmer and Sydney W. Palmer, Waynesboro.

JESSE CAMPBELL PALMER, SR., s/o Ida W. Boyd and John T. Palmer was b. July 9, 1893. His father was b. Apr. 10, 1867 and d. at the early age of 28. His elder brother, John T. Palmer, was b. Apr. 7, 1892; his second brother, Ernest, was b. in 1895, d. 1906, at 11 years old; and a sister, Madeline, who lived but one month. His mother remarried, but his father's death made it necessary for him to work early.

He went to Waynesboro and established the City Pressing Club. After several years he entered Emory and sold the pressing business. But the very next year he bought back the business, and the pressing club became a partnership, Palmer and Farrar, with a new place under the Armory.

He joined the First National Bank of Waynesboro on June 5, 1912 as an Assistant Cashier and in 1914 was made Cashier. On Oct. 7, 1914, he md. Bessie Thomas (b. Feb. 22, 1893), the d/o Eula Redd and Jethro Beauregard Thomas. In addition to his bank job he began farming the land of his father-in-law and was a good farmer. In time he enlarged his ownership of land acreage.

He was County Tax Commissioner from 1916 to 1932. He has served as a Deacon in the First Baptist Church of Waynesboro. He is a member of the Rotary Club and a past pres. of the club.

He became a member of the Burke County Board of Commissioners during 16 years and was Chairman of the Board 13 out of the 16. He also was a member of the State Board of Education. On Jan. 17, 1930 he was elected President of the First National Bank of Waynesboro and Chairman of the Board of Directors. He also was later a member of the Burke County Hospital Authority and the County Library Board.

In 1924 he and his elder brother, John Turner ("Teddy") Palmer organized the Palmer Hardware Co., Inc. at the Vinson's Old Stand. The business prospered.

His wife, Bessie Thomas Palmer, d. June 28, 1956, and is interred in the Waynesboro Magnolia Cemetery. They had three children:
1. Carolyn Palmer was b. July 24, 1915; md. Wilkes Aiken Law, Jr., on June 11, 1934. They had four children:
    (a) Wilkes Aiken Law, III, b. Aug. 9, 1935, d. May 21, 1949 at age 13.
    (b) Palmer Law, b. Nov. 24, 1941, md. Donald Uppham Ellsworth. They had three children: Donald Uppham Ellsworth, Jr. b. Nov. 25, 1965; Wilkes Robert Ellsworth, b. Dec. 8, 1966; and Campbell Benson Elsworth, b. Dec. 6, 1970.

      (c) Carolyn Law, b. July 9, 1946, md. James Lee Day. They had two children: James Lee Day, II, b. June 7, 1970; Shelly Benson Day, b. Apr. 24, 1973.
      (d) Joseph Robert Law, b. Apr. 15, 1950. Md Carolyn Sapp. They had three children: Carolyn Paige Law, b. Sept. 29, 1971; Leslie Ann Law, b. June 5, 1975 and Joseph Robert Law, Jr., b. Mar. 23, 1977.

   Carolyn Palmer Law d. Mar. 19, 1969 and is interred in the Waynesboro Magnolia Cemetery.
2. Jesse Campbell Palmer, II, was b. Aug. 31, 1918. Md. Betty Fulcher Lewis, d/o Clifford McElmurray and Preston Brooks Lewis, Jr. They have two children:
   (a) Jesse Campbell Palmer, III, b. July 28, 1946. Md. Carol Marie Hughes. Two children by this marriage: Jesse Campbell Palmer, IV, b. Aug. 9, 1972, and Ashley Louise Palmer, b. June 4, 1976.
   (b) Betty Pamela Palmer, b. July 19, 1950. Md. John Emile Hummel, Jr. They have one child: Pamela Brooke Hummel, b. Nov. 8, 1978.
3. Jettie Thomas Palmer, b. Oct. 4, 1926. Md. Roy Crederic Owen, Jr. One child, Leigh Palmer Owen, who md. Alan Jackson. No children.

On Feb. 2, 1957, Jesse Campbell Palmer, Sr., md. Ruth McElmurray (Cothran), b. in Waynesboro, Apr. 3, 1894. She was a widow with grown sons and a daughter (in Atlanta). She lived until Oct. 23, 1971 and is interred in the Waynesboro Magnolia Cemetery.

In June, 1972, the First National Bank of Waynesboro observed his 60th anniversary with the bank (June 5, 1912 to June, 1972). Mr. Palmer's most recent service to the county and state was his Chairmanship of the local drive for the Richard Russell Memorial Fund.

On Mar. 15, 1973, the State Transportation Board (formerly the Highway Board) honored Jesse C. Palmer, Sr. for his service on the Board for a five-year term which began Apr. 15, 1968. On the Board he represented the First Congressional District from his home county of Burke.

JESSE CAMPBELL PALMER, JR., s/o Bessie Thomas and Jesse Campbell Palmer, Sr. was b. Aug. 31, 1918. Educated at the Waynesboro H.S. (graduated 1935) and Vanderbilt Univ., A.B. (June, 1939). Member Phi Delta Theta fraternity.

He served in WW-II. Entered Sept. 1941; graduated in Officers Candidate School, Ft. Bragg, N.C.; Field Artillery Ranger School, Camp Forrest, Tenn.; European Theater. Five campaign stars: Bronze Star with Oak Leaf Cluster. Discharged Dec. 25, 1945 with the rank of Captain.

Md. Betty Fulcher Lewis on Sept. 8, 1943, the d/o Clifford McElmurray and Preston Brooks Lewis, Jr.

He is a stockholder, a director and president of the First National Bank of Waynesboro, Ga. He also has diversified farming interests: Cattle, soybeans, peanuts and pecans. The plantation is 14 miles west of Waynesboro on Highway 80.

His church membership is with the First Baptist Church of Waynesboro; A former Chairman of the Board of Deacons.

He has served as President of the Waynesboro Rotary Club; former Pres. of the Waynesboro Development Corp.; member of the Burke County Hospital Authority; former member of the Central Savannah River Authority and of the Ga. Real Estate Board. For such a man, his recreation includes hunting, fishing and boating.

Children and Grandchildren:
1. Jesse Campbell Palmer, III, b. July 28, 1946. Md. Carol Marie Hughes b. June 19, 1948. Children by this marriage: Jesse Campbell Palmer, IV, b. Aug. 9, 1972 and Ashley Louise Palmer, b. June 4, 1976.
2. Betty Pamela Palmer, b. July 19, 1950. Md. John Emile Hummel, Jr., b. July 4, 1948. Children by this marriage: Pamela Brooke Hummel, b. Nov. 8, 1978.

JOHN TURNER PALMER, SR. b. April 7, 1892 in Telfair Community, Burke Co., Ga. Educated at Telfair School. Sgt. Batry "C" 118th Field Artillery 31st Div. A.E.F. Served in Mexican Border Conflict before WW-I. After WW-I, Jesse Campbell Palmer, brother, and John Turner Palmer bought Hardware store on Liberty St. from Gary Vinson (Vinson Hardware) in 1922 and Palmer Hardware Co., has been in continuous operation since then. Now being owned and operated by John Turner Palmer, Jr. and grandson John Turner Palmer, III. John Turner Palmer, Sr. was Deacon and Elder in Presbyterian Church U.S. and for 30 years Superintendent of Sunday School. She was Chairman of Draft Board during WW-II, Pres. of the Rotary Club, a Mason, instrumental in helping organize Amer. Legion Post 120 and in helping to raise funds for the Amer. Legion Home on Liberty Street. On Feb. 24, 1918, was md. to Maud Evelyn Long of Comer, Ga. He died on May 23, 1956.

Maud Evelyn Long, b. Dec. 6, 1887 in Madison County, Comer, Ga. Father, Thomas Wilson Long, was first cousin to Dr. Crawford W. Long, who discovered ether. Attended school in Comer, Ga. then graduated from Ga. Normal Institute in Milledgeville, Ga. Taught school in Madison County, later in Waynesboro Public School. Also, was a Clerk in Office of Burke County Tax Commissioner. She died on Mar. 2, 1936.

JOHN TURNER PALMER, JR. was b. Dec. 11, 1921, in Waynesboro, Burke County, Ga. Educated in Waynesboro Public School and attended Presbyterian College in Clinton, S.C. Was drafted into WW-II while a senior at P.C. While at P.C. he was initiated in the Pi Kappa Alpha Fraternity.

Received training in Air Corp as an Aerial Armament gunner assigned to a B 24 Four Engine Bomber group attached to 8th Air Force in England. Transferred to 15th Air Force, flew 22 missions over Northern Italy and Europe, and on Dec. 28, 1943 on 22nd mission was shot down. Spent 17 months a prisoner of Germans at Stalag 17B, Krems, Austria, liberated by Gen. Patton's Army May 3, 1945 in Austrian-Bavarian Alps.

Upon discharge from Air Corp became employed with father in Palmer Hardware Co. Became owner of store in 1961. Returned to Europe in 1977 and had the opportunity to go back to the site of Stalag 17B where he had been imprisoned. Needless to say, everything was changed. Recognized only the railroad station which was there when he was brought to the prison camp. Well received by the fine Austrian People in Krems, Austria, and was shown every consideration during his visit there.

Served as a Deacon and then an Elder in Waynesboro Presbyterian Church U.S. Now a member of Waynesboro Presbyterian Church of America. Charter member of Waynesboro Exchange Club serving as President, member of American Legion Post 120 and Veterans of Foreign Wars. Purchased Palmer Hardware building on Liberty St. in Aug., 1979, from the McElmurray Estate. Md. Mildred Ann Millis Aug. 14, 1945. Chairman of local school board, 1964-1970.

Mildred Ann Millis was b. July 17, 1920, fifth d/o Charles Gloston and Hattie Tomlinson Millis Thomasville, N.C. Received education in Thomasville Public Schools. Works with husband and son at Palmer Hardware Co., Inc. as bookkeeper, secretary and treasurer. Member of Waynesboro Presbyterian Church of America.

ATTON PEMBERTON, b. 1776 in England and d. in Burke County, Apr. 17, 1841, at 65 years.

"Emigrated to this country in his youth and consistently sustained his reputation of a just man, charitable in all his relations to his fellowmen; by his unswerving honesty he imprisoned the principle that an honest man's the noblest work of God".

He md. the widowed mother of James Madison Reynolds. All his property was left by will to two step-sons, Wm. Henry Reynolds and James Madison Reynolds, Jr.

EDWARD ALONZO PERKINS, M.D., s/o Francis Ann Scarborough and Dr. David Simpson Perkins, was b. in Burke County on Mar. 8, 1849. As was the case with many others of his age, his education was interrupted by the Civil War. He had the benefits only of a h.s. instruction, but, by diligent application, has acquired, since the War, an education that fits him well for his profession.

When Sherman made his famous march to the sea, through Ga., young Perkins was attending school at Whitesville, 30 miles above Savannah. He was cut off from home by the Fed. forces, and, though not 16 years of age, he made application to join the service, and was received as a member of Pruden's Battery of Artillery, from Milledgeville, serving with the same in the fortifications around Savannah, and subsequently made the march through S.C. to Augusta, where he was taken ill with typhoid fever and carried to his home.

After the War, Edward A. read medicine, and entered the Medical College of Augusta in Nov., 1868, graduating on the first day of March, 1870, seven days before he was 21 years of age; since which time he engaged in the practice of medicine in Burke County.

On the 29th of Sept., 1870, he was md. to Miss Julia E. Jackson, d/o Geo. L. Jackson, a prominent Baptist minister, of Burke County.

Dr. Perkins was a Democrat, as were his father and grandfather before him.

With the Hons. Samuel A. Corker and W. F. Walton he ran for the Legislature in 1876, and was elected by a very large majority. After the adoption of the New Constitution in 1877 he ran again, with the same ticket, and met with like success in 1879 and again in 1880.

He was personally popular for his courteous bearing and his sterling character. He d. July 27, 1893; she lived until 1922.[1]

---

[1] Samuel A. Echols, Biographical Sketches, Georgia Assembly of 1878, Atlanta, Ga. See also Donald E. Perkins, History of the Perkins Family of Perkins, Ga. (1979), pp. 92-93.

JOHN HARRELL PERKINS, was b. in Burke County on Dec. 17, 1849, the s/o Sarah F. Harrell and Brinson Leary Perkins. His grandfather emigrated from N. C. to Burke County in 1800.

He began farming for several years but in 1879 he engaged in the lumber business in Burke County. Over a 30-year period he became one of the prominent lumbermen in the State. He began with Perkins Manufacturing Co.; later identified with the Sylvania Lumber Co., Toy Lumber Co. in Effingham County, and in 1908 he became one of the chief promoters of the Savannah Valley R.R.

He was twice married: his first wife was Eliz. Anthony Ward (b. Mar. 5, 1854; d. Feb. 1, 1897), was the d/o Joannah H. and Dr. Thomas A. Ward of Burke County. His second wife was Emma Smith, d/o F. M. Smith of Tattnall County, Ga. From these marriages there were seven living children: Percy H., John H., Alma T., Sheppard E., Jr., Sallie Joe Pierpont, Vivian and W. C. Perkins.

He was a staunch adherent of the Democratic party, and represented Burke Co. in the Legislature of 1886 and 1887.

Mr. Perkins' life was one of steady and unflagging industry, combined with strictest integrity and conscientiousness. He was an industrialist who saw keenly the need for lumbering railroads, and manufacturing companies to serve the growth of towns and cities. He was also a patriot with profound convictions. He worked by his writings to build up and improve the educational system in the rural districts to make country life more attractive to boys and girls. He d. on Aug. 5, 1913 and was buried in the Brewton Cemetery at Hagan, Ga.[1]

---

[1] Excerpts from Donald E. Perkins, History of the Perkins Family of Perkins, Ga. (1979), pp. 67-70.

HEMAN HUMPHREYS PERRY was b. Apr. 13, 1835 in Burke County, the s/o Mary Fryer (a native of Burke County) and his father, Hardy Perry (born in Va.). Both of his grandfathers were Rev. War patriots.

He studied at Georgetown College in the Dist. of Columbia, graduated in 1857 at the Univ. of Va. He studied law in Waynesboro and was admitted to the Bar in 1861.

When the Burke Sharpshooters left for Va., Apr. 19, 1861, Perry was the first sergeant. By 1863 he had been promoted to Capt. and had moved up to brigade headquarters as Capt. and Ass't Adjutant-Gen. Subsequently Brig.-Gen. Sorrel requested that Perry be sent to the 3rd Brig. in A.P. Hill's 3rd Army Corp. This placed Perry at Appomattox. Perry was the officer who met under a truce with Gen. Seth Williams of Grant's Staff which was the first step to the Conf. surrender.

After the War was over, he went back to Waynesboro to practice law. In 186? he was made Judge of the Burke County Court and held his Judgeship until the County Court was abolished in 1902.

In 1868 he md. Miss Charlotte Eliz. Carter, d/o Angelina Carpenter and R. Edward J. Carter. At H. H. Perry's death, he left one daughter, Miss Angie Reynolds, wife of Mr. Joseph P. Reynolds, and several grandchildren: Misses Charlotte and Barbara, and Masters Joseph, Herman and Oliver.

He was a member of the 1877 Constitution Convention and was made a State Senator (1878-79). Later he was one of the Committee appointed by the Gov. to assist in the unveiling of the Ga. Monument at Chickamauga, and his name appears on the monument.

Judge Perry was a very versatile man, even beyond his patriotism--and his soldiers' feats during many battles in Northern Va. He was a lawyer, jurist, poet, artist, violinist, and newspaper editorial writer. His beautiful paintings were true to nature in their minuetly details, and the exquisite notes of his violin only express the deeper thought and feeling of a brave, tender, classic and poetic soul. During 15 years he was editor-in-chief of The True Citizen. He died Feb. 14, 1908 and is interred in the Old Cemetery (the Waynesboro Confederate Memorial Cemetery).

RODERIC PETTIGREW, a native of Waynesboro and the grandson of the late Mr. & Mrs. Edward Phinazee of Waynesboro, has been admitted to the Univ. of Miami School of Medicine with a status that carries exemption from the first and second years. Dr. Pettigrew was one of 28 finalists chosen from a field of 600 national and international candidates for the program.

Dr. Pettigrew is the nephew of Mr. & Mrs. A. K. Phinazee, owners of Phinazee Funeral Home in Waynesboro. His mother, the former Miss Edwina Phinazee, was a teacher in the Burke County School System for several years. His father is Dr. C. W. Pettigrew, president of Ft. Valley State College.

Pettigrew's selection resulted from his high level of performance at the Mass. Institute of Techn. where he was recently awarded the Ph.D. degree in nuclear engineering with a concentration in applied radiation physics. His work there centered on a new adaptation of two irradiation theories made applicable to a more finely tuned method of excising cancerous tissues.

The fast paced and innovative plan of Miami is programmed so that inductees must do in 24 months what the traditional medical course requires 48 months to do.

Dr. Pettigrew holds the Master of Science degree in nuclear physics from Rensselaer Polytech. Institute in Troy, N.Y., and the B.S. degree in physics from Morehouse College. He is a Merrill Scholar, and Atomic Energy Commission fellow, a winner in international science fair competition and has been cited by the U. S. Air Force for his work in nuclear missiles and areodynamics. He has completed special post graduate studies at Columbia Univ. and the University of Vienna, Austria. [1]

---

[1] T.C., Nov. 16, 1977.

LOUIS PINTCHUCK, was a native of Rome, Ga. He was a graduate of the Univ. of Ga. at Athens and a veteran of W.W.-I. For many years he lived in Waynesboro and operated a department store prior to his retirement.

Rabbi Norman Goldberg knew Pintchuck. He saw a very special kind of person--outgoing, exhuberant, friendly, open-hearted and open-handed, generous. Louis and the Rabbi would often go to the Rotary together and he caught some of the enthusiasm which he imparted. It was translated into hard work and good deeds for the Club and for the community. Deservedly, he was a highly respected citizen of Waynesboro. The good and welfare of the community was close to his heart. He was an indefatigable and enthusiastic worker.

He was never one to say "no" to projects designed for the betterment and improvement of life. And, he had that wonderful capacity of transmitting the enthusiasm. When he closed his store in Waynesboro, it was a sorrowful event for myriad friends and customers, who had been with him through the years. It was like the end of an era.

The Rotary slogan is "Service above Self"--and Louis Pintchuck might have written it for it is a terse but accurate reflection of his philosophy of life. We shall miss him, indeed.

Pintchuck d. on Dec. 24, 1976. The funeral services were held on Monday, Dec. 27, at the Bon Air Retirement Club. He was interred at Westover Memorial Park Cemetery in Augusta.

Survivors include a son, Louis Pintchuck, Jr., Indianapolis, Ind.; two daughters, Mrs. Terry L. Green, Atlanta, and Mrs. Hariett P. Goldberg, Indianapolis; and one sister, Rose P. Goldberg, Indianapolis.

THOMAS POLHILL, the s/o Hannah Barksdale (Miller) and Nathaniel Polhill, II, was b. Jan. 12, 1760 in Chatham County, Ga. He held the following public offices: Warden, Savannah, Apr. 29, 1788; lumber master, Savannah, May 28, 1789; Comm'r. Effingham County, Feb. 21, 1796; Senate, Effingham Co., 1797, 1798, 1800, 1802-03; Constitutional Awarding Convention, 1795; Constitutional Convention, 1798; Justice Inferior Court, Apr. 11, 1798, Feb. 14, 1799, Nov. 25, 1800 and Nov. 3, 1813. On Dec. 23, 1794, he was Capt. of a Battery Co, Effingham County.[1] He had two sisters and one brother.

He md. first June 13, 1782, Rachel Patton (d. Mar. 29, 1783); second md. Jan. 18, 1785 Mary Anderson (b. May, 1769, d. Jan. 10, 1804); third med. Rebecca Hamilton, July 19, 1809.

In 1789, listening to the preaching of a black man in Burke County, he was converted and was baptized at Black Swamp by Rev. Alexander Scott, his step-father. Nearly two years following the death of Mary Anderson, the mother of his eight children, he was ordained a minister (Dec. 9, 1805). He became a Baptist minister late in life; his ministry covered only some nine years. He was known as Rev. Thomas Polhill, but also "Major" Polhill.

He authored a treatise on baptism entitled, A Reply to, A Vindication of the Right of Infants, to the Ordinance of Baptism by the Rev. James Russell, M.M.E.C. It was published in 1812. In the controversy with the Methodist minister, Rev. Polhill displayed a sound mind and respectable talents.

He was a delegate from the Savannah Church to the first Baptist Convention of Ga., held at Powelton in 1803; a member of the committee to establish a Baptist College, and sec. of the Board of Trustees of Mt. Enon Col.

His father was a preacher in Mr. Whitfield's, probably at the Orphan Home. But having embarked for England from Episcopal ordination, the ship was swallowed up in the Charleston harbor by a violent whirlwind.

Children:
1. Thomas Polhill, II, b. Mar. 17, 1783 in Savannah, Ga. His mother was Rachel Patton. His next wife, Mary Anderson, bore eight children:
2. Nathaniel Polhill, IV, b. Jan. 25, 1787 in Newington, Ga.
3. Hannah Polhill, b. Jan. 8, 1789 in Savannah.
4. James Polhill, b. June 14, 1791 in Effingham, Co.(He became a judge of a Superior Court).
5. John Goldwire Polhill, b. Oct. 16, 1793 at Newington, Ga. (He also became a judge of a Superior Court). Md. a niece of Pres. Zachary Taylor.
6. Benj. Polhill, b. Mar. 1796, d. July 26, 1800.
7. Joseph Polhill, b. Apr. 2, 1798 in Effingtham, Ga.
8. Rachel Eliz. Polhill, b. Jan. 7, 1801.
9. Mary Ann Polhill, b. May 17, 1803.
10. Rebecca Dixon Polhill, b. Dec. 4, 1810, d. 1812.
11. Sarah Eliz. Polhill, b. Feb. 22, 1813, d. 1816.

---

[1] Refer to a book by A. M. Hillhouse, The Miller, Polhill and Other Families, 1936, pp. 57-58.

REV. JOSEPH POLHILL, s/o Mary Anderson and Thomas Polhill, was b. Apr. 2, 1798 in Effingham County, Ga. Md. Julia Jemima Guion (b. Feb. 19, 1799), in the year 1819. She was a descendant of Louis Guion of LaRochelle, France, a Huguenot, who four years before the Revocation of the Edict of Nantes (oct. 22, 1685), fled with his family to England. From there they emigrated in 1687 and settled in New Rochelle, N.Y. Julia was the d/o Jemima Hackett and Frederic Guion. Joseph met Julia Guion in Savannah when she was teaching school there. Their life together was spent in Burke County.

Joseph Polhill was trained as a Baptist minister and was ordained Nov 3rd and was his life-time work. Warren Grice once wrote in The Christian Index that Rev. Joseph P. was "of high standing and great usefulness." His pastorates were all within the Hephzebah Baptist Assn. area. For 19 years he was the Clerk of the Assn. and was its Moderator at the time of his death. He kept, over his active years, a memorandum book which recorded all the Baptisms, his assistance in the constitution of new churches; the ordination of ministers and Deacons, and the number of marriage ceremonies.

A letter on parental obligations, written by him, was sent out to all of the churches in Hephzibah Baptist Assn., and was published in the Minutes (1853). "A New Church Formed" was printed in The Christian Index in 1832 and reprinted a second time in The Index. A picture of Rev. Polhill appeared in The Christian Index (Dec. 25, 1920).

The family had a plantation, inherited from his father, and this was their home all the years. The house now is gone and the small cemetery is near by. Rev. Joseph died on Dec. 2, 1858 and Julia J. on Jan. 23, 1863.
Children:
1. John G. Polhill, b. July 30, 1820 md. first May 28, 1848 Susan M. Sharp (d. Mar. 8, 1873); second, June, 1874, Sallie V. Moore. He opened a school in Jeff. Co. and taught there 1840 and 1841. In 1844, graduated from the Med. Col. of Ga., and after practicing medicine for many years, he was ordained in 1869.
2. Cornelia Ellet Polhill, b. Jan. 30, 1834; md. Dr. B. B. Miller, d. June 6, 1922.[1]
3. Josephine R. Polhill md. Joseph Smith.
4. Augustas Polhill of Jeff. Co. md. Mary Williams.
5. Julia J. Polhill md. Nov. 22, 1855, Rev. James M. Cross[2], b. Sept. 9, 1854.
6. Louisa Polhill md. F. J. Holcombe.

---
[1] See the sketch of Dr. Baldwin B. Miller in this book for her husband and children. A picture of her is in Austin Croch, Memorials of the Baptist Hall of Fame, 1913-1923, p. 192.

[2] See History of the Baptist Denomination in Georgia (1881). The Christian Index, pp. 159-160 for an account of his life.

JOHN POWELL, was elected in 1788 to represent Burke County in the State House of Representatives and again in 1789.[1] He was chosen Speaker of the House for 1789.[2] Over its long history Burke has provided only three Speakers of the House: John Jones in 1781; John Powell in 1789; and Abraham Jackson for five terms, 1802-1806.[3] Powell was also chosen, together with Edward Telfair and George Walton (who did not live in Burke), to represent Burke in a Constitutional Convention by the Governor to take under consideration the changes in the State Constitution which would be necessary upon ratification by some states of the Fed. Constitution.[4]

---

[1] Official Register 1961/62, p. 1220; The Georgia State Gazette or Independent Register, Dec. 29, 1787 and Dec. 6, 1788.

[2] Official Register 1961/62, p. 1195.

[3] Ibid.

[4] The Augusta Chronicle and Gazette of the State, Apr. 18, 1789.

WILLIAM HENRY POWELL was b. Feb. 10, 1895, s/o Moselle Griffin and Henry Cater Powell, near Girard in Burke County. He graduated at the Girard H.S.. On _____ he married Lillian Lewis, d/o Lillian Fulcher and Preston Brooks Lewis, Sr.

"Will" Powell was an engineer with Stone & Webster (Engineering Co.) for many years on contracts in Fla., Kansas, Mich. and Va. He returned to Ga. soon after the 1930 depression set in. He worked with the WPA Program and then joined the Ga. State Health Dept. as a sanitarian for Burke, Jenkins and Screven counties. At age 70 years he retired in 1965. He was a Mason.

He was a very interesting man. His hobbies had long been the Savannah River, and the river's lakes. When he was growing up he also stored a lot of lore about interesting pilots, the different Savannah River boats and their cargoes and landing stations. He loved fishing, gardening (both flower, and vegetables), birds and Nature in general. After his retirement he did more writing about his lore but it was not published. He used his writings as material because he was often invited to talk about the Savannah River and on many other interesting Nature subjects.

They had two sons, William Henry Powell, Jr. and Ralph Lewis Powell. The elder son was in WW-II, had md. Frances McNair, and had one son, Wm. Henry Powell, The elder son and his 14-year-old son lost their lives in the crash of an Eastern Airlines flight in the Atlantic Ocean approximately six miles off shore from Jamaica, N.Y. in the evening of Feb. 8, 1965. This was a great blow to the Powell-Lewis families. Wm. Henry Powell, Sr. lived until Mar. 4, 1971. He is interred in the Magnolia Cemetery beside his elder son and their young grandson.

JOHN CARTER POYTHRESS, the s/o Hetty Carter (the d/o Alexander Carter, Esq.) and Maj. Geo. Poythress of Va. Maj. Poythress md. a second time, so that John C. had a half-sister, Mary Eliz. Poythress. She md. Addison Mondell. Their son was Geo. A. Mandell, h/o Mrs. Mary E. Mandell. John C. md. a Miss Morris, a sister of Wm. S. C. Morris.

In his will, Will Bk A, 207-209, John C. excluded his nephew Geo. A., and left his property to his wife's niece, Maria B.M. McIntosh (the d/o Wm. S.C. Morris), and to his nephew's wife, Mrs. Mary E. Mandell and her daughter, Annie R. Mandell (Munnerlyn). In the settlement of John C's large estate, the historic Carter-Poythress House, with all its fine silver and furniture, passed into the hands of Mrs. Mandell and ultimately to Mrs. Munnerlyn. Thus, the house for decades became known as the Munnerlyn House.

Poythress was a pillar of the Bath-Waynesboro Presbyterian Church. He was a generous man. The Poythress Volunteers that went early to the War was named for him. He died Sept. 12, 1862, so never lived to know the defeat of the Confederacy.

JAMES LAWRENCE PUGH, a Representative and a Senator from Ala.; b. in Burke County, Ga., Dec. 12, 1820; moved with his parents to Ala. in 1824; pursued an academic course in Ala. and Ga.; studied law; was admitted to the Bar in 1841 and commenced practice in Eufaula, Ala.; also engaged in agricultural pursuits; Democratic presidential election in 1848, 1856, and 1876; elected to the 96th Congress and served from Mar. 4, 1859 to Jan. 21, 1861, when he withdrew; during the Civil War joined to Eufaula Rifles, First Ala. Regiment as a private; elected to the Confed. Congress in 1861 and re-elected in 1863; after the War resumed the practice of law. President of the Democratic State Convention in 1874; member of the convention that framed the State Constitution in 1875; presidential elector on the Democratic ticket of Tilden and Hendricks in 1876; elected as a Democrat to the U. S. Senate to fill the vacancy caused by the death of Geo. S. Houston; re-elected, and served from Nov. 24, 1880, to Mar. 3, 1897; was not a candidate for re-election; retired from active business and resided in Washington, D.C. until his death there on Mar. 9, 1907; interment in the Fairview Cemetery, Eufaula, Barbour County, Ala.[1]

---

[1] Biographical Directory of the American Congress (1774-1949), pp. 1707-08.

ELLA MARY RAINWATER has for 20 years run the Anthony Wayne Hotel in Waynesboro. Prior to the Arlington Hotel, owned by Mrs. Inez Wilkins Jones, this was the best hotel. About 1925 Mrs. Jones sold the whole block to Mr. Enon Chance, the largest real estate transaction ever in the city. The hotel was rebuilt and the hotel became the Anthony Wayne Hotel. The hotel had 35 rentable rooms and a fine lobby and dining room.

At the grand opening Mayor Frank Palmer praised Mr. Chance richly:

'One more step in Waynesboro's march of progress is evidenced by the opening of the beautiful Anthony Wayne Hotel. No town in Ga. twice or triple the size of Waynesboro can boast of a finer or more modern hostelry... It is the town's best advertisement and outstanding asset and the pride of us all.

Today the hotel is a quiet glimpse of the past, where not much seems to have changed in many years.

Mrs. Rainwater has been running the hotel for 20 years. Since the death of her husband, Ivan Rainwater, nine years ago, the full responsibility has been hers alone. The dining room where breakfast and lunch time has served daily has been known for its good food. It is the favorite meeting and eating place in Waynesboro. It becomes on Sunday a large reception after church. Before Sunday all persons must have had reservations in advance. She knows her business and is well beloved.

Mrs. Rainwater was b. in Tennille, Ga., the d/o Susie E. Mann and Clarence G. Peacock. Ella Mary Peacock md. Ivey Vason Rainwater on Nov. 20, 1912 Mr. Rainwater was the s/o Letitia Williams and Joseph Henry Rainwater. Ivey was b. Aug. 11, 1889 and d. Oct. 14, 1971. He is interred in the Zeta Cemetery, Tennille, Ga.

Children and Grandchildren:
1. Ivey Vason Rainwater, Jr. was b. Oct. 21, 1913. Md. Frances Boutchard on Sept. 18, 1938. He d. Sept. 12, 1967.
2. Mrs. Rainwater from the marriage by her son, has seven grandchildren: Mary Frances; Ivey Vason, III; Peggy Ann; James Donald; William Bruce; Dianne; and Joseph Henry Rainwater.

KATE THOMAS (WILKINS)(DOWELL)(RAUERS), d/o Ruth M. Miller and Charles Henry Thomas, was born Jan. 14, 1883 at Waynesboro, Ga. She graduated at the Hepzebah H.S., then studied at Monroe College.

At age 19 she md. first, Maj. Wm. A. Wilkins, the leading merchant in Burke County. He was retired after his first wife died (June 16, 1898). He was b. in Liberty Co., Ga.; he studied law and practiced in Louisville, Ga. but he shifted to business and was highly successful. He was civic-minded, highly intelligent, cosmopolitan, and a very generous man. He was 65 yrs. when they md. Her mother did not approve of Kate's marriage because of the wide difference in ages. The wedding was at the Thomas home and only the two families were invited.

She was a beautiful young lady and moved into the new Wilkins home. He had wooed her on his 94-foot steam yacht, under chaperon (usually Dr. & Mrs. R. L. Miller), and made a longer trip by liner to European countries after married. The Maj. also had one of the first automobiles in Augusta or Waynesboro. He d. Feb. 14, 1907 at age 71 years.

She was a widow for some four years. The Maj. had provided for his grown children. If his second wife remarried, she would lose the home, but his will provided that she would receive a fixed amout every year, which was charged against land owned by the Neelys. But for four years she enjoyed the new home, and her automobile was a great delight.

On a boat trip with Mrs. R. L. Miller (her aunt by marriage) they went to Cuba. As they were leaving, a U.S. Lieut. saw her on the railing of the liner, but he was on the dock. However, he learned of her address (probably from the hotel), and he began corresponding with her. After some months he invited her to come to Ft. Russell, Wyoming, where he was stationed. Again Mrs. R. L. Miller was the chaperon; they took the trip and the couple became engaged.

On April 14, 1910, they were married at the Waynesboro Baptist Church. The maid of honor was Miss Bessie Wilson and the best man was Lieut. Delbert Reordan.

The couple lived several years at Ft. Russell. Here their only child was born, Cassius McClellan Dowell, Jr., on Jan. 24, 1914. His father was sent to the Mexican border where there were skirmishes with the Mexican forces of Gen. V. Huerta. Soon thereafter the Dowells were transferred to Washington, D.C., where he studied and received a law degree from Ga. Washington Univ. When the USA entered the WW-I, Capt. Dowell was sent overseas. He served in combat in France and received the Purple Heart and the Distinguished Service Medal. Upon his return from the War he attended the War College in Washington, D.C. Maj. Dowell was then transferred to Ft. Leavenworth as an instructor at the Command and General Staff School. After four years at Leavenworth the Dowells were stationed at Ft. Sam Houston in San Antonio, Tx. They were then transferred to Berkeley where Col. Dowell was Assoc. Prof. of Military Service and Tactics at the Univ. of Calif. In 1929 the marriage ended in divorce.

Kate Dowell returned to Ga. briefly before moving to the South of France where she md. James McHenry Rauers in 1930. He was b. in Savannah in Nov. 21, 1885, and she was a lifelong friend of the brothers and sisters of the Rauers' family.[1] They returned to the U. S. in 1933 and lived in Monterey, CA, before moving to Santa Barbara, where he died in May, 1948.

Kate Rauers lived subsequently in Riverside, CA, Raguna CA, and Oakland, CA. Cassius, Jr., did his college work at the Univ. of Cal. at Berkeley. She d. on Jan. 8, 1965 and is buried next to Mr. Rauers in the Bonaventure Cemetery in Savannah, Ga.

Harry Rauers had a beneficiary trust fund established by the estate of Joanna Mc D. Rauers at the Savannah Trust Co. There were two sisters and a brother, Donald. The family names in Savannah that are closely related are Oemler and Rauers.

---

[1] In WW-I Rauers was a Naval veteran. He was the youngest of the late Mr. & Mrs. Jacob Rauers.

JOSEPH JONES REYNOLDS, JR. was b. Feb. 6, 1893, the s/o Joe J. Reynolds and Angie Carter Perry, and grandson of Judge Heman H. Perry. He had two sisters, Charlotte and Barbara. Charlotte md. first Sydney McCathern. They had one daughter, Marcia. After Sydney's death Charlotte remarried David M. Garvin of St. George, S.C. after Garvin's death, the family moved to Lakeland, Fla. Barbara md. J. Frank Rackley and they had one son, J. Frank Rackley, Jr.

Joseph Jones Reynolds, Jr. attended public school in Waynesboro and in 1908 attended Bingham Military Academy at Asheville, N.C. (a prep school); attended also the prep school to Ga. Tech. in Atlanta. He also transferred to The Citadel in Charleston, S.C.

Joseph began work as helper at the Southern Cotton Oil Co. in Waynesboro for two years. He moved to The Citizens Bank and was employed as a Teller and Ass't Cashier and was advanced to an Auditor in the Bankers Trust Co. of Atlanta. The fiscal agent of the Witham Chain of Banks which included The Citizens Bank of Waynesboro. Later he was returned to the Citizens Bank as Cashier. Aleck Murphey, was called to duty with "E" Co., and the Waynesboro Co. went to the Mexican border. Joe remained with the Bank until joining The Naval Reserve, serving as Paymaster. At the end of the Mexican problems he returned to Waynesboro as an accountant for R.C. Neely Co.

In 1920 Reynolds organized the Planter Warehouse Co., the warehouses were at the S & A Railroad. Mr. E. E. Chance was Pres. until his death. Reynolds managed the company during the time of organization, until moving up to the time when Mr. Chance died. In 1958 he retired at the age of 65.

Mr. C. W. Skinner, Sr. and Charles W. Skinner, Jr. both had stock in the Warehouse and were loyal supporters.

Joseph J. Reynolds, Jr. was given in 1936 the Chairman of the Burke County Board of Education by the County Grand Jury. For the past 27 years, he carefully attended the monthly board meetings in the cramped little room beneath the courthouse stairs. There he presided with ease and concern for the best interest of the county's complex educational system.

His interest and concern for the education of the children of Burke County did not dimish although the last of his own children had graduated from the local school system some years ago.

His years of service were marked with his unusual ability to deal fairly with everyone and solve problems which sometimes took on proportions of magnitude.

Mr. Reynolds, whose family has been associated for generations with Burke County's cultural and educational life, served as his forefathers. His service was marked with fairness, understanding, patience, and wisdom. His incredible range of knowledge was put to use in settling problems that ran the gamut from curriculum to what kind of paint lasted longer on a classroom wall.

Mr. Reynolds was unfailingly courteous. His sense of humor and detached personality saved many a situation from becoming involved and firey.

As chairman, he took great care to see that petitioners really understood why they were denied their request, if it was impossible to accommodate them and although the meetings were necessarily long, he never watched the clock.

An astute businessman, Mr. Reynolds used the county funds to good advantage and made the limited amount stretch to include all school systems. His impartial concern for all the schools was uppermost, when decisions were made.

Mr. Reynolds leaves a big gap to be filled by his successor. His 27 years of service is studded with progress and growth.

We join people all over Burke County in saluting Mr. Reynolds for his unselfish service to the people.

Joe Reynolds ia a man who has lived with sports and hobbies all his life. Hunting dogs and horses were his most beloved sport. He also played golf, tennis and boating. He held an office of the Waynesboro Country Club for about 60 years and was also active for 50 years in the Ga. Field Trial Assn., serving as Sec. He was also a Director of the First National Bank of Waynesboro, retiring at age 84.

He also kept his beautiful ground around his house and became a good wood-worker, including reproductions of old furniture and remodeling rooms in his home by paneling one room of lumber found in the old Munnerly House where George Washington slept.

His courtesies extended to those who came down from the North. Reynolds came to know many of the Pittsburg men who came down to enjoy the Ga. Field Trial Assn. One of the prominent Pittsburg men was Mr. J. C. Lozeor, who had a beautiful home in Augusta and had built kennels and a home for his trainer. He was one of the finest and a liberal friend. Though Joe also got to know Andrew Meldon, the Sec. of the U. S. Treasury, and his son-in-law, David Bruce, Dick's brother-in-law is Allen Scarfe. On a few occasions, President Nicholas Murray Butler of Columbia Univ. joined in the men from Augusta.

On Nar. 26, 1919 Joseph md. Tommie Barron Quinney, d/o Alice Gray and Thomas Quinney. Tommie was b. Dec. 11, 1895.

They had three children:
1. <u>Alice Gray Reynolds</u>, b. Aug. 2, 1920. She md. Wm. Brinson; now retired as Col. U. S. Air Force. They live at Taxonville, Fla. They have no children.
2. <u>Joseph Jones Reynolds, III</u>, b. Nov. 24, 1924. Graduated from Waynesboro H.S., was Eagle Scout. Entered V.M.I. joined Navy in his sophomore year. Returned to V.M.I. at Wars end. Graduated in electric engineering and now is employed as District Engineer by Southern Bell.
3. <u>Thomas Lazear Reynolds</u>, b. May 6, 1935. Attended public school at Waynesboro. Later returned to Waynesboro, operated planters until Liquidation. Then started his own business.

MARGARET STORY (RIORDAN) was b. Nov. 4, 1911 in Augusta, Ga., Richmond Co., d/o Ida Gresham and Samuel Gaines Story, II. She graduated from the Waynesboro H.S., the Burke Co. Jr. Col. and from the Univ. of Ga., with a BA Cum Laude in Journalism. She taught English and Latin in Girard Union H. S. (1 year), two years 4th grade in Waynesboro, and next year worked for the Resettlement Administration in Washington, D. C.

On Feb. 15, 1936 she md. Forrest Heth Riordan, Jr., s/o Edith Bayer and Forrest Heth Riordan, Sr. Her husband had a six-year old son, Forrest Heth Riordan, III. Two years after marriage her husband (a 2nd Lt.) was sent to the cavalry school at Ft. Riley, Kansas. Next they were moved to Philadelphia where Samuel Gresham Riordan was b. Jan. 28, 1940.

In 1941 Forrest H. was sent to the Command and Gen. Staff School at Ft. Leavenworth, Kansas, for three months, then transferred to Camp Lee, Va. (now Ft. Lee). After Pearl Harbor he was promoted and transferred to Ft. Monmouth, N.J. to teach at the Signal School. The family moved again. Six months later he was transferred (the family had only four hours notice that time) to Cal. where he helped set up headquarters for a Theater of War in the Southwest. Then to San Francisco for six months; then to Ft. Crook, Neb. (now AFD.)

During the War he served two years in the China-Burma-India Theater: One as Regimental Commander, running communications and lines through the Burma jungles and once was the executive officer for Gen. King in New Delhi. The family stayed in Cal. After the War he was in the army of occupation and the family moved to Japan for a year on Hazuki AB on the island of Kyushu.

Finally the strain was too much. In 1956 they were divorced and Margaret took up the thread of being her own person, by teaching again for a year. Then she obtained a job in the Civil Service at Norton AFB Cal. in San Bernardino. She settled in Redlands for 12 years. During this time Samuel Gresham served in the Navy during the Vietnam conflict. He was lucky and came home well and fit.

After Norton AFB closed in 1966 Margaret transferred to McClellan AFB in Sacramento where she now lives. She worked as an "Inventory Management Specialist" for most of the 26 years in Civil Service. She retired Feb. 29, 1980.

Margaret keeps in touch with her step-son, Forrest III and his charming wife, Patricia. Forrest III graduated from Stanford Univ. and is an orthopedic surgeon in Rockford, Ill. They manage a house call to Cal. every year.

Samuel Gresham Riordan graduated from the San Francisco Art Institute and is now a commercial artist in San Diego. As an undergraduate he had a one-man ceramic show at Valley College in San Bernardino. He received honorable mention from the San Diego Museum of Art, Southwest Regional Crafts Show, for one of his sculptures. Margaret received an engraved invitation from the museum to a reception given for the artists. She was overwhelmed to see the Sculpture, which had been in the corner of the living room for weeks, as a pedestal in the rotunda of the museum, the first thing you saw as you entered.

Samuel Gresham md. Carol Alexandra Campbell, d/o Jeanne Carol Yarnell and Alexander Boyle Campbell. Carol attended San Diego State Univ. In 1967 she taught children's theater at the Actors Lab School in San Francisco. She also took the role of "Mother Courage" in Bertolt Brecht's play at a playhouse in San Francisco. She designed the costumes. Samuel had the part of a soldier and designed the armor, swords, shields, breast plates, as well as the scenery. He designed and built the wagon which was the home of Mother Courage. Of the wagon a San Francisco Chronicle wrote: "it seemed to be a living thing with a personality of its own."

Their children are:
1. Loren Jeremy Riordan, b. Oct. 1, 1970
2. Rachel Eliz. Riordan, b. July 21, 1973

Margaret's grandchildren are both in love with music, poetry, stories, drama, camping, sailing, river rafting, theater, swimming, baseball. They are talented, imaginative, perceptive, adaptable and stimulating to be with.

Forrest H. Riordan, Jr. retired as a full Col. and had a colorful life. But at age 43 she had no life of her own at all. She started her career and from that date she considered herself very, very fortunate. She has lots of time left to enjoy living.

GRATTAN WHITEHEAD ROWLAND[1] was b. Jan. 27, 1898, s/o Marian Wallace Whitehead and Clarence Leonard Rowland,[2] at the home of his grandfather, Dr. Amos Grattan Whitehead. His mother died when he was 1½ years old. On Dec. 27, 1900, his father remarried, Mary Edith O'Connell of Little Rock, when Grattan was almost three years old.

He grew up in Waynesboro and attended public school through the first high school grade. He then attended Richmond Academy in Augusta, living with his uncle on the Hill. Two more years completed his high school at two preparatory schools in Tenn.[3]

He studied at Ga. Tech four years; joined the S.A.E. fraternity. For two months he was at Camp Gordon (Training School), Oct. 1 to Nov. 30, 1918. He then did a nine-month graduate training under B. G. Laemm, Ch. Engr. for Westinghouse Electric & Mfg. Co. at East Pittsburgh, Pa. For two years he was with Duquesne Light Co. in Pittsburgh before he moved to Chattanooga, Tenn. where he worked nine years with Tenn. Electric Power Co., advancing to Ass't Electrical Superintendent.

The Great Depression forced a change from utility to sales engineering, and in 1931 he went with James R. Kearney Corp. of St. Louis, with most of the Southeast as his sales territory. He spent 33 years with this firm. He was a professional Electrical Engineer, registered in Ga. #1377.

On Dec. 22, 1934, Grattan md. Florence Clarice Mewborn (b. Nov. 29, 1906). They have two sons: Grattan Whitehead Rowland, Jr. (b. May 26, 1937) and Clarence Leonard Rowland (b. Sept. 27, 1941). They also have two grandchildren, Grattan Whitehead Rowland, III and Catherine Eliz. Rowland.

---

[1] He was christened Amos Grattan Whitehead, but he dropped the "Amos" before leaving high school.
[2] His father and mother were second cousins, both being descendants of William Whitehead and Susannah Dowse.
[3] Bell Buckle, Tenn. and Fitzgerald and Clark, Tullahoma, Tenn.

Grattan has lived in Atlanta since 1932. He is a member of Druid Hills Presbyterian Church and served as a Deacon for several years. He is a life member of the Ga. and National Societies of Professional Engineers, and the Ga. Engineering Society. Before he was md. he held a Transport Pilot's license #4287 which qualified him as under the first 5000 pilots in this country.

On a visit to Mrs. Susan Whitehead Belt many years ago, he learned that she had important genealogical material on the Whiteheads and upon his retirement he turned his energy to genealogy. He has become a vigorous and highly competent genealogist. In years to come, more and more Whitehead descendants will rise up and realize how much he has done. His books have already enriched a number of genealogical libraries. At age 78 after publishing three books on Grandparents' diaries during the Civil War, he started his The Whiteheads of Burke County, Ga. He has completed five sections. He has also researched the Rowlands of Fairfield, Conn. and the McKinnes of Augusta, Ga. Both he and his wife are members of the Ga. Genealogical Society. He is also a member of the Huguenot Society of South Carolina, the South Carolina Historical Society and the Fairfield Historical Society of Fairfield, Conn.

JOHN WESLEY SANDERFORD was born Mar. 5, 1847 in Burke Co., near Waynesboro, Ga. He was educated at the best schools this section afforded: Pine View Academy, Bacon in Screven County, Waynesboro and later Dr. A. C. Thompson, a well-known educator at Habersham. Schools in those days were in session for short periods each year and a boy was fortunate to get even an elementary education.

At the age of 17 he enlisted in the Confederate Army. He served in the A.R. Wright Brigade. He was wounded early in his career but stayed in the hospital only one night. He served until the end of the War and surrendered at Appomattox Court House with Gen. Lee. He came back to Burke County and labored most where he was needed, as a farmer and carpenter, helping to build and enrich his native county.

Sanderford came to Midville, then known as Station 9½. His first work was as a school teacher and the only school then was on the Cross plantation, later owned by S. A. Jones. Later the school was moved near the Station, on the lot then owned by J. L. Parish. While Sanderford taught, he farmed between the school terms and lived on his farm at the Barton place.

After teaching for five years he md. Miss Beatrice Murphree, d/o Eliz. T. Jordan and Augustus Wm. Murphree. They began with a small house on the site of the present Sanderford Hotel. In fact, this house was the beginning of the Sanderford Hotel.

At that time Midville had only two stores, Evans and Carswell, and Davis and Marks. Sanderford kept books for Evans and Carswell, and went into business with S. C. Evans, always farming in connection. In 1880 Mr. Sanderford, Robert Burton and S.C. Evans organized the Methodist Church and built the church building, that was used for many years.

The Sanderfords lost three infants, a girl and two sons. Their next son, Ralph Herman Sanderford, was b. Nov. 3, 1890. He md. Grace Smith. Ralph lived until Jan. 31, 1956.

John Wesley Sanderford lived 77 years; dying on Dec. 19, 1924. His wife followed him by 50 days, on Feb. 7, 1925.

GEORGE W. SAPP was b. in Burke Co., Nov. 22, 1843. He served through the Civil War with Co. D, 2nd Ga. Regiment. He was md. to Miss Julia E. Martin of Madison, Ga. He was a type of the old school of Southern gentlemen. One of his friends remembered that the beautiful flowers sent were appropriate for he had scattered flowers along the pathway of many that had made their lives brighter. Mr. Sapp was a Mason and a member of the Grove Level Baptist Church.

He was well-known in Burke Co. and over a long period visited his friends there. For many years he resided at Broad Acres near Dalton in Whitfield Co. and spent winters in South Ga., especially Burke County.

The funeral exercise was conducted from the residence of his son, William M. Sapp. Mr. George W. is survived by his wife; four sons: Messrs. W.M. Sapp; Judson C.; Philip B.; Richard H.; and Miss Sadie C. Sapp, all in thic county.[1]

---
[1] From the Dalton Argus, Sept. 26, 1908.

THE WILLIAM SAPP FAMILY. William Sapp and Zylpdia(Dill) Sapp of Ireland and md., ran away and reached America in the early or middle part of 1700. They were of pure Irish stock. They went first to North Carolina and later moved to St. George's Parish, which became Burke County in 1777. He was the "Squire" Sapp mentioned in the Sardis Church records (Jan., 1809) when the Baptists chose a site, "a mount on the Savannah Road near Squire Sapp's to build the church". In 1810 the church house was named "Sardis", and the town took the same name. Wm. Sapp, Sr. joined the Sardis Church in Jan., 1809 and became a strong Baptist and for some time was a licentiate minister. He was one of the trustees of the church.[1]

Zylpdia became a widow in 1827 (noted in an 1827 Land Lottery). Both William Sapp, Sr. and his wife, were probably interred in the Sardis Cemetery, but their markers have not been found.

Children of William and Zylpdia (Dill) Sapp were:
1. Dennis Dill Sapp was the eldest. He received bounty land in 1784 for his Rev. War service. A list of the First Battalion of the Burke Co. Militia in 1792 listed him as Capt. Dill Sapp of the 3rd Co with 48 men, a 1st Lieut. Wills Davies and 2nd Lieut. Henry Bryant.[2] Dill Sapp died in Burke Co., 1804.
2. Hardy Corneil Sapp md. Eliz. B. Bowers. He spent his life principally in Muscogee, later Chattahoochie C., moving there from Augusta (1831 or 1832). He d. in 1846. His children:
    (a) John Marion (1825-1897). He lived in Lauderdale Co., Tenn.
    (b) George Henry (1833-1907) in Cusseta, Ga.
    (c) Wm. Alexander, b. 1837.
    (d) Harriet C. md. Dr. J. D. Trammell.

---
[1] Sardis Church Records (beginning Sept., 1803). State Archives, Atlanta (microfilm).
[2] Rev. George White, Historical Collections of Ga. (1854), Pudney & Russell, NY, p. 284.

3. John Sapp (died 1860). Married _____. His children:
   (a) Hansford
   (b) Augustus
   (c) Elizabeth, md. Bargeson
   (d) Kesiah md. Bell
   (e) Mary md. Brookins
   (f) Emily md. Jenkins
   (g) Sarah md. Perkins
   (h) John

   John Sapp married, second, Elizabeth _____.

4. Zylpdia md. Joseph Bush. Little is known of her. She was apparently a widow in 1836, for her father acted as agent and paid taxes for her. She had at least one daughter, Zylpdia, who md. Henry Stringfellow in 1842 and lived in Chattahoochee Co., and a son, Thomas, who also lived in Chattahoochee Co.

5. William Sapp, Jr. was b. Feb. 7, 1789 in N. C. In 1826 he md. in Burke Co., Sarah Hankinson (1799-1857), a widow of Barnwell District, S.C. Sarah had a little daughter, Emily Jane Leslie (1818-1888) who md. Minis H. McElmurray. William Sapp, Jr. was baptized in 1828.

   William's home was known as the "Sapp House" also "Indra House" after a Hindu god. It was built about 1810 and remains a fine old Colonial Manor house. The house was near Old Buckhead Baptist Church and there in 1832 Mercer Univ. was born. William later became a Mercer Trustee (1855-63). We do not find a record of his gifts to church and education, but he is said to have been liberal.[3] His fine portrait hangs in the Mercer Univ. Library at Macon, Ga.

   The estate called "Alexander" was the house of the Sapps, one of Burke Co.'s early large plantation families. They owned all the land between Alexander and Sardis, from Beaver Dam Creek to Briar Creek. The vastness of the original Sapp holders and affluence of the family can be shown by the fact that as late as 1860 it required the labor of 138 slaves to operate the plantation. Wm. Sapp, Jr.'s success as a planter enabled him to maintain his family and his establishment in exceptional comfort. He is said to have been uncommonly humane in the treatment of his slaves.[4]

   When Sherman's Army went through Ga (1864), the Sapp House was saved. The father was ill, but George W. Sapp was exceedingly polite, talkative and affable. The Brigade Headquarters wagon was not yet up. Young Mr. Sapp, however, volunteered to get supper for the Brigade Commander and staff and they soon sat down to a smoking hot supper of sweet potatoes, corn bread and ham. He said that there were no knives and forks ("the Yankees had taken them all") but pocket knives and fingers served in lieu of the missing cutlery.[5]

   After the Civil War, William Sapp, Jr. built a summer house in Whitfield Co., near Dalton, Ga. Later they made this home permanent. William's wife, Sarah, d. May 12, 1857 and was buried in the Sardis Cemetery. Until the death of his daughter, Caroline Eliz. (Sapp) (Hines) (Jones), in 1869, he spent some time with her at her home on the Magnolia Springs site. Later he began to spend more and more months near Dalton. He d. Jan. 25, 1875, age 86, and was buried beside his wife in the Sardis Cemetery.

---

[3] B.D. Ragsdale, Mercer Univ., Benfield Record & Related Interests, Vol. I, published by author.
[4] Ibid.
[5] Southern Unionist, item from James Moore Wayne, 92nd Ill. (Union Army).

Children of Sarah Hankinson and William Sapp, Jr. were:
1. Caroline Eliz. Sapp md. first, Dr. Henry C. Hines. He d. Jan. 15, 1856. Her second marriage was to Batt Jones, who lived only to Dec. 18, 1862; Caroline d. June 28, 1869 without children.
2. Richard Hampton Sapp (1830-1865) represented Whitfield Co. in the State Legislature, but about 1856, after the death of his wife and his little son, he moved to Cal. He d. 1865 in Helena, Mont.
3. Judson C. Sapp was b. Oct. 27, 1837. D. Sept. 19, 1863 at Martinsburg, Va., after losing an arm at Gettysburg, Pa. He is buried at Fredericksburg, Va. He had studied law at the Univ. of Va. Law School. When Judson was wounded, his devoted brother, George W., stayed with him to nurse him, but both were captured. Judson was a 1st Lieut. in the Burke Co. Sharpshooters.

4. When he was captured Aug 1, 1863 he was exchanged, 1864, and detailed by order of Sec. of War to superintend farms in Burke Co., Ga. and continued in that capacity until the close of the War. Later he engaged in agriculture, and in 1872 upon his marriage to Julia Martin, they made their home at Broad Acre in Whitfield Co. He died Sept. 21, 1908, in Dalton, Ga. and is buried there.

George Washington Sapp was b. Nov. 22, 1843 in Burke Co. In 1865 he md. Julia S. Burney (1842-1866) of Madison, Ga. He brought her to Waynesboro. She d. March 23, 1866 and also the twin sons. All three are buried at Madison, Ga. In 1872 he md. Julia Elvira Martin (1853-1924) of Madison. Julia Martin was a niece of Julia S. Burney, his first wife.

Children of George W. and Julia (Martin) Sapp were:
(a) Judson Council Sapp (1874-1917). He was their only child b. in Burke Co.
(b) William Martin Sapp (1876-1941)
(c) Philip Bryan Sapp (1878-1938)
(d) Richard Hampton Sapp (1882-1949)
(e) Sarah Cornelia Sapp (1888-1965)

For a time after the Civil War George W. held intact the large farm lands which his father owned. At one time George W. owned the Magnolia Springs site. He was an interesting man. A relative once said that George had the fine traits of a Robin Hood. He often visited Burke and Jefferson counties; loved to hunt and fish and he was always welcomed. During the Civil War he risked his life in the attempt to nurse his brother back to health. By his affability and hospitality the Yankees did not destroy the Sapp House. An old gentleman in Waynesboro once remarked: "My father knew George Sapp. He was a talented and likeable man. It is true that the county is full of Sapps, but there was never but one Sapp and that was George. When he entered a gathering he was the center of the group."[6]

---

[6] The author is much indebted to Mrs. W. B. Farrar of St. Petersburg Beach, Fla. for portions of the genealogy of her family. She is a granddaughter of George W. Sapp.

FLOYD LAWSON SCALES of the Waynesboro Bar, departed this life on Apr. 26, 1906, in the city of Baltimore, where he had gone for medical treatment. His remains were brought to his home and two days later interred with civic and military honors. The deceased was a s/o Robert and Frances R. (Martin) Scales. He was b. in Waynesboro, July 15, 1871. But on Dec. 12, 1872 his father d. in Waynesboro and left his mother a widow.[1] Floyd attended the Waynesboro Academy until he was sixteen years of age, after which he read law in the office of Judge Phil. P. Johnston, and was admitted to the Bar when he was 19, entering the firm of Lawson and Callaway, composed of Judge Edw. F. Lawson and Judge E. H. Callaway. This partnership existed until the appointment of Mr. Callaway as Judge of the Augusta Circuit, when he retired, leaving the firm of Lawson & Scales, which existed until the death of Capt. Scales. Owing to the impaired health of Judge Lawson, the large business of the firm has devolved chiefly upon Mr. Scales for several years past. The firm was a represntative clientage and extensive practice, numbering on its clientele many prominent eastern persons and corporations having interests in Burke County. Mr. Scales is a staunch adherent of the Democratic party. At the time of his death he was serving a second term as Mayor of Waynesboro.

He is a member of the Methodist Episcopal Church South, and in a fraternal way is a Royal-Arch Mason; a member of the Knights of Pythias, in which he is past chancellor; the Benevolent and protective Order of Elks, and the Independent Order of Odd Fellows, in which last he is Noble Guard of his lodge. He was a Director of the Bank of Waynesboro. For 15 years he was an officer in the Burke Light Infantry and was several years Capt. of his company. He later was Capt. in the Nat'l Guard of Ga. He was universally popular, and on the occasion of his funeral, business was suspended and the entire people met to pay tribute to his memory. As a lawyer he was successful to an unusual degree, and he carried into his professional work that zeal and ability which characterized his life and made him a leader in all undertakings with which he allied himself.

By his untimely death, coming in the years so full of promise, the Ga. Bar has lost one of its best members.[2]

---

[1] Robert W. Scales was a brother of ex-Gov. Alfred M. Scales of N.C. Mrs. Frances R. (Martin) Scales is a representative of an old and influential N.C. family, and her father, Robert Martin, was an uncle of the wife of Hon. Stephen A. Douglas, Mrs. Douglas having been a Martin.

[2] The Annual Report, Ga. Bar Ass'n (1909), p. 131; a portion of Cyc of Ga., Vol. III, p. 244.

HENRY JACKSON SCHLEY, s/o Mrs. Eliza Sarah Hargrove and Hon. Wm. Schley (1786-1858), was b. in 1825 at his father's home some six miles from Augusta, Ga. Henry was in the Class of 1845 at Franklin College (now Univ. of Ga.), but did not graduate. His father was an able lawyer in Augusta, a representative in the Gen. Assembly, a U. S. Congressman and Governor of Ga.

In 1846 Henry md. Frances Virginia Miller (b. July 30, 1828), d/o Dr. Baldwin B. Miller and his first wife, Rosa Anderson, widow of John Morrison. They had four children:
   1. Baldwin Miller Schley, b. about 1847. Came to manhood in Texas;
      d. at his grandfather's plantation in Burke Co. at the age of 23 yrs.

2. Eliza Schley, b. Mar 5, 1848; d. Oct. 29, 1851.
3. Henry Schley, b. Apr. 22, 1850; d. Sept. 7, 1850.
4. Rosa A. Schley, b. Sept. 7, 1854; d. Aug. 13, 1855.

Henry's plantation "Buckhead", some 1412 acres in Burke Co., was 12 miles north of Midville. Before the Civil War he went out to Texas to visit his elder half-brother and there bought some 2,630 acres in Wharton Co., Tex. At the outbreak of the Civil War, he returned to Ga. to settle his business affairs. When Dr. B. B. Miller sponsored the Miller Volunteers in 1861, the company voted Schley the Capt. The co. served on the Ga. coast near Brunswick.

In 1866 Henry returned to Tex. and lived the rest of his life in Wharton Co. He was a large planter and also a surveyor of most of the land in four counties, including Wharton Co. On Oct. 20, 1893, while he was surveying, he dropped dead, not far from his home. He is buried in the Wharton Cemetery. His widow d. on July 20, 1901, and rests beside her husband.[1]

---

[1] See Grave Markers of Burke County, pp. 184-185, and Myers', The Children of Pride, p. 1670.

ROBERT LEE SCOTT, JR. Air Force Officer and author. Was b. Apr. 12, 1908 at Waynesboro, Ga., the s/o Ola Louise (Buckhalter) and Robert Lee. Education: Mercer Univ. (1924-25); B.S., U.S. Military Academy (1932); graduated Air Corps Training Center (pilot) 1933. Md. Catherine Rita Green, Sept. 1, 1934. One daughter, Robin Lee.

Commd. 2nd Lieut. Air Corps (1932) Advanced through grades to Col. (Feb., 1942). Service in 99th Squadron, Mitchell Field; 78th Pursuit Squadron, Canal Zone; flying instructor, Randolph Fields Tex (1937-39). Commanded Cal-Aero Academy (1939-1941). Commanded 23rd Fighter Group (1942-43); fighter Comdr. for Gen. Chennault (1943-45); dept. Nat. Comdr, Civil Air Patrol (1947-48); Wing Comdr. Jet Fighter School, Williams Field, Ariz. (1948-50); Commanded 36th Fighter Bomb Wing Furstenfeldbruck Air Base (1950-53); Nat. War College, assignment since 1953.

Awarded: Silver Star with oak leaf cluster for gallantry; Air Medal with two oak leaf clusters; Distinguished Flying Cross with two oak leaf clusters; Special citation from Chief of Staff, U.S. Army, 1943 (US); Order of Cloud Banner; Yum Hwei, Ten Star Dragon Medal (China); Special War Cross from U.D.C.

Member Md. Order of World Wars; Mark Twain Society; Royal George Soc. (London). Clubs: Explorers; Kiwanis (hon); Macon, Ga. Republican, Episcopalian.

Author: God Is My Co-Pilot (1943); Damned to Glory (1944); Runaway to the Sun (1945). Address: Care Air Judge Adj.-Gen., Dept. of Air Force, Washington, D. C. [1]

---

[1] Who's Who In America, Vol. 28 (1954-55). Other books added to the 1960-61

ADIEL SHERWOOD - Rev. Dr. Adiel Sherwood, Baptist minister, educator, and author of the famous "Gazetteer of Georgia," was b. at Ft. Edward, NY, Oct. 3, 1791. His great-grandfather, Thomas Sherwood, came from England and settled in NY in 1633.

Dr. Sherwood had good educational advantages and graduated from Union College at Schenectady, NY, in 1817. He then studied theology in Andover Theological Seminary, and in 1818, was preaching at Savannah. He taught school for two years at Waynesboro, and was ordained to the Baptist ministry at Bethesda, in Greene County.

At a meeting of the Sarepta Baptist Ass'n, held at Ruckersville, Elbert Co., he offered the resolution which led to the organization of the Ga. State Baptist Convention, and in 1823, at the triennial convention in Washington City, he offered the resolution which resulted in the organization of State conventions all over the country.

Dr. Sherwood served as pastor of churches at Penfield, Milledgeville, Macon, Greensboro, Griffin, Monticello, and Greenville. He was a great educator and promoter of education. At his suggestion Mercer Institute was established at Penfield, and from it, eventually, Mercer Univ. developed. He also established a Manual Training School at Eaton.

After the establishment of Mercer, he served three years as professor of sacred literature while he was pastor of a church at Penfield.

In 1837 he was a professor in the Columbian College, Washington, D.C. In 1841 he was president of Shurtleff College, Alton, Ill. In 1848-49 he was president of the Masonic College, Lexington, Missouri. In 1857 he was back in Ga., and was president of Marshall College at Griffin. Union College, from which he graduated in 1817, conferred on him the degree of Doctor of Laws.

Dr. Sherwood's "Gazetteer of Georgia," like White's "Statistics of Georgia" and White's "Historical Collections," was a compendium of great value, in which historical material and statistics of the early half of the 19th century in Ga. were assembled and preserved.

Dr. Sherwood was a man of commanding appearance, highly intellectual, but pious, simple in his manner and modest, though learned in many ways, and it has been well said that he was one of the early giants of the Baptist Church in Ga. His creative mind originated much of the progress and many of the progressive movements of his time. He had a very wide acquaintance with eminent men, knew every president from Washington to Grant, 20 Ga. Gov's, from Mitchell to Jenkins, and 19 U.S. Senators were his friends. He was the credit of having aided in the education of 30 young Baptist ministers.

In 1821 he md. the widow of Gov. Peter Early of Ga., who lived only a short while, and in 1824 he md. Miss Herriot, of S.C. He d. in St. Louis, Mo., Aug. 18, 1879, when he was in his 88th year.[1]

1
The Story of Georgia, p. 735.

BURKE SHEWMAKE, eldest son of Judge John T. and Lizzie P. (Jones) Shewmake, was b. in the city of Augusta, Ga., June 16, 1859. He studied at home until 12 years of age and then attended the private school of Prof. J. Alma Petot, in the city of Augusta, two years later becoming a student at the old Richomd Academy at Augusta, from which he was graduated, in 1876, with the degree of B.A. He then attended the Virginia Military Institute, at which institution he made a most remarkable record, never receiving a mark of discredit as a cadet, and was graduated with the rank of adjutant, in the course of Bachelor of Arts. Returning to Augusta, Ga., he immediately entered the employ of Z. McCord, the largest grocery house in that city, as chief clerk and occasionally acted as traveling salesman. He remained in the employ of Mr. McCord for five years, resigning at the end of that time in order to organize the firm of Beane, Shewmake & Savage. Three years later he withdrew from that firm and organized the firm of Moore & Shewmake, which continued until the organization of the present firm of Shewmake Bros., three years later. The present firm conducts quite an extensive business and commands a generous patronage among the citizens of Augusta and vicinity. Burke Shewmake, senior member of the firm, is Maj. of the 6th Ga. Reg't, Volunteers, and has received the third degree of Masonry.[1]

---

[1] Memoirs of Georgia, Vol. II (1895), p. 809.

JOHN TROUP SHEWMAKE was b. in Burke on the family plantation near Alexander, Jan. 23, 1826. His parents were Joseph Shewmake and Anna Lassiter. He studied at home until his 18th birthday, then entered the College of N.J. (now Princeton Univ.). After graduation (1847) he entered Judge William T. Gould's Law School in Augusta and after one year was admitted to the Bar. Initially he practiced in Waynesboro, but subsequently moved to Augusta, which was his home for the remainder of his life.

In 1851-55 he was Attorney-Gen. (the later title is Solicitor-Gen.)[1] of the Middle Judicial Circuit; he represented Burke in the State Senate, 1861-63; and in 1863 he was elected to the Second Confederate Congress as a Rep. from the 5th Ga. Dist.

After the Civil War he resumed his law practice. From 1874-79 he served as President of the Augusta Board of Educ., and was again in the State Senate, 1877, from Richmond Co. Death came on Dec. 1, 1898.

On Dec., 1850 he md. Eliz. Penelope Jones, the d/o Henry Philip Jones, owner of the Birdville Plantation. They had eight children:
1. Burke Shewmake. Senior member of Shewmake Bros., Augusta, Ga.
2. Henry Philip Shewmake (Hal), Shewmake Bus., Dublin Ga.
3. John T. Shewmake, Jr., d. in youth.
4. Claude Shewmake (prominent businessman of Atlanta). A daughter, Anna Harriet md. Admiral Rufus Thayer.
5. Anna Virginia Shewmake md. James Whitehead (Warren Co. Attorney), the s/o John T. Shewmake's classmate at Princeton, James Troup Whitehead.

---

[1] For many years (actually until 1868) so long as the State Capitol was in the Middle Judicial Circuit, the Soliciter-Gen. of the Circuit was *ex-officio* the Attorney-Gen. of the State. The Capitol was moved out of the Circuit to Atlanta in 1868. Jones and Dulther, Memorial History of Augusta, Ga. (1896) p. 192.

6. Lena Penelope Shewmake, md. Philip P. Johnston, lawyer and judge in Waynesboro.
7. William Jones Shewmake, Shewmake Bros., Augusta, Ga.
8. Marshall Augustus Shewmake. The oldest s/o Marshall A. Shewmake (John Troup Shewmake, president of the Southwestern Electric Co. of Dallas, Tx.)

CHARLES W. SKINNER, SR. was b. May 23, 1863, s/o Sarah Tabb and John J. Skinner. He came to Waynesboro years ago from farming as a young man. He became a member of the firm Cates and Skinner. Later he bought Mr. Cates' interest in the firm.

On Mar. 8, 1900, he md. Miss Minnie Caraker of Milledgeville, Ga., the d/o Eliz. Bayne and Jacob Monroe Caraker.

He was in business for 40 years. He became one of the largest merchants and cotton buyers in the county, having large farm interests. He became Pres. of the Bank of Waynesboro for 25 years. He was a director of the Savannah & Atlanta Railway; Vice-President of the Planter's Bonded Warehouse and owned the land where the Brinson Railroad had its depot. He owned two brick buildings on Liberty Street; at one time he was Dir. of the Ga. Tax Revision Association.

He was a member and steward of the Waynesboro Methodist Church and a handsome man. He d. at age 68 on Jan. 16, 1931. He was interred in the Magnolia Cemetery. Surviving was his wife, a nephew, John Jones Skinner, his two sons and two grandchildren:
1. Charles W. Skinner, Jr., b. Apr. 21, 1901; d. Mar. 26, 1955. He was Pres. of the Bank of Waynesboro after his father. He md. Henrietta Boyer (b. Feb. 22, 1907), b. of Lena McKenzie Lovejoy and Mirabeau H.) They had one daughter, Joy Skinner, who md. Spencer L. Wiley, NY City.
2. Franklin Monroe Skinner, b. Nov. 20, 1907. He md. Mary Brinson, d/o Sarah McElmurray and Frank L. Brinson, Jr. They had a son, Franklin Monroe Skinner, Jr., (b. Oct. 3, 1931). He lives in NY City. His father died Nov. 5, 1953.

Mrs. Minnie Caraker Skinner d. Apr. 29, 1940 and is interred in the Magnolia Cemetery in Waynesboro.

FRANKLIN MONROE SKINNER, JR. was b. Oct. 3, 1931 at Waynesboro, Ga. His schooling began in the kindergarten that Mrs. Roger Fulcher ran. He adored her, called her "Aunt Mary-Sally". She convinced that he had a gift in his hand and much imagination. Perhaps, child-like, she was his friend and he took everything she said as gospel. After many years he still considered her one of the many magnificient women in his life, after his own Mother.

Every minute of the Waynesboro Grammar School he hated and his record showed it. His high school was at the Ga. Military Academy (G.M.A.) in College Park just outside of Atlanta. He hated G.M.A., too but he could go to the High Museum of Art.[1] He loved Atlanta and spent as much time at this Museum as he could. At the Univ. of Ga. there were some teachers who inspired and encourage him, and most probably a few at G.M.A.

From his memories, he also had the inspiration and encouragement from his Mother and her closest friends: Messes Joel Chappell, Henry Daniel, Shelly Griffin, A. W. Welborn, and Louis Pintchuck. They were unaware of their talents and reveled in sharing with each other and with others. He learned something by listening.

At the Univ. he was granted a B.A. degree and was a member of the Pi Kappa Alpha Frat. Again he did not know how he earned his degree. He was already involved with projects he set for himself, usually intricate stage and motion picture settings.

Starting with his first exposure to the city of Atlanta, New York loomed as Olympus was and still is! He loved it. After six months he joined the N.B.C., actually it was a big reservoir of young employees for future placement within the company as needed. He won the David Sarnoff Fellowship to study scenic design at Yale Univ. at New Haven, Conn. R.C.A. (Radio Corp. of America owns N.B.C. Gen. Sarnoff was Chairman of R.C.A. at that time. There was a competition for the Fellowship to all R.C.A. employees, N.B.C. included. Franklin M. Skinner won with photographs, or his minerature work done at G.M.A. and Ga. for Hamlet, The Pirate and Gone With the Wind.

He spent a year at Yale "in Heaven". N.B.C. gave him a choice of a second year at Yale but he thought that he was ready to work successfully. He was given the job of its youngest Art Director. He never regretted that decision. On Feb. 7, 1980 he had been with the N.B.C. a full 25 years and at age 48 was the oldest Art Director.

Based in NY, he has also had assignments in Hollywood, Washington, D.C., Chicago, London and Paris. His assignments have run the television gamut. The following is a run-down of his career. A few of the persons and companies with whom he has worked. They follow:

    Today Show: with Frank McGee, Barbara Walters and Tom Brokaw
    Commercials: Sinclair Oil; Campbell Soups; Goodyear (10 years); Kraft
        Foods (12 years); American Express; Cotton Incorporated; Kellogg Foods;
        Revelon; Pan American Airlines,(over 500 in all).
    Home Show: with Arlene Francis
    Soap Operas: Another World
    Game Shows: What's My Line; To Tell the Truth
    N.B.C. News: Weekend, Prime Time Saturday,(and endless news specials)
    N.B.C. Opera: The St. Matthew Passion; Amahl & The Night Visitors.
    Musical Comedy: Carol Burnet; Florence Henderson; Lena Horne; Rise
        Stevens; Judy Garland; Beverly Sills; Leontyne Price; Sam Pierce;
        Robert Merrill; Frank Sinatra; Rudolf Nureyev; Margot Fonteyn;
        Richard Rodgers; Oscar Hammerstein; Irving Berlin; Julie Andrews,
        and others.
    Children's Shows: Exploring (a series)
    Drama-Specials: Richard Burton; Elizabeth Taylor; John Gielgud; Ralph
        Richardson; Julie Harris; Greer Garson; E. G. Marshall; Bette Davis;

Fritz Weaver; Peter Ustinov; Vivian Leigh.

He enjoyed working with Vivien Leigh and Judy Garland more than any other of the actresses.

HENRY HANSEL STEMBRIDGE, JR., the s/o Maude Foreman and Dr. H. H. Stembridge, Sr., was b. Nov. 14, 1906 at Waynesboro, Ga. He grew up in Waynesboro, graduated from the Waynesboro H.S. Studied at Mercer Univ. and received his A.B. at the Univ. of Southern Cal. (Los Angeles); was graduated from the Southern Baptist Seminary in Louisville, Ky. Later he received a D.D. degree from Union University.

On Sept. 5, 1933, md. Lois Sawyer (Stembridge), d/o Nellie Watson and Louis Shelton Sawyer, Sr.

His pastorales began in Barnswell, S.C. in 1933 and continued in Cedartown, Ga. (1935-37); Paris, Tenn. (1937-1944); Paducah, Ky. (1944-46); Forest City, N.C. (1946-1957); Lynchburg, Va. (1957-62); Daly City, Cal (1962-70); and Columbia, S.C. (1975-79).

Dr. Stembridge served as Chairman of the Board at Gardner Webb College and the Southern Baptist Convention School Board. He was an outstanding speaker.

Children:
1. Jane Shelton Stembridge
2. Hnery Hansel Stembridge, III

He d. July 9, 1979, and is interred at Magnolia Cemetery, Waynesboro, Ga. "Dr. Stembridge was a devout and humble servant of Jesus Christ. He lived his life as an offering to the Church, to the community, and to his family. His reward in Heaven must surely be great."

MAJOR JOHN R. STURGES, s/o Rachel Lowrey and Samuel Sturges, b. in 1827 at Waynesboro, Ga. He was first a teacher, studied law and was in the firm of Jones and Sturges. The writer of Maj. Stuges' death (Col. H. H. Johns, Ass't Ed. of The Southern World) was fortunate because it was his privilege to meet one of his comrades in arms who was within a few feet of Maj. Sturges when he fell and was conversant with all the facts. Maj. Sturges was comm'der of the 3rd. Ga. Reg't.

It was the 1st of July, 1862, and the battle of Malvern Hill had raged from noon until the sun was dipping beneath the murkey horizon. Charge after charge had been made up the steep hillside to carry the strong works on the summit, and often repulsed, with heavy loss, by the enemy. But our gallant boys would take shelter and recover breath in an adjacent ravine, and then, reforming, again rush to the onset with loud cheers. At length, however, they were demoralized from the continuous hail of grape and canister which decimated their stricken ranks.

It was at this juncture, as the day was closing, that Maj. Sturges once more rallied his shattered regiment, and with stirring words of cheer and encouragement, clad in a new and conspicuous uniform, put himself at their head and rushed to meet the foe.

With waving sword he was fully 30 yards in advance of his command, when a fatal minie ball perforated the centre of his forehead, and he fell dead, prone upon his face.

The next morning the intrepid Maj. was found, his sword still tightly clasped in hand, and lying in a pool of blood. Gen. A. R. Wright, the brigade commander and beloved friend of the departed hero, immediately sent the remains in an ambulance to Richmond, distant 17 miles, where they were placed in a casket to be forwarded to Ga. Owing to some unforeseen cause, however, transportation could not be had for them, and the body of the gallant Sturges was interred in a gentleman's garden at Gen. Longstreet's headquarters, three miles from Richmond. There it slumbered until about six years ago, when loved hands removed the last relics of the dauntless soldier to their final resting place in Waynesboro, the home of his ancestors.

Among the hecatomb of victims sacrificed to the "lost cause" in Ga. during the late War, there was not one more precious, more excellent, more noble than John R. Sturges. In the Church, at the Bar, in the Senate of Ga., and in private life he was alike distinguished, respected and beloved. The writer, who knew and loved him well, asks the indulgence of the reader for this passing tribute to the memory of a good and brave man.[1]

John R. Sturges, a graduate of Yale College and a lawyer, entered the service of the Burke Guards, which became Co. A., 3rd Ga. Regt, A.R.Wright's Brigade. He shared the achievements of Roanoke and Sawyer's Lane, but upon the reorganization of the Regiment he was promoted to Maj. and commander of the 3rd Ga. Regt.

Brig.-Gen. A.R. Wright included in his Report to Maj-Gen Benj Hugen (July 12, 1862) a paragraph which ended with this sentence: "In the fall of this young officer, the regiment which he commanded has sustained an irreparable loss and the country loses one of its most deserving and competent officers."[2]

---
[1]
The Southern World, May 1, 1884
[2]
Official Correspondence

SAMUEL STURGES, s/o Samuel and Abigail (Lewis) Sturges, was b. Nov. 5, 1774 at Fairfield, Conn.[1] He left his hometown and may have reached Ga. as early as 1795. By 1803 he was living in Waynesboro, Ga., and, on May 3, 1804, md. Rachel Lowrey. She was b. in Ga. (Oct. 18, 1786) and bore him eight children: Abigail Eliza,; Jane Robinson; Nathaniel Lewis; Sarah Ann; William Urguhart; Samuel; Julia; and John R. Sturges.

For many years Samuel Sturges was the Ordinary of Burke County. He was elected as one of the five members of the Board of Town Incorporators, and was elected as one of the first five commissioners to govern the new Town.

William Stone, Samuel Sturges and Southward Harlow consisted a committee to draft rules and regulations for the Board of Commissioners. Samuel d. Oct. 6, 1831 and Rachel in 1837. Both of their graves are no longer marked. They rest in what was the Old Cemetery, but is now the Waynesboro Confederate Memorial Cemetery.

Their first child, Abigail Eliza Sturges (b. about 1805) md. twice: 1st md. Samuel Dowse in 1827. No children by that marriage; 2nd md. Henry Hart Jones. They had one child, Ella Struges Jones (b. 1851), but d. from croup (Nov. 28, 1854) and is interred in the Midway Cemetery. Henry Jones had two children before his second marriage. Henry d. 1893 and she d. 1897.

The second child of Samuel and Rachel, Jane Robinson, was b. Nov. 30, 1809 and d. Aug. 17, 1817. William Urquhart was b. 1816 and was a resident in Waynesboro all his life. He d. May 7, 1884. He md. Georgia Anna Ward (b. 1826; d. Feb. 18, 1905). Their two children who lived to maturity were Philoclia Whitehead Sturges (b. 1853) and William Ward Sturges (b. 1855). One marker for both children read "Sister and brother". William Ward lived until about 1870 or 1880.

John R. Sturges (b. 1827), the last child of Samuel and Rachel Sturges, was a Civil War hero. He d. July 1, 1862. See his Sketch.

Philoclia Whitehead Sturges, the granddaughter of Samuel and Rachel Sturges, was b. 1853 and d. Jan. 31, 1931. She never md. She was a music teacher in the Waynesboro Academy; later on the staff of Lucy Cobb Institute, Athens, Ga., and Agnes Scott College, Decatur, Ga. She lived in Decatur nearly 20 years. She was widely known as "Miss Philo".

With the death of Lt. Col. John R. Sturges and "Miss Philo", neither of whom was married, this branch of the Samuel Sturges line ended.

---

[1] His older brother, Nathaniel Lewis Sturges settled in Augusta, Ga.

THOMAS F. TANHAM, a native of Brooklyn Heights, N.Y. Mr. Tanham's first wife was the late Irene Kilpatrick, d/o the late Mr. & Mrs. George Kilpatrick of Waynesboro. He was former owner of Frank Tanham Co. He attended the Presbyterian Church and was a WW-I veteran.

He d. in NY City on Jan. 6, 1977 and services were held at the Magnolia Cemetery at Waynesboro by the Rev. Dr. Roderic L. Murray officiating on Saturday, Jan. 8. He was buried by his first wife, Irene Kilpatrick Tanham.

Survivors include his widow, Mrs. Allyne Mathews Tanham; one son, Dr. George K. Tanham, Middleburg, Va.; one daughter, Mrs. John Z. Speer, Augusta; and one sister, Mrs. Fred Schmidt, Venice, Fla.

BEN JAMES TARBUTTON, Railroad Executive. Born at Sandersville, Ga., May 14, 1885, s/o Ben James and Mary (Bangs) Tarbutton. Student at Emory College. Md. on Nov. 22, 1928 Rosa McMaster, d/o Rosa Moore and Dr. H. B. McMaster of Waynesboro, Ga. Children: Ben James Tarbutton and Hugh McMaster Tarbutton.

Gen. Mgr., Sandersville Railroad (1914-1926); President since 1926; President of Central of Ga. RR Co. since 1951; owner of the Savannah (Ga.) Hotel; President of the Ocean S.S. Co. of Savannah. Director: of the Citizens and Southern Nat'l Bank, Wrightsville and Tennille R.R. Co., Wadley So. Ry Co.; Louisville & Wadley R.R. Co.; Sylvania Central Ry Co.; Savannah & Atlanta Ry Co.; Central of Ga. Motor Transport Co.; Augusta and Summerville R.R.; Birmingham, Ala.Terminal Co.; Chattanooga Sta. Co.

Mayor of Sandersville 1938-1941; Member Ga. State Senate since 1947. Member Phi Delta Theta frat.; Methodist; Mason (Shrine) Club; Traffic (NYC); Capitol City (Atlanta); Yacht and Country; Oglethorpe (Savannah, Ga.) Home; Savannah Hotel; Savannah and Sandersville Office 227 W. Broad Street, Savannah, Ga. [1]

---

[1] Who's Who In America, Vol. 28 (1954-55), p. 2630.

ANDREW E. TARVER. Mr. Tarver was b. in Burke County, Ga., on the 23rd day of Nov., 1817, and was the youngest s/o Samuel B. and Charlotte Tarver. In 1822 his parents removed from Burke and settled in Jeff. Co., where Mr. Tarver was reared, and where he still lives.

His education was received principally at "old-field schools." In 1842 he md. Miss Julia Ann Daniels, of Washington Co.

His principal occupation during life has been farming, though he has also been successful in merchandising and stock-raising.

While serving as Judge of the Inferior Court, in 1858, he was elected to the State Senate of 1859.

Mr. Tarver was not in military service during the late war, but he ministered to the comfort of the soldiers and their families, many of whom were left in a destitute condition. He was elected to his present position in the House by almost the unanimous vote of the county. He is a strong adherent of the Golden Rule, and benevolence is the prominent feature of his character.[1]

---

[1] Samuel A. Echols, Biographical Sketches, Georgia Assembly of 1878, Atlanta (1878) See p. 208.

CHARLES F. TARVER. His friends describe him as energetic, witty, an excellent craftsman and a gourmet cook. That's Charles F. Tarver of Waynesboro who celebrated his 90th birthday Mon., Apr. 3, with a dinner party at the Waynesboro Shrine Club. Hosts were his children Maj. Charles F. Tarver, Jr. of Miami, Fla., and Mrs. Seymour Friess of Bethesda, Md.

A native of Savannah, on his retirement from the Central of Ga. RR where he was a Yard Master of the Railroad Yard in Athens, he and his wife, the former Miss Nancy Gibson of Macon, moved to Waynesboro in 1947. They bought the home of his aunt, Mrs. Edward Blount at 532 Jones Ave. where they resided until Mrs. Tarver's death in 1965. Since then he has made his home in an apartment in the home of Mrs. Lee Manley on Liberty and Fourth Streets in Waynesboro.

Every morning come rain or come shine Mr. Tarver walks the three blocks to town where he joins the other members of the Quinney Club at the local drug store. After a game of pitching pennies, the loser buys the cokes. When any member has a birthday it calls for a party to celebrate and most of the time Mr. Tarver serves as cook.

In his spare time he canes chair seats in intricate patterns for himself, friends, family and antique dealers.

Does this sound like a 90-year-old man? Not to Mrs. Manley either. She said he has the most vivid memory and the most jovial nature she has ever heard of.

In addition to his pride in his children, he is especially proud of his grandchildren, Phillip Friess and Martin Friess of Bethesda, Md., and his step-grandson, Richard B. Brock, of Atlanta.[1]

---

[1] "Ninety Years Young and Proud of It", article by Gloria Cochran in The True Citizen, April 3, 1972.

ETHELRED THOMAS, emigrated from N.C. to Burke Co. in Ga. and took up farming land in the Northwestern part of Burke Co. He was a faithful member of the Brushy Creek Baptist Church.

He md. Axalina Clark (b. July 16, 1799). They had four children: Richard; Celia; Jethro (b. Mar. 4, 1823); and William. Ethelred Thomas d. about 1825, and left Axalina with small children. Subsequently, Axalina Clark (Thomas) md. (Sept. 1, 1827) James Robinson. They had one daughter, Eliza Eliz.,Robinson d. about 1835. Axalina Clark (Thomas) (Robinson) md. the third time (about 1837) to Stephen Wm. Blount (his second marriage). This marriage produced two Blount sons, Edwin Fitzgerald (b. Jan. 7, 1838) and Robt. Broadnax (b. Apr. 15, 1841). Axalina d. Apr. 2, 1856 and Stephen Wm. Blount died Dec. 16, 1858.

GEORGE C. THOMAS was the s/o Jane Blount and Jethro Thomas. Jane Blount was the d/o Eliz. Wynn and Stephhn W. Blount. She d. sometime before 1854. George C. was reared by his father and his step-mother, Mary Davenport Thomas.

He was admitted to the Bar in 1873 at age 24. <u>Martindales Directory</u> as late as 1922 indicated that he and his son, Wm. Milton Thomas, constituted the firm of Thomas and Thomas.

In 1912 <u>Annual Report</u>, George C. was Vice-President of the Athens Bar Ass'n. Mamie Thomas was the only daughter.

Judge Thomas was elected Mayor of Athens on Nov. 23, 1921. He had run on cleaning up the City Hall "gang". The former Mayor's office was in the Clayton pool room. The Police Force was fired and a new force recruited. No bootleg was allowed to be sold on the streets. The new Mayor set up his office in the City Hall.

The George C. Thomas family were the friends of the W. Leslie McElmurray and his family in Waynesboro.

<u>JETHRO THOMAS</u>, s/o Axalina Clark and Ethelred Thomas, was b. Mar. 4, 1823. He farmed in a western part of Burke Co. For many years he was a member of the Rocky Creek Baptist Church. For years he was a Deacon. He md. first, Jane Blount, the d/o Eliz. Wynn and Stephen Wm. Blount. She d. sometime before 1854. They had children but only one, George C. Thomas, survived.

Jethro Thomas' 2nd md. Nancy Cates (Davenport), b. Sept. 13, 1831, d/o Araminta Hodges and Joseph Cates. The s/o Jane Blount, George C. Thomas, was reared by his father and step-mother. The other children were:
1. Charles Henry Thomas   b. Oct. 13, 1854
2. Kate Thomas   b. Apr. 12, 1856
3. Jethro Beauregard Thomas   b. Oct. 4, 1861

Jethro Thomas was not only a farmer but also a merchant in Waynesboro on the southeast corner of Liberty and Peace Streets. He, like Simeon A. Gray, was well established in business before the Civil War. He was an upright man; a Baptist Deacon (first in the Rocky Creek Church) who put his Deaconate above everything else, and if elected to a county or town office he met his obligations. He served on Grand Juries, was a commissioner when Waynesboro was only a Town, and a member of the Inferior Court. John W. Carswell was elected Chairman of the new County Board of Education for four years. Jethro Thomas followed him for the next four years. He opposed and worked to ban the sale of liquor in Waynesboro.

When the Waynesboro Baptist Church was organized, he was one of the first 20 members. A beautiful window in the present building was dedicated both to Jethro Thomas as the first Deacon and Rev. W. L. Kilpatrick, the first Pastor of the new church.

When Sherman's Army started to the Sea, Jethro joined Wheeler's Cavalry (Co. D, 5th Ga. Cavalry), despite the fact that he had four small children. When the advance Union Cavalry reached the western boundary of Burke, he was a "Paul Revere", warning the plantation families in advance. Unfortunately, he was caught by the Union forces and was sent to Point Lookout, Md., a Union prison. When the War was over he was very ill. Without a horse it took him nearly a year to reach his home. But for Ranson Y. Saxon, also a prisoner at Pt. Lookout, who stayed with him, nursed him, and helped him on the long journey, Jethro might not have lived.

He and his wife, Nancy, are both interred in the Old Cemetery (now the Waynesboro Confed. Mem. Cemetery). Jethro d. Apr. 25, 1885; his wife, Nancy, lived until Oct. 2, 1911.

Some years after Mr. Thomas had d., Mr. Thomas Quinney wrote in The True Citizen. He said, "Mr. Jethro Thomas was a man after my own heart. While he was my senior by many years, yet I claimed him as an intimate friend. When there was preaching sometime on Saturday, he would close up his store to attend divine worship. Worldly people thought it would break him, but he was living for another world to the recompense of this reward."

A good many years ago Brother Thomas was carrying on a protracted meeting here and I said to him: "I could not talk in church". He said: "If you did no good it would have to be by the life you live. You could do a great deal of good that way. If God be for us who can be against us".

J. PINKNEY THOMAS - Upon the resignation recently of the Hon. S. A. Corker, one of the members elected from Burke Co., for the purpose of running for Congress in the First Dist., an election was held to fill the vacancy caused by this resignation. Mr. Thomas was nominated by the Democracy of Burke Co., and after a hard contest, in which he was opposed by Mr. D. Ashton, and subsequently by James T. Palmer, Esq., he was elected by a majority of 200 out of 1,300 votes. This is the first instance in several years when a nominee of the Democracy in Burke Co. has been elected to the Legislature; and it strikingly illustrates Mr. Thomas' popularity with his people, and it is all the more evidenced by the fact that it is the first time that he has ever been a candidate before the people for the office. While ever having been an ardent Democrat, and one of the most valiant of those who have fought against the Radical supremacy, he has preferred others to wear the honors of victory, being content himself to pursue quietly his vocation of planting. He was for years a member of the Co. Exec. Committee, and is now a member of the First Congressional District Executive Committee, and one of the Commissioner of Roads and Revenues of the Co. of Burke.

Mr. Thomas was b. in the county in which he now resides, on the 29th of April, 1839 and is the s/o Joseph D. Thomas, who formerly represented Burke Co. in the Legislature, and who was, before the War, a Gen. of the military of the State. At an early age Mr. Thomas entered school in Richmond Co., and subsequently took a collegiate course at Davidson College in North Carolina, which institute he left after passing through the soph. class, and entered the Univ. of Va., attending during the sessions of 1857-8 and 1858-9.

Upon the call to arms in 1861, he joined the Richmond Hussars from Augusta, in which co. he served as private until 1862, being wounded in Nov. of that year at the Battle of Little Washington, in Va. He still has in his breast a ball received in that battle. From this wound he was in bed four months and confined for six months to his room. Upon his return to the army he was promoted to the position of Aid-de-camp on Gen. P.M.B. Young's staff, 1st Cav. Brigade, Army of Northern Va. with the rank of Capt., which position and rank he held until the close of the War. He continues at times still to suffer from that wound. The charge in which it was received was one of the most gallant made during the war. It was led by the gallant Col. Deloney, of Athens.

Returning home in 1865, Capt. Thomas gave his entire attention to his planting interests and has continued to do so up to this time.

He md. in Feb., 1860, Miss Mary L. Clanton, 3rd d/o Col. Turner Clanton of Augusta.

Capt. Thomas is genial in social intercourse, a gentleman of culture and of commanding personal bearing. He has a host of friends throughout the State as well as in his own immediate section. He has been for years Capt. of the "Wilkins Cavalry" of Burke Co., and said to be one of the finest Cavalry companies in the State, and Capt. Thomas himself is complimented as being one of the finest of commanding officers.[1]

---
[1] Samuel A. Echols. Biographical Sketches General Assembly of 1878 (Atlanta) 1978, pp. 94-95.

PEYTON WADE THOMPSON, 68, former Waynesboro mayor, banker, d. unexpectedly Wednesday, Aug. 2, at his residence, 847 Liberty Street.

Mr. Thompson was b. Aug. 8, 1893 in Savannah, the s/o the late Wall Tattnall Thompson and Josephene Wade Thompson of Quitman. Mr. Thompson came to Waynesboro in 1919 and was md. to Miss Florence McElmurray of Waynesboro.

He was a Capt. during WW-I serving in France. For many years he was Capt. of the 118th Field Artillery of the National Guard. He was in his early years associated with the Bank of Waynesboro. He built and managed the Waynesboro Gin Co. for 25 years. He served as sec. and treasurer of the Production Credit Assn. In 1925 he established the Thompson Insurance Agency. For a number of years he served as chairman of the board of education, and also served as city councilman and mayor of Waynesboro. He was a member of the Burke Co. Hospital Authority, past president of Rotary Club, the Amer. Legion, Veterans of WW-I, and a Mason. He was a member of the Presbyterian Church and clerk of the Session First Presby. Church.

Besides his wife he is survived by two daughters, Mrs. Rowland P. Bolton and Mrs. Melvin Nussbaum, both of Bainbridge; one son, Judson McElmurray Thompson of Waynesboro; nine grandchildren, several nieces and nephews. Another son, Peyton Wade Thompson, Jr., 2nd Lieut., Co. 120 Inf., 30 Inf. Div., was killed in WW-II in action near Mortain, France, and is buried in the American Cemetery there.

Funeral services were held Fri., Aug. 4 from the First Presby. Church by the Rev. Wm. Hines, assisted by the Rev. John Richardson, pastor of the First Presby. Church of Macon.

Burial was in Magnolia Cemetery. Pallbearers were H. C. Hopkins, Jr., H. H. Gray, W. H. Walters, Dr. J. M. Byne, Jr., J. C. Palmer, Jr., S. A. Gray, Jr., Donald Blount, L. M. Martin, McKinley Franklin, Quinton Rogers, and Mayor Holder Watson.[1]

---
[1] The True Citizen, Aug. 6, 1961.

WALL TATTNALL THOMPSON was b. Dec. 7, 1913 at Quitman, Ga., the s/o Jane Cone Thompson of White Springs, Fla. and Wall Tattnall Thompson, II of Quitman, Ga.

He attended the Univ. of Fla., served with the U. S. Marine Corps, Pacific Theater, WW-II.

Md. Lidie Mills Nesbitt, Jacksonville, Fla., Mar. 12, 1938, the d/o Anna Mary Clark and MacGregor Nesbitt. They had three children:

1. Rene Telfair Thompson, b. Feb. 23, 1939. Md. May 7, 1960, s/o Grace Kelly and Eugene Joseph McManus, II
   Children:
   (a) Eugene Joseph McManus, III, b. Sept. 2, 1961
   (b) Peyton Merriweather McManus, b. Sept. 14, 1966
   (c) Porter Telfair McManus, b. May 2, 1968
2. Wall Tattnall Thompson, IV, b. July 26, 1949. Md. April 23, 1977 Charlotte Howell Hampton, b. May 6, 1953, d/o Charlotte Vance Elliott and C. L. Hampton, Galax, Va.
3. Ann MacGregor Thompson, b. May 3, 1953, Md. Oct. 7, 1977, Craig McKay Fletcher of Bainbridge, Ga., s/o Marian Wall and Hugh McKay Fletcher.

The Thompsons live at Lake Bluff in Waynesboro, Ga. He is the Executive Director of the Waynesboro Housing Authority, East Sixth Street, Waynesboro, Ga. Past Pres. of Ga. Ass'n of Housing Authorities; Ex. Sec. Burke Co. Industrial Authority; past member of Burke Co. Hospital Board; member of St. Michael's Episcopal Church, past Sr. and Jr. Warden; member of the Vestry for 16 years. Past Chairman of CSRA Planning and Development Comm.; Past Chairman of the State Advisory Board on Area Planning and Development; Chairman of the Burke Co. Board of Elections.

MEMORY KING TUCKER was b. Sept. 19, 1897 at Statham, Barrow Co., Ga. He was the s/o Udora Rachel Amanda Lanier (b. Nov. 19, 1863) and James Tucker (b. May 12, 1852), both in Walton Co. His grandfathers Richard Overstreet Tucker were b. in Westmoreland Co., Va. and O.W.N. Lanier (b. Dec. 12, 1830) in Jackson County, Ga.

On Feb. 20, 1916 he md. Margaret Jeanette Hill (b. Oct. 19, 1896 in Drone, Burke County), d/o Mary Ann Whitehead and Leonard Dozier Hill. They md. in Gough where he had been employed at the Bank of Gough since 1914. They moved to Waynesboro when King was next employed by the First Nat'l Bank of Waynesboro where he became Exec. Vice-Pres. before June 1, 1940. He bought substantial stock in the Bank of Waynesboro and became the bank's President. There he remained as Chief Executive Officer until June, 1976.

Their marriage ended in divorce on Nov. 15, 1956. Their children were born, md. and all grown up in the Waynesboro Presbyterian Church where Mr. Tucker was currently serving as Trustee.

Besides running a bank, he was a member of the Waynesboro City Council (1935-36); a hand in establishing the Waynesboro Radio Station; Mayor of Waynesboro (1938-42); member of the Board of County Commissioners (1944-52); for a time a merchandise business under the firm, Tucker & Wheeler; chairman of the Hospital Authority, and Representative from Burke County (1959-64) in the Ga. House of Representatives.

Children:
1. Margaret Hill Tucker, b. Feb. 23, 1918; d. May 7, 1919.
2. Susan Whitehead Tucker, b. June 29, 1920. <u>Md</u>. Feb. 7, 1943, Reuben Luckie Rockwell, Jr., He d. May 24, 1963.
3. Margaret Lanier Tucker, b. Mar. 25, 1923. <u>Md</u>. Oct. 13, 1945, Carl Ashton Blount, Jr., M.D. (b. Nov. 14, 1922).
4. Mary Elizabeth Tucker, b. May 10, 1927. <u>Md</u>. Charles Andrew Evans, II, b. Oct. 10, 1926.

JOHN TWIGGS, a hard-fighting Rev. War officer, was b. June 5, 1750. He emigrated from Maryland to Ga. about 1765 and settled in St. George's Parish, where he learned the carpenter trade. As a young officer in his middle 20's he rose rapidly to the rank of Col. during the early years of the War, and became one of the illustrious Ga. leaders of partisan American forces. He ranks among such men as Colonels Elijah Clarke, John Jones, Benjamin Few, William Few and Dooly. He distinguished himself at the Battle of Burke County Jail (Jan., 1779) by his defeat of the Tory Daniel McGirth at Isaac Lockhart's place (Aug., 1779) and in many other engagements, 1779-1782. [1]

During the dark days when the new provisional State Government had to move its capitol frequently because of British and Tory harassment, Twiggs served in the State Assembly as a representative of Burke, 1779, 1781, and 1782, [2] and on the Governor's Supreme Executive Council from Dec. 3, 1779 to Jan. 7, 1780. Council meetings were at Augusta under Richard Hawley, President and Acting Governor. [3]

After the War Col. Twiggs moved to Augusta. He represented Richmond County three times in the State Senate (1791, 1804 and 1804-06), and once in the Assembly (1800). [4]

David Emanuel, Jr. and Twiggs were brothers-in-law. Twiggs' son, David Emanuel Twiggs, b. in 1790, was the oldest Gen. in the Confed. Army. He had served with distinction in the Mexican War, continued an Army career and at the time of the Civil War was next in seniority to Gen. Winfield Scott. He was made a Major-Gen. in the C.S.A., but because of age and infirmity soon had to retire. He d. Sept. 15, 1862 at Augusta and is buried at the old family cemetery ten miles from Augusta.

1
Maj. McCalls history

2
Official Register 1861/62, p. 1219

3
Ibid, pp. 995 and 1005.

4
Ibid, pp. 1154 and 1355.

KATE C. WAKELEE, a Northerner, b. in Conn. (1829), came to teach school in the South and to be near a cousin from Conn. who had md. Augustus Seaborn Jones. Miss Wakelee was an able teacher, and a young lady of some literacy talent, contributing frequently and acceptably both to the Augusta and Waynesboro press. One of her poems, written for The Waynesboro News, was a sparkling pen picture of a number of prominent young men in Waynesboro and other sections of Burke, giving to each a sobriquet, suggested by some personal characteristic. One of the victims to whom the title of "Bank Bill" had been applied, responded in rather a sarcastic vein. Unfortunately, we do not have the original caricature in verse nor "Bank Bills" reply; only her dignified but touching effort to make amends.

BANK BILL

"Dear 'Bank Bill' I am worried and puzzled tonight;
'Tis hard to be blamed when the heart is all-right;
I thought with sly mischief to tease a few friends
And then by acknowledging all make amends,
But I find some are wounded, who never were meant,
A misprint has thwarted the kindest intent,
So with errors of printing and errors of guessing
I'm in a dilemma that's almost distressing.
        X X X X
I wait a true penitent, am I forgiven?
Each penitent tear is a pure pearl in Heaven.
With this 'buenos noche' dear Mr. 'Bank Bill'.
Pleasant dreams, happy wakings. Melanie Maxwell."

That she never married, we know from A Lost Arcadia, so we fear the worst happened (if it were a real interest in dear "Mr. Bank Bill"). The mind cannot help turning to, "it might have been".

After the first Battle of Manassas she wrote a very pretty tribute in verse to the memory of Gen. Francis S. Bartow, which was published in the Augusta Constitutionalist. She also secured a prize offered by the Field and Fireside for the best story written for its columns.

She was a teacher by profession and an optimist by nature. She never seemed to see the dark side of anything or anybody. She was always bright and witty and a charming correspondent. Sometime after she had retired she came one winter for a visit to the home of Mrs. Ida Jones, and her death was a very sad one. Sitting in her room before a glowing fire and busied with her pen and paper, her dress became in some way ignited and before aid could reach her she was fatally burned.

She is buried in the Fair Haven Methodist Church Cemetery alongside members of the Birdsville family. Her grave marker contains the dates: b. 8-27-1829; d. 2-5-1905.

THE GEORGE WALKER FAMILY

George Walker and his brother, Thomas Walker, together with their sister, Mary, and her husband, John Dallas, whom she md. in Ireland, came to America from Ireland in 1750. John Dallas and his wife settled on Sassafras River in Delaware. The connection was not kept up between the families. Thomas after a few years spent in S.C., settled in Richmond Co., Ga., near Hephzibah in 1756 and raised a large family. Some of his descendants live in that county.

George Walker settled on Brier Creek in Burke Co., and in 1756 md. Mary Gerhardt Duhart, d/o John Duhart. They had 12 children born to them: 1st Mary was b. Dec. 10, 1757; she md. Gen. William Byne and had five children: Martha, Margaret, Elijah, Enoch and Mary. There are no living descendants of this branch.

2nd, Esther b. Feb. 29, 1759. She md. Isaiah, Apr. 27, 1792. They had two children. Mary md. Wm. Stone of Milford, Conn. He was first a teacher, then a Waynesboro merchant, and member of the first town council. The first meeting was in his house. Margaret md. Welcome Allen, a native of N.H. They lived in Augusta, Ga. where he was a prosperous merchant.

3rd, John Walker, b. Sept. 5, 1760. He md. Frances Byne, a sister of Gen. Wm. Byne and had four children: Isaac, Edmund, John B., and Eliza Dawson.

4th, Elizabeth Walker, b. Dec. 25, 1761. She md. John Jones, lived in Burke Co. and had seven children: Mary, George, Esther, Eliza, Rebecca, John and Margaret A. Some descendants are now living in Burke County.

5th, George Walker, b. Nov. 14, 1763, settled in Longstreet, in Pulaski Co. He had nine children: Joel, Rebecca, Polly, George, David, Thomas B., Charles, Sarah, and Betsy.

6th, William Walker, b. Sept. 5, 1765. He settled first in Putnam, then moved to Harris Co. He had seven children: Dr. Austin M. Thatcher, Virgil, David E., William, George, Lucian, and Polly.

7th, Rebecca, b. Oct. 5, 1767. She md. Henry Byne and had three children, Thomas, Edmund and Henry. This branch is now extinct.

8th, Thomas Walker, b. Feb. 3, 1769. Nothing known of him; whether he ever md. or even reached maturity.

9th & 10th, David Walker, b. Nov. 3, 1771 and Enoch Walker, b. Jan. 23, 1773. These brothers lived together on a farm on Little River in Morgan Co. Neither ever md. They each d. in their 44th year. They are buried beside each other and their brother, John Walker, in the old Walker grave yard in Morgan. Co.

11th, Margaret, b. Jan. 30, 1775, md. Reuben Reynolds in Burke Co. and had five children: Thomas, Walker, Margaret, Reuben Y. and John A.

12th, Moses Walker, b. May 2, 1776, had six children: Frank, Moses, Margaret, Maria, Alex and Isaiah.

The trunk of the tree represents Georgia Walker, originator of the family in America. His children are represented by the twelve main branches whose names and date of birth are shown in this synopsis.

The Walker Family Tree. The original steel engraved was owned by the late Mrs. Wylie Gresham (DeForest McElmurray Gresham). A copy belongs to Miss Ruby Davis on Water Street, Waynesboro, Ga.[1]

---

[1]This synopsis of the George Walker family tree was given to A. M. Hillhouse in 1970.

JOHN WOOLFOLK WALKER was b. in Augusta, Ga. in 1907, the s/o John W. Walker and Mattie P. Walker. He attended elementary school and high school there and in 1927 graduated from the Univ. of Ga. After college he engaged in the banking, investment security and insurance businesses in Augusta.

In 1935 he md. Marion Neely of Waynesboro and Augusta and they had two children, John Walker, Jr., and Louise P. Walker.

In 1942 he moved to Waynesboro and worked with his father-in-law, Robert C. Neely, Jr.,in the cotton warehouse, ginning and fertilizer businesses.

In 1977 he ran for City Council in Waynesboro and was elected and again in 1979 he was re-elected to this body.

Retirement from active business was effected in 1979 and at the present time, in addition to his councilman duties, he is serving as Sec.-Treas. of the Waynesboro Development Corp., which is an industrial promotion organization aimed at attracting new industry and business to Burke Co. and to Waynesboro.

THOMAS H. WALL, JR. - Carrying on extensive scholastic activities down to the present, Thomas H. Wall, Jr., is superintendent of the schools of Pulaski. His work has been markedly beneficial to the people of this dist., and has caused him to be honored and trusted in a wide circle of acquaintance.

Mr. Wall was b. in Midville, Ga., a s/o Thomas H. Wall, a former banker and merchant; a former mayor and chairman, for 16 years, of the school board, of Midville, and Vashti (Hughes) Wall, his wife, also of Ga.

The public schools gave Thomas H. Wall, Jr., his preliminary education, and afterward he became a student at Mercer Univ., in Macon, there being graduated in 1928 with the degree of B.A. Taking up teaching, he was engaged first of all in the schools of Sylvania, one year as principal and three years as superintendent at Collins, continuing there until he accepted his present post of superintendent of schools at Pulaski, succeeding a Mr. Garner in this office. His achievements as head of the local school system have been such as to add substantially to the cultural life of his community.

He is, moreover, one of the most popular residents of Pulaski. Eagerness to do everything in his power for civic betterment and to promote prosperity and general welfare has been a quality that has consistently stood out among his characteristics. Pulaski itself stands in the midst of a large farming area, and Mr. Wall does not, for that reason, belong to many clubs and civic organizations, as do some teachers and school administrators, but he is none the less widely known and beloved. He holds memberships in several fraternities that he joined in his student days, but mostly he gives his time and attention to his work of education and school management.

In 1932 Thomas H. Wall, Jr., md. Jimmie Lee Overstreet, of Sylvania, Ga. They are the parents of one son, Thomas H. Wall III, who was b. Dec. 20, 1933. [1]

---

[1] The Story of Georgia, p. 601.

W. T. WALTON. Mr. Walton represents the county of his nativity. He is a s/o Hughes and Rebecca Walton, and was b. Sept. 15, 1839. He attended school at Grove Mound, Burke Co., and afterwards took an irregular course at Emory College.

He was engaged in farming; his present avocation, from the time of leaving school until the outbreak of the War, when he entered the Army as Private in the Burke Sharpshooters - the first co. that left his county. His first service as at Tybee Island. Withdrawing from the Sharpshooters, he joined a co. of cavalry from Chatham Co., of which he was elected 2nd Lieut. and which formed a part of the 5th Ga. Reg't, under the command of Col. R. H. Anderson. For quite a while his regiment was in service on the coast, but it was subsequently ordered under Gen. Wheeler's command, joining him at Kennesaw Mt. Afterward he was in Gen. Hampton's command, and with that command was paroled, upon the surrender of Gen. Johnston's Army, in N. C.

In 1865, he was md. to Miss Ida E. Gordon. Mr. Walton was elected Capt. of the Burke Hussars, a cavalry co. which he commanded for about five years before resigning his commission. This co. was awarded the prize at Augusta at the reunion of Hampton's Brigade in that city, over all competing co's from Ga. and S. C. Gen. Fields, an old army officer, remarked on that occasion, that Mr. Walton was the best drilled cavalry officer he had ever seen, and Gen. Hampton seconded the compliment paid by Gen. Fields.

Mr. Walton's political life began with his election, in 1866, to the Sheriff of his county, which office he held 18 months and then resigned it. He was elected to the Legislature in 1876, and re-elected in 1877 by a majority of about 900 out of about 1,600 votes.

GEORGE O. WARNOCK was b. Jan. 29, 1842 in Burke Co., s/o Nancy E. Moore Warnock. His father d. when George O. was only six months old. His mother lived until 1888. One brother, William, was killed at Sharpsburg and the other was severly wounded in the same battle, but he lived until 1886.

"Judge" Warnock was a gallant Confed. soldier. He enlisted with Co. B, 7th Ga. Volunteers. He was made 2nd Lieut. in this organization. He served with that co. for six months, and then organized a co. known as the 21st Ga. Cavalry, being in active service for two years. He then became a Lieut. in the Seventh Cavalry until he was wounded at Trevillian Station, Va., where he was captured and taken to Ft. Delaware until the close of the War. At one time he was Commandant of Camp Gordon, U.C.V. in Burke Co.

He took an active interest in Waynesboro and Burke Co. governments. His charities and church work were large and he was a pillar in the Waynesboro Methodist Church.

He was Clerk of the Burke Superior Court, a board member of the County Commissioners, an Alderman (city); also connected with the First National Bank and the Bank of Waynesboro and a member of the Board of Stewarts; member of the Waynesboro Lodge No. 274 F & AM. Dr. McFerrin for six years was very close to him. He financed a Sunday School Room. He practiced the principle of stewardship in life.

Judge Warnock had an estate of $100,000 to $125,000. His will established a fund of $35,000 for helping worthy white boys and girls to get a college education. Initially Gray Quinney, Joe Law and Evans Heath were the first Trustees of the Educational Fund. They were to make reports to the Grand Jury as to its distribution.

He d. on Sat., Dec. 20, 1924 and was buried in the Magnolia Cemetery.

ELI WARREN was b. in Burke Co. in Feb., 1801. The father, Joseph Warren, removed to Lawrence Co..where he and the mother died while Lott (his brother) and Eli were two of a large family of children and were reared in Wilkinson Co. by their brother-in-law, Rev. Charles Culpepper, who educated them in the country schools, neither ever having been at school in a town or village.

Eli, like his brother, Lott, never drank intoxicating liquor, never chewed or smoked tobacco. Eli, when a youth spent two years in Miss., but returned to Ga., and in the office of his brother, studied law and was admitted to the Bar in 1823. He served many years as a member of the Legislature of Lawrence Co., in the House and Senate; and was often elected without opposition. He later resided in the beautiful town of Perry in Houston Co., and practiced law.[1]

---
[1]
Herbert Fielder, A Sketch of the Life and Times and Speeches of Joseph E. Brown, Springfield, Mass (1883), p. 48.

LOTT WARREN, a scion of one of the old and honored families of Ga., lent distinction to his native state through his able services as a jurist, a member of Congress and a citizen of sterling character. He was b. in Burke Co., Ga., Oct. 30, 1797, his ancestors having come from England and settled in Va., whence his father, Josiah Warren, removed to N. C., from which latter state he came to Ga. The early education of Lott Warren was secured under the tutorage of several private instructors, and in 1816 he became a clerk in a retain mercantile establishment in Dublin, Laurens Co., Ga. Shortly afterward he was drafted into the state militia, for service in the Seminole War and was elected 2nd Lieut. of the Laurens Co. He served with distinction during the campaign and on his discharge again became identified with business affairs.

Having long cherished the ambition of becoming a lawyer, he applied himself to technical study, and in 1820 entered the law office of Daniel McNeil, a prominent lawyer of Dublin. In the same year was solemnized his marriage to Miss Jane Desaubleaux, d/o a French general who came to America to assist the colonies in their struggle for independence, and who was an active participant in the war of the Revolution. In 1821 young Warren was admitted to the Bar, forthwith opened an office in Dublin and entered upon the practice of the profession for which he had well fortified himself. In 1825 he removed to Marion, Twiggs Co., and in the following year received from Gov. Troup appointment to the office of Solicitor-General.

He became very prominent and influential in the legal circles of the State, and in 1830 was elected to the State Senate. In the same year he was elected Judge of the Superior Court of the Southern Dist. of Ga., for a term of three years. In 1834 he resumed the active practice of law, in Americus, Sumter Co., and in 1838 he was elected a Representative in Congress, being chosen as his own successor in 1840. His career in Congress was distinguished and on the return from his service in the National Capital he was elected to the bench of the Superior Court of the Southwestern Dist. of the State in 1843, and re-elected in 1847. He d. in 1861, in the court house at Albany, while defending a client charged with murder, his death being the result of a stroke of appoplexy.[1]

---

[1] Cyc of Georgia, Vol. III, pp. 527-528.

AMOS GRATTAN WHITEHEAD, was b. July 11, 1811 at "Spread Oak" in Burke Co. His parents were Susannah Dowse (b. Jan. 27, 1777) and William Whitehead (b. Nov. 29, 1773). He was always known as Amos. He with his brother both were reared by some members of the family as both parents had died when the two boys were respectively three and five years old.

Amos entered Franklin College (now Univ. of Ga.) in the sophomore class of 1827 and graduated in 1830 in the middle of his class. He belonged to the Phi Kappa literary society and later became a quiet country gentleman and a planter.

In 1835 he md. Elizabeth McKinne, oldest d/o Ann Galphin and Barna McKinne.

The family were Presbyterians of the highest order, but while he attended church regularly, he never joined. As often said, Elizabeth looked after the household matters, medical and others, as well as religious, while Amos rode over the plantation and gave directions to the overseers. Their plantation was known as "Ivanhoe" and it remains today owned by some of his descendants, the Paul Dyes.

He was named after Sir Henry Grattan, English statesman and member of Parliament because his father admired his political views.

Amos served with the state troops around Atlanta in 1864. During the Civil conflict his wife was actively in hospital work, spending most of her time at the "Wayside House" in Millen, Ga. from the time it was opened in 1862 until it was "laid waste" by Sherman's Army, Nov. 1864.

The two brothers, despite their inheritance was not fully legally documented because most papers perished in the Burke County Court House fire of 1856. But they seemed to be prosperous at a very early age, because they rode to Baltimore, MD on horseback and ordered two identical sets of English china. When the china arrived by boat at an east coast port, a wagon was dispatched to pick up the china. One set marked (each piece) "Amos Grattan Whitehead (Ivanhoe)" and the other set, "John P. C. Whitehead (Waverly)", their plantation homes.

Ivanhoe burned in 1870 and everything of the china was destroyed except a cup and saucer and two silver tablespoons engraved "Ivanhoe" and Amos Grattan Whitehead. This remnant is now owned by Grattan Whitehead Rowland.

Amos named his oldest son John P. C. Whitehead and was known as J.P.C. W. II from Amos's brother.[1]

---

[1] This sketch is from Grattan Whitehead Rowland, The Whiteheads of Burke County, Georgia (Section 30), 1977, # 30-4.

AMOS GRATTAN WHITEHEAD, MD. was b. Feb. 14, 1841 at "Spread Oak" plantation in the same room his father and grandfather were born. His mother was Mary Ann Wallace Dent, d/o Dr. John Dent, one of the founders of the Medical College of Ga. He was sent to the Univ. of Ga. at the age of 13 and graduated at 19.

At the beginning of the Civil War, he joined the celebrated "Clinch Rifles" Co. and served one year. He was then appointed aide-de-camp in the staff of Gen. Montgomery Gardner and later commanded a battery of artillery. After the War he continued his studies at the Medical College of Ga. in Augusta and after receiving his M.D. degree, began in March, 1866 active practice in Waynesboro which he continued until his death in 1903.

He md. in 1871 Tallulah Gilbertine Neyland whose father was John Prioleau Neyland and her mother was Agnes C. Cline of Savannah. Her grandfather was Rev. Gilbert Neyland who md. Charlotte Prioleau, great-granddaughter of Elisha Prioleau, the first Pastor of the French Huguenots of Charleston, S.C.

He was president of the Med. Ass'n of Ga. for one term and was given a solid gold-headed walking cane engraved with his name and the year 1886. He was a 32nd degree Mason, member of the Knights of Honor, the American Legion of Honor, the protected home sole, the Royal Arcanam and the United Confed. Vets.

He md. (2) Mrs. Florence (Byne) Routzahn, d/o Edmond and Charlotte (Young) Byne in 1887. The Byne family was of French Huguenot lineage.

For many years he was not a member of any church, but a few years before his death he joined the Episcopal Church in Waynesboro.

Among the heirlooms inherited by his only grandson [1] are his gold watch from his father, his Whitehead china cup and saucer, two silver spoons, his solid gold-headed walking cane and the Priorleau creamer engraved J.P. & E.B., meaning John Prioleau and Elizabeth Broadbelt, his wife's great-grandparents.

He was always notably chivalrous, as insisting everyone precede him through any door or walkway. Later, Mrs. Dan I. MacIntyre (#34-25) [2] often told how

---

[1] Grattan Whitehead Rowland
[2] A cousin of Gratten Whitehead Rowland

provoked she was when she often visited Dr. Whitehead and his wife, Tallulah. When as a young girl it was customary to sleep late the mornings after a dance or party. However, Cousin Tallulah would tiptoe up the stairs and beg her to put on something and come down stairs as Cousin Grattan was pacing the floor and refusing to sit down to his breakfast until she was present.[3]

---

[3] This sketch is from Grattan Whitehead Rowland, The Whiteheads of Burke County, Georgia (Section 30), 1977, #30-13.

FLORENCE BYNE (ROUTZAHN) (WHITEHEAD) was b. Dec. 19, 1847, the d/o Charlotte Young and Edmund Byne. On her mother's side she was a granddaughter of Gen. Willis Young. She grew up with a class of six girls who were taught by a fine private teacher, Mrs. Kate M. Davis. The school closed in 1861.

She md. first, Lewis H. Routzahn, a merchant who settled in Waynesboro from N. C. They had three children: Bertha R., md. George M. Gordon; Haidee R., md. Judson S. McElmurray, and Madeline R., md. Jas. H. Whitehead.

She was a charter member of the Woman's Club and was devoted to the Waynesboro Presbyterian Church. As a young girl she provided the music for the Sunday School. Later she directed the choir and played the organ. Her gift of music furnished the church music over some 53 years. She was also at ease with the harp.

Mr. Routzahn d. Aug. 1, 1885. Subsequently, she md. Dr. Amos Grattan Whitehead. The doctor d. on March 23, 1904. She lived until Feb. 9, 1925. She is buried in the Waynesboro Confed. Memorial Cemetery (the Old Cemetery).

She was survived by one daughter, Haidie (Mrs. Judson McElmurray); two grandchildren; Mrs. P. W. Thompson, Mrs. Bannon, and several great-grandchildren.

JAMES HARPER WHITEHEAD was b. Nov. 19, 1866, the s/o Margaret Ireland Harper and John P. C. Whitehead, in the old family "Spread Oak" plantation. He was descended from one of the first families in Burke Co. His education was received at Milledgeville and at the age of 16 he entered business in Waynesboro as a clerk in one of the mercantile establishments. A few years later he entered business for himself and was most successful.

Mr. Whitehead md. three times. First, he md. Carolyn McElmurray, d/o Annie E. Shewmake and John F. McElmurray, on Nov. 27, 1895. Sadly, she d. in June, 1898. Second, he md. Madeline Routzahn, d/o Florence Byne and Louis H. Routzahn. She lived only seven years. Third, on Dec. 2, 1919, he md. Nora L. Edmonston from Savannah. She d. Aug. 31, 1920. He was crushed.

Mr. Whitehead served his city as Mayor and was interested in all things pertaining to its progress. He was president of the Waynesboro Gin Co., president of Hatchers Mill Fishing Club, president of the Waynesboro Country Club, the Exchange Club, ex-president of the Citizens Bank of Waynesboro, member of the County Board of Education and served as Chairman for eight years. In every way he was interested in the business affairs of the city and county. He was a successful merchant and cotton buyer, and contributed much of his time and talents to assisting in every way in the city's development.

During the past few years he became interested in the Waynesboro Country Club, and aided in the development of this pleasure resort into one of the finest swimming pools, club house and pleasure grounds.

He worshipped in the Waynesboro Presbyterian Church and took an active interest in the welfare of the Church. His charities were large and many whom he helped never knew the source of their beneficence.

Mr. Whitehead's business career in Waynesboro was marked by a ruggedly honest life, nothing shady ever being tolerated by him in any business transaction. His public life was marked with the same stripe and his home life was most lovable. He was loved and esteemed by all with whom he came in contact and he was one of the highest and truest types of citizenry in the county. Truly his place in the community will be hard to fill.

The funeral was held at his late residence at 11:00. Rev. G. W. Tollett, assisted by Rev. Willis Howard and Rev. George Acree. Business was suspended during the funeral. Interment was in the Waynesboro Magnolia Cemetery. He died July 23, 1928.

JOHN PHILPOT CURREN WHITEHEAD, II.was b. at Ivanhoe, Burke Co., July 18, 1837, the s/o Elizabeth McKinne and Amos Grattan Whitehead. He began law practice in Augusta. But a legal card in The Waynesboro News (1858) showed that he was an attorney in Augusta, but that he "paid particular attention to the practice in Burke." Also he contributed some poetry under the name of "Briefless Barrister", and to a continued story, a short novelette, "Rosina, A Story".

In April, 1861 he went to War with the "Burke Sharpshooters". The co. was ordered to Tybee and Brunswick for training. He was elected 1st Lieut. Later Brig.-Gen. Marcellus A. Stovall chose Whitehead for his Assistant Adjutant-General in Stovall's Brigade, Cheathams Division. He was promoted to Captain. On April 29, 1862 he md. Catherine E. Fitzsimons. Nine times Capt. Whitehead was mentioned in the Official Records. Only three will be mentioned here. At the struggle over Missionary Ridge, near Chattanooga, Oct. 3, 1863, Stovall commended Whitehead and two others: "Who displayed great coolness and daring during the conflict, and to them I am much indebted for valuable services rendered".[1] Again while Stovall's brigade was supporting Wheeler's Cavalry in Northern Georgia (May 29-June 2, 1864), Capt. Whitehead (and two others) were praised by Stovall "all three of them had their horses shot from under them and were conspicuous for their coolness under fire".[2] On May 29, 1864, Capt. L. P. Thomas, commanding the 42nd Ga. Regt. wrote: "and before closing I must return my thanks to Capt. Whitehead, Lts. Cahal and Dearing of Stovall's staff, who were constantly moving among us

---
[1] Series I, Vol. XXX, Part II, Oct. 3, 1863.

[2] Series I, Vol. XXXVIII, Part III, p. 826.

in the different engagements, and on the march, going where duty called them, and where the fighting was severe, around showers of bullets and shells, and were encouraging deeds of daring and glory."[3] Whitehead was with Stovall's Brigade until the end of the War.

After the War ended, he was made the Solicitor-General of the Ga. Middle Circuit. In 1870 he went to Texas and settled first in Homestead until 1876 when he moved to Austin as City Attorney. Later in 1882 he became Sec. of the Texas State Senate, and announced for the office of State Attorney-General, but had to withdraw due to his health. Later he moved to Laredo and was elected City Attorney. He came to Dallas in 1884 where he was made Assistant City Attorney.

On Dec. 14, 1906 he fell on slick pavement, just north of the courthouse, and without regaining consciousness from the fall, died at the City Hospital six days later on Dec. 20, 1906.

At the time of his death his wife was with the U. S. Treasury Dept. in Washington, D. C. She died Sept. 1, 1930 and is interred in the Cottage Cemetery in Richmond County.[4]

---

[3] Ibid., p. 828.

[4] Much of the sketch is from Grattan Whitehead Rowland, *The Whiteheads of Burke County, Georgia*, Section 30 (1977), # 30-7.

WILLIAM DOWSE WHITEHEAD, s/o Elizabeth McKinne and Amos Grattan Rowland, was b. April 3, 1841 at Ivanhoe Plantation in Burke Co. He entered the Univ. of Ga., Aug. 1, 1856 with the class of 1861. Member of the Phi Kappa literary society. Left college Aug., 1860.

He was a planter at the time he entered the War in April, 1861, Co. D., 2nd Ga. Reg't. He was Color Bearer and was killed July 2, 1862 at Malvern Hill with the flag of his Regiment in his hand. He had been promoted to Corporal a few days before.[1]

---

[1] This sketch is from Grattan Whitehead Rowland, *The Whiteheads of Burke County, Georgia*, Section 30 (1977), # 30-9.

EZEKIEL WILLIAMS, b. 1806 and d. in Burke Co. on Jan. 1, 1867. He was a successful planter. He remained a bachelor. In his will he provided for his half sister: Mary Prescott and her two daughters; a sister, Sarah Williams, w/o William Allen of Houston Co., Ga., and her four daughters. And one niece, Sarah Ophelia Allen, who md. William Cox, was included also in his will.

He sponsored a Confed. Co, known as the "Williams Volunteers", when the War broke out. His contribution was important for the War. After the co. returned in April or May, 1865 he had some months yet to live. He must have praised each soldier he met and bolstered their spirits.

ROY F. CHALKER, JR., was b. Oct. 31, 1946, attended Waynesboro High School and Emory University. On Sept. 14, 1969, he married Kimberly Cibulski of Girard, Ga. They have two daughters:

1. Anne Neil, b. Sept. 20, 1972
2. Jennifer, b. Aug. 7, 1976

He has been active in the City of Waynesboro and Burke County through a number of several clubs and societies. President of West Burke Civitan Club (1975); Waynesboro Rotary Club (1976); President of Burke County Chamber of Commerce (1978). He has served six years in the Georgia National Guard.

Member of the Georgia Bicentennial Commission (1972-79); member of the Georgia State Democratic Committee; member of Burke County Democratic Committee; Delegate to the 1976 National Democratic Committee; member Inaugural Staff of President Jimmy Carter, Jan.,1977; member of Waynesboro City Council (1974-75); Mayor of Waynesboro (1976-80). At the age of 29, he was the youngest person ever elected to the Mayor's Office in Waynesboro. He first won the two-term beginning Dec., 1975; again a second race in Dec., 1977.

Improving the housing opportunities for low-income residents of the city is his proudest achievement. He said that:

"We've torn down over 200 (substandard houses) since I've been in office. Some were abandoned or had to be evacuated after sustaining fire damage."

Chalker stresses that no one was thrown out of a home; no matter how retched, just to keep the Urban Renewal drive on schedule.

"We were obligated by the federal government to see that these families had a decent and sanitary place to move to and we had to pay their moving expenses as well."

His father has stepped down and now he is the Editor and Publisher of The True Citizen. As far as the near future is concerned, Chalker, Jr. sees himself concentrating on his business ventures and leaving the world of politics, at least for awhile.

For other of his successes in the Mayor's Office during four years, see The True Citizen, Jan. 9, 1980.

WILLIAM H. (BILL) CRAVEN, JR. was b. in Bamberg, S.C. on Nov. 1, 1929, the son of William H. Craven and Marion Easterling Craven.

The son of a County Agricultural Agent, Craven never forgot his heritage, as he has spent his adulthood in an effort to make the earth more fruitful for a growing world population.

Educated in the public schools of Bamberg, Craven graduated in the spring of 1946 and in that autumn entered Clemson University to pursue a Bachelor of Science degree in Agronomy and a commission in the U.S. Army Reserve. He accomplished both in June of 1950.

While at Clemson, Craven was active in many student organizations. He was a member of Senior Council, the University's student governmental body; Alpha Zeta, the honorary agricultural fraternity; and Alpha Phi Omega, the honorary fraternity for former outstanding members of the Boy Scouts of America.

Upon graduation from Clemson, Craven was employed as an agronomist for the Epting Distributing Company of Leesville, S.C. After two years with this agribusiness firm, Craven was called to active military duty with the U.S. Army during the Korean War.

At the conclusion of his military duties, Craven began his duties as an Assistant County Agent in Edgefield, S.C. with the Clemson Cooperative Extension Service. There he served for two-and-one-half years until he was promoted to County Agent in Saluda County, S.C.

Serving in Saluda County for 14½ years, Craven helped change the county's agriculture from one dominated by crops to one led by a livestock economy. All the while, the county's farm income, both gross and net, was soaring. He chaired many community activities while in Saluda. Two noteworthy ones were the Saluda County Agricultural Building Committee which remodeled and doubled the size of the county's agricultural center, and the Boy Scout Memorial Building. The latter was South Carolina's finest local troop Boy Scout facility.

In May of 1971, Craven came to Burke County as her County Agricultural Agent. He found a bustling agriculture. It was one marked by a rich heritage and bright future. County Agent Craven has been an active part of that agriculture since his arrival in Burke County. The University of Georgia honored Craven in 1980 with her Distinguished Public Service Award.

He has brought the latest in scientific farming to the county and has prevailed upon the farmers to employ the newest techniques on the land. Burke's agriculture has blossomed during the years of Craven's service. It is today, in many different areas, Georgia's leading farm county.

In 1951, Craven married the former Lois Anita Kearse of Olar, S.C. She was a graduate in music from Winthrop College in Rock Hill, S.C.

From this marriage came two children. William H. Craven, III was b. in April of 1955. He graduated from the University of Georgia in 1978 where he studied Landscape Architecture. Pamela Ann Craven was b. in Oct., of 1957. She finished Clemson University with a Bachelor of Science degree in Microbiology in 1979 and was granted her Master of Science degree in Microbiology from the same institution in 1981.

Craven has been active in many civic and community endeavors over the years. He has served as District Governor of Lion's International. The Boy Scouts of America have bestowed upon him their coveted Silver Beaver Award. The people of Saluda County, S.C., honored him with a "Bill Craven Day" in 1971. A similar day was his in 1974 in Burke County when the Bill Craven Scholarhip was established for graduate study in agriculture.

Early in his County Agent career Craven began to write a weekly farm column for the county newspapers. He has continued that over the many years of his service. Three times in the 1970's the column was termed the nation's top farm column. His accompanying news photos have also been thrice declared the nation's best.

Craven chaired the committee responsible for the funding and building of the Burke County Office Park. This spacious office and auditorium complex has added greatly to the economic and cultural life of Burke. Additionally, Craven originated, and largely photographed, the idea of The Pictorial Panorama of Burke's Rural Past and Present. The one hundred color canvases hang upon the corridor walls of the Burke County Office Park and richly illustrate the story of Burke's varied rural life.

HENRY J. FULLBRIGHT came to Waynesboro in about 1892-1895. He had attended Young Harris College and had graduated in 1892. He first went into the office of Judge William H. Davis. Later he founded a partnership with W. R. Callaway which lasted from Oct. 1, 1899 until 1901. Then another partnership was formed with Judge P. P. Johnston, which lasted five years.

In 1897 he married Miss Chessie Dobbs and they set up a home in Waynesboro. His friends urged him to run for the House of Representatives and he won. Mr. W.R. Burton was the other Representative. In 1909 and 1910, Fullbright soon showed that he could carry committee loads much beyond others. His record was tremendous: Amendments to the Constitution; counties and court matters; education; general judiciary; hygiene and sanitation; labor and labor statistics; the penitentiary; public property; temperance; University of Georgia & its' branches; Ways and Means; and in addition, was Chairman of the special judiciary, which later committee was to have considered more bills than any other committee of the House, having reported during the Session of 1910, 135 bills. Nearly one-fourth of all the bills introduced during the term was referred to his Committee as it was known as the "working committee" and the Chairman being present and presiding at every meeting of the Committee during the session. In 1912-13 his friends with the House wanted him to run for the Speaker's Race, but he declined.

During World War I he was appointed to handle two matters. He was appointed to supervise the food administration and he was a part of the government's appeal agent on the Draft Board.

On Dec. 1918, he was appointed State Tax Commissioner to succeed Judge John C. Grant. He moved then to Atlanta, this was the post he held some seven years, from 1918 to 1925. Fullbright suggested to the next Governor that a Tax Review Board would be a good idea, but the new governor did not accept his advice.

He returned back to Waynesboro in 1925 and established a new law firm, Fullbright and Burney on Sept. 1, 1925. His father had died on Aug. 15, 1914, and was buried in Columbia County. His father had friends earlier in Waynesboro and was a Confederate Veteran.

The Atlanta Georgian picked up the fact that Fullbright had been placed in Who's Who in America and the reporter in 1929 wrote a fine article on Fullbright as one of the finest public officials in the State Government. He had already received a place on the Board of the North Georgia Agricultural College and was also made a Trustee of Emory University.

While Fullbright was in State Government, he had a small feud with Thomas B. Felder, a lawyer born in Burke County. Felder had placed in The Augusta Chronicle that he seeks only notoriety. Fullbright's position on temperance explains his position and did so in a well-worded communication. He was not making a fight for political preferment. Mr. Felder boasts that he was the council for a number of years for the Wholesale Liquor Dealers of America. He, Fullbright, at the same time only prosecuted violations of prohibition law in his county, when asked to do so by the citizens thereof.

The Fullbrights had four children and all four were achievers. Iris Fullbright was the first woman graduate in her class from Lagrange Female College.

Miss Eloise Fullbright married Supt. White of the Lawrenceville schools, also distinguished herself as a student at the same college. Miss Sarah Fullbright received her Master of Arts from the Ferrum Training School in Virginia, and Henry J. Fullbright, Jr., graduated with a B.A. degree and a LLB from Emory Univesity. He became a fine lawyer.

CHARLES GRAY GREEN, SR. was b. Feb. 6, 1921, the son of Alice Barron Gray and Walter Gresham Green, Jr.

He attended public schools in Waynesboro, Ga.; graduating in 1937. Following graduation he attended Emory-at-Oxford and Emory University. He received medical education at the University of Georgia School of Medicine; graduating in 1943. He served his internship at the University Hospital, Augusta, Ga.

In 1944 he married Mary Juanita Gaston of Blacksburg, S.C. They have two children: Charles Gray Green, Jr., and Mary Alice Green Colley.

He served as medical officer in the U.S. Marines, 1944 to 1946. He started practice of medicine in Waynesboro, Ga. in 1946.

CHARLES GRAY GREEN, JR., M.D. was b. the son of Dr. & Mrs. Charles Gray Green, Sr., Nov. 11, 1948, at Waynesboro, Ga. He graduated from the Waynesboro High School, University of Georgia, B.W. (1970), M.D. Medical College of Ga. (1974).

Internship Parkland Memorial Hospital (July 1974-75); Residency: Parkland Memorial Hospital and Stanford University Hospital (July 1975-Sept. 1977). Certified: American Board of Internal Medicine, June 1977. Licensed: #10384. Narcotic: AG7535531; SS: 255-74-9816.

Private Practice: Internal Medicine Diabetes, Sept. 19, 1977, to present. Attending Physician: University Hospital, Augusta, Ga., St. Joseph Hospital, Augusta, Ga., Doctors Hospital, Augusta, Ga., Eugene Talmadge Memorial Hospital, Augusta, Ga.

Post Graduate Work: Diabetes Mellitus in General Medicine Seminar, Mayo Clinic, Oct., 1978; Endocrine Society, Annual Post Graduate Seminar, Mayo Clinic, Oct., 1979; Fellow in Metabolism and Endocrinology, Medical College of Georgia, Augusta, Ga., 1979 to present.

Honors: Cum Laude graduate of University of Georgia, 1970; Phi Beta Kappa, 1970; Who's Who in American Colleges and Universities, 1970; AOA Honor Society, 1973; UpJohn Physician's Physician Board, 1974; Assistant Clinical Professor of Medicine, Medical College of Georgia, 1977. Elected to: Texas Chapter of American College of Physicians, June 1977; American College of Physicians, March, 1978; President, Augusta Area Diabetes Association, 1979-80; President, Augusta Diagnostic Associates P.C., 1979-80.

Membership: American Diabetes Association; American College of Physicians; First Presbyterian Church, Augusta, Georgia.

Presentations:

1. Organophosphate Poisoning, the Parkland Experience and a Review of the Literature, 1976, Parkland Hospital, Dallas, Tx.

2. Coccidioidomycosis, Case Report and Review of the Literature, 1976, Texas Southern School of Medicine, Dallas, Texas.

3. Fundiscopic Manifestations of Systematic Disease, 1977. Dallas V.A. Hospital, Dallas, Tx.

4. Speaker at "Advances in Internal Medicine", Changing Concepts in the Etiology, Genetics and Classification of Diabetes Mellitus." 1980.

Charles G. Green, Jr., married Margaret Graham Orr in June, 1970. She was b. in Lexington, Ky., on Jan. 5, 1947. She was educated in public schools in Lexington, Ky.; graduated from University of Georgia; Phi Beta Kappa, 1969; graduated Medical College of Georgia; AOA, 1973; Opthamology Residency at Texas Southwestern Medical School 1974-1977; private practice in Augusta, Ga. in Opthamology

Children:

1. Caroline Parker Green (4)
2. Walter Gresham Green, III (2)

JOB GRESHAM, JR. was b. July 20, 1781, the son of Job Gresham, Sr., and Mary Byne of King & Queen County, Virginia. Sometime before 1800 his father moved his family to Lincoln County, Ky. When Job was not more than 18 or 19 years old, he decided to go to Burke County, Ga. He struck out on his own with one companion to go to Georgia where his grandfather, the Rev. Edmund Byne lived. Each one was leading a pack mule with all their earthly possessions. Job went to work for his uncle, Thomas Byne.

He married Mary Jones, b. July 10, 1785, the daughter of John and Margaret Walker Jones, about 1800-1801. They had three children. One was a daughter, who died in infancy. They had then two sons, Edmund Byne Gresham and John Jones Gresham.

Edmund Byne Gresham stayed in Burke County and John Jones Gresham was born on Jan. 21, 1812. After graduating from Franklin College with first honors in 1833, John Jones Gresham studied law in Augusta, practiced briefly in Waynesboro, and in 1836 settled in Macon where he was for many years a successful planter, lawyer, banker and businessman. He married on May 25, 1843, Mary E. Baxter, daughter of Thomas W. Baxter of Athens. He organized the Macon Manufacturing Company, the first steam cotton factory in the South and was president from 1851 to 1869. He was twice Mayor of Macon (1843; 1847), Judge of the Inferior Court (1860) and State Senator (1866-67). For nearly 50 years he was an elder of the First Presbyterian Church. In May of 1859, he was commissioner to the General Assembly of the Presbyterian Church meeting in Indianapolis.

They had two children. He died suddenly in Baltimore the 16th day of Oct., 1891, at the residence of his daughter, Mrs. Arthur W. Machen and was buried beside his wife in Rose Hill Cemetery in Macon.

(See *Testimonials to the Life and Character of John Jones Gresham*, John Murphy and Company, Printers, Baltimore, Md. (1892).)

EDMUND BYNE GRESHAM was one of the three delegates from Burke who voted for the Ordinance of Secession in 1861. He was b. about 1803-04, the son of Job and Mary Jones Gresham.[1] Although a de facto resident of Brothersville (later Hephzibah) where he owned a home, he retained his citizenship in Burke and several times represented Burke County in the General Assembly.[2] At the time of election to the Secession Convention he was a large planter, 57 years old, and the owner of 99 slaves.[3]

Walter A. Clark in *A Lost Arcadia* wrote this of him as a person:

"A successful planter and a man of kindly, genial nature and gentle, generous heart. He confessed to me once that he never made a horse trade in his life without worsting himself, and this was perhaps to his credit. On one occasion I heard him say, 'Do a man a wrong and you'll hate him for it all your days,' and I am sure through all his years he never had occasion for such a cause to bear ill will to any human being."[4]

After his death in 1872, the family remained for a time at Brothersville, but later sold the home and moved to Waynesboro. Mrs. Gresham was the former Sarah M. Anderson, daughter of Elisha Anderson, Jr. and Jane McCullers Anderson. Eight children were born of this union. One of his sons, Job A. Gresham, served as a young man for three years with the 48th Regiment of Georgia Volunteers in the Army of Northern Virginia under Gen. Robert E. Lee and was at the surrender at Appomattox Courthouse on April 9, 1865.

Children:

1. Mary Jane Gresham married first Jesse Green and after his death, she married Dr. G.B. Parnell: Jesse and Walter Green, and Lewis Parnell was the third son.
2. Sarah Adeline Gresham. She never married; known as "Miss Addie" and a beloved teacher in the Hephzibah High School and the Waynesboro Academy. Born 1841; died 1927.
3. Job Anderson Gresham, CSA, and Annie Lassiter. Their children included:
   a. Ida Gresham b. May 21, 1876. Married Samuel Gaines Story, II.
   b. Emmett Burdell Gresham b. March 7, 1875; d. May 17, 1936.
   c. Margaret Gresham Godbee b. Nov. 26, 1882; wife of Simeon A. Godbee. Died May 12, 1958.
   d. Oscar Milledge Gresham, W.W.-I, b. 1889; d. 1964.
4. John Jones Gresham, CSA, b. 1845 and d. 1910, married Ella Lassiter. Children:
   a. Mary Gresham, wife of John Milledge, b. Dec. 8, 1869; d. Aug. 16, 1944.
   b. Orrin Lassiter Gresham married Mary Dye b. 1875; d. 1946.
   c. Helen Gresham, wife of Seaborn H. Jones, b. Dec. 15, 1873; died Dec. 8, 1943.
   d. Arthur Gresham, husband of Ruth E. Jones, married June 23, 1915. Born Aug. 15, 1888; d. Oct. 10, 1953.
5. Harriet Gresham Burton b. 1851; d. 1935, wife of Robert H. Burton, CSA. No children.
6. Mary Gresham married Richard Milledge and lived in Atlanta. Their children were: John, Kate, Hattie, Richard, Rosa and Adeline.
7. Leora Scales b. Dec. 10, 1856; d. Dec. 23, 1934. Daughter of Francis Rebecca Martin and Robert Watt Scales. Wife of first Oscar R. Gresham. They had two children: Wyly and Fannie. Second husband--H.J. Davis.
8. Margaret H. Gresham was b. 1859. She lived 18 years; not married; d. Oct. 7, 1877.

---

[1] His mother was the daughter of John and Margaret Walker Jones.
[2] Elected to the House in 1847 and 1849-50 and to the State Senate in 1853-54 and 1857-58. Official Register, 1961/62, pp. 1221 and 1045.
[3] 1860 Census for Burke.
[4] A Lost Arcadia, p. 162. His picture and an excerpt from a letter which he wrote to his wife the day the Secession Convention took Georgia out of the Union, were reproduced in the Civil War Centennial Edition, The True Citizen, April 20, 1961.
[5] For ramification of this family, see Clark, A Lost Arcadia, pp. 162-163.
[6] Civil War Centennial Edition (T.C. op. cit.), p. 11B.
[7] Edmund B. Gresham in Dec., 1843 was made a Colonel in the Governor's Staff.

JOHN JONES GRESHAM, CSA, was b. March 25, 1845, the son of Sarah M. Anderson and Edmund Byne Gresham. He was a member of one of Burke County's oldest and most honored families. He passed away quietly at his home on Myrick Street in this city, Monday morning. Mr. Gresham was a native of Burke County and at the time of his death had reached the age of 65. When quite a young man he enlisted in the Confederate Army to fight for his beloved Southland. He served in Wheeler's division, 5th Georgia Cavalry and in Captain Marsh's Company. The memories of the confederacy and its many hard-fought battlefields were ever dear to him and he loved to mingle with his comrades and recount the glorious victories of the boys in Gray. He loved to attend the reunions and other gatherings of the Confederate Veterans.

And though his feeble condition often would not warrant his attendance, still with that persistent pluck and undaunted carage which characterized him as one of the South's bravest soldiers, he was always present and took and took an active part in making these occasions delightful for all.

After the war Mr. Gresham returned to his native county to take up the important duties of citizenship and gave his every effort to rehabilitating the Old South. By his thrift, intelligence and upright conduct, he early established himself as one of Burke's most representative citizens. Mr. Gresham was a man of remarkable memory and a most gifted conversationalist. It was a rare treat to hear him recount his many recollections of the War times. He d. June 6, 1910.

The funeral occurred at the residence 4 o'clock Tuesday afternoon, and was attended by many friends and relatives and Gordon Camp Veterans of the 60's. The internment was at the Magnolia Cemetery and he was placed to rest in the bosom of his native land covered with Dixie's choicest flavors.

Mr. Gresham was survived by his wife and four children: Mrs. Mamie Milledge, Mrs. Seaborn Jones and Messr's Orrin and Arthur Gresham.

CAPT. RICHARD H. MILLEDGE married Mary Gresham, a daughter of Sarah M. Anderson and Col. Edmund Byne Gresham, and from Burke County. They lived at Forsyth, then moved to Atlanta. They had two sons and four daughters: John, Kate, Hattie, Richard, Rosa and Adeline.

Richard ("Dick") Milledge was the descendant of a Colonial family. He was a Confederate veteran and a businessman in Atlanta some 30 years. He died at the residence of his daughter, Mrs. Emery H. Patillo of No. 11 Candler Street. He was interred in the Forsyth, Georgia Cemetery.

Capt. Milledge had a wide circle of friends and acquaintances. He came of distinguished ancestry. His father, Col. John Milledge, was one of the foremost citizens of Augusta in ante-bellum days. A grandson of the John Milledge of Athens, a former Governor of Georgia, who gave 600 acres of tract of land for starting the State University. His great-grandfather was Joseph Habersham, a colonial governor of Georgia.

EMMETT BURDELL GRESHAM was b. March 7, 1875, the son of Annie Lassiter and Job Anderson Gresham, CSA. He grew up in Burke County; studied in the Waynesboro Academy and graduated at the University of Georgia.

Since his father had served in the Civil War, he was interested in forming the Burke County company. In 1908 he was elected Captain of Co. E. On May 7, 1910, Capt. Gresham, Lts. M.C. Cohen and H.P. Jones went to Atlanta for ten days instruction in military matters at Fort McPherson.

On June 24, 1908, Emmett married Nona Johnston, the daughter of Lena Shewmake and Philip P. Johnston, Attorney. The billiant marriage included Mrs. James Whitehead, the matron of honor; the maid of honor was Lena Johnston, the sister of the bride. Miss Ida Story and Master John Shewmake preceded the bride, leaving the bride to lean on the arm of her father, Judge Philip P. Johnston, and was met by the groom and his best man, Mr. Orrin Gresham. Rev. Dr. Scruggs pronounced the ceremony in the Methodist Church (Waynesboro).

E.B. Gresham and H.C. Hatcher were in the Georgia House of Representatives in June 25, 1921. On Nov. 4, 1922, Emmett Gresham resigned the position of the Georgia Legislature to Governor Hardwick to seek the position of the Burke County Agricultural Agent. On Dec. 9, 1922, Mr. Gresham was elected the Agricultural Agent. He interviewed many cotton farmers who were watching the movement of the boll weevils toward Goergia and Burke County. The farmers knew that within two years the boll weevil would have to be fought. He also organized Boys Clubs in each school to help the farmers.

On Aug. 1, 1925, Mr. Gresham had again become the Superintendent of the County Schools. He was also placed on the State School Book Commission.

Mr. Gresham, before he left the County School Superintendency, he began back into the model book kept by County Superintendent J. H. Roberts, which showed the progress that was made under Roberts and other County School Superintendents. The 25 years while Mr. R.C. Neely was head of the County Board of Education he also worked for the greatest strides. Mr. Gresham, almost every week, placed in The True Citizen a new insight from the past.

Mr. Gresham was much disappointed that the Burke County Junior College at Waynesboro was closed after an early good start.

Mr. Gresham was very proud of his young daughter, Lena Shewmake Gresham. She finished her A.B. at the University of Georgia in three years. She was 15 years old and a freshman at Wesleyan College and finished there by 16. After two regular terms, plus two full summers, plus her freshman year, she was able to graduate at the end of Aug., 1929. She went to New York City to study dancing.

Mr. Gresham died at the age of 61 years on May 17, 1936, and was interred in the Magnolia Cemetery. His wife outlived him. She died April 28, 1964. While the Exchange Club was working hard to build a library in Burke County, she gave her service, and she had had considerable experience in libraries. She lived until April 28, 1964, and is also interred in the Waynesboro Magnolia Cemetery.

Their children:
1. Job Anderson Gresham b. March 25, 1911; d. Jan. 4, 1966.
2. Phil J. Gresham
3. Lena Shewmake Gresham
4. Emmett B. Gresham, Jr. b. May 25, 1923; d. Feb. 25, 1954.
5. Dolly

OSCAR MILLEDGE GRESHAM was the last of the fourth children of Annie Lassiter and Job Anderson Gresham, CSA.

He was known as "Scrap". He studied at the Waynesboro High School and then graduated at Georgia Tech (Institute of Technology) in Civil Engineering, and his first job was with the L & N Railroad.

Because Mexico had been disturbing the borders along Texas and U.S. soldiers were necessary to stop their raiding borders and destruction. Captain M.C. Cohen had been appointed as a recruiting officer. 2nd Lidt. O.M. Gresham, 1st Lidt. A.T. Murphey, and Capt. E. Howell McElmurray were the three first officers. The strength of Co. E was 64 soldiers. Milledge had come back to Waynesboro to do his duty. Their first barracks were at Macon, Ga., and then on to the U.S. Mexica borders

Another war was brewing. Germany began sinking American vessels by submarines and in Feb., 1917, the first of American Expeditionary Force (AEF) landed in France on June 26. Later Co. E from Waynesboro saw battle service. In 1919 they were back at home.

Later O.M. Gresham was promoted to Captain. He became the head of the Burke Light Infantry (BLI) and Post of the American Legion.

On Oct. 4, 1924, Milledge went to Europe and returned from his tour. It was most delightful and he enjoyed many familiar scenes which thousands of men did who saw service "over there".

When the boll weevil hit in 1924 and 1925 the farmers of Burke County wanted Milledge's older brother, Emmett B. Gresham to ask the Governor to let him fill the County Agriculture Agency, and Milledge served two terms as the County School Superintendent.

The year 1940 for O.M. Gresham was one full of changes. He was made Commander (Captain) and headed the BLI Post American Legion. Later the same year he was named Chairman of the Red Cross Roll Call.

On July 15, 1940, Porter W. Carswell resigned as the Editor of The True Citizen. On August 8, 1940, Milledge replaced Carswell and he held that post for several years.

On Nov. 14, 1940, his father, Job A. Gresham, died at age 98. On April, 1940, his father was not able to be at the celebration, but had his food served to him at the Millen Hospital. He was the last of the old Confederates in Burke County.

The death of Joseph Law (54 years) on Nov. 22, 1940, the Judge of the Ordinary Court of Burke County, opened up the post. O.M. Gresham, as Senator-Elect of the 17th Senatorial District, asked Gov. E.D. Rivers to allow him to resign. This allowed him to run for the Ordinary Judge of Burke County. The two seeking the post were F.S. Burney and O.M. Gresham. On Jan. 9, 1941, Burney had 628 votes and Gresham 601.

But Gresham had his Editorial post. And it was not long before many changes in the Local Board of Selective Service (W.W.-II) were made, and he was helpful to Col. H.C. Hatcher at the Judge-Advocate post in Atlanta.

Milledge Gresham never married, but he had sisters and especially he was fond of his nieces in the Story and Emmett Gresham families. He died in 1964 and was interred in the Waynesboro Magnolia Cemetery.

LENA SHEWMAKE GRESHAM (STEVENSON), the daughter of Nona Johnston and Emmett Burdell Gresham. She grew up in Waynesboro, Ga., and finished the Waynesboro High School and one year in the Burke County Junior College. She studied one year in Wesleyan (Macon) and graduated from the University of Georgia (A.B.). After Athens, she went to New York to learn dancing.

She taught school for many years before changing over to a school librarian. She married Bernard Stevenson, B.S., M.S., who built the partnership, Stevenson and Associates, B.S., M.S., They live in Fort Myers, Fla. Her husband started out as a science teacher, but eventually set up his own engineering business. They have three daughters:

Children:
1. Nona Stevenson is married to John T. Balfe, who directs plays and teaches theatre at a Junior College. They live in Brooklyn Park, Minneapolis, Minn., and have four children: Julia, Mark, Gary and John.

2. Sarah (Sally) Stevenson, married to Lt. Col. Roger V. Gossick, U.S. Air Force. They are presently stationed at San Antonio, Texas, at Randolph AFB. They have two children: Eric and Lena.
3. Lena Stevenson (their last child) is married to John A. Herce who works for Exxon Oil Company. They live in Houston, Texas, and have two children: Heather and Michael.

EVANS VIRGIL HEATH, JR. was b. May 22, 1923, the son of Florence Fulcher and Evans Virgil Heath, Sr. His father died on Aug. 8, 1926, when Evans, Jr. was three years old. His sister, Mary Heath, was born Oct. 18, 1920.

The two Heath children both had fine education. Mary and Evans both graduated from the Waynesboro High School. He went to the Georgia Institute of Technology in Atlanta. He graduated as an electrical engineer in 1943. He worked himself up in the AT&T Company. He became the Engineer Director of the Plant Implementation. He married Joy Pillitiers of New Orleans, La., b. March 3, 1927. They had two children:
Children:
1. Baby boy who died at birth, Dec. 20, 1950.
2. Rachel Joy Heath was b. Feb. 4, 1967.
Mary Heath married Earl Massie of Glasgow, Va.
Children:
1. Mary Earl Massie b. June 12, 1947, in Glasgow, Va. Now lives in Richmond, Va. Divorced.
2. Evans Heath Massie b. June 11, 1949, in Glasgow, Va. He and his wife Becky are expecting their first child in May, 1981.
3. Suzanne Massie b. on Sept. 10, 1961, in Glasgow, Va. She is not married. She lives in N.C. while in college.

Florence Fulcher Evans married the second time to James H. Oliver of Waynesboro, Ga. They had a son, James H. Oliver, Jr. See the biographical sketch of Dr. James H. Oliver, Jr.

PRESTON BROOKS LEWIS, JR. was b. March 20, 1891. The son of Lillian Fulcher and Preston Brooks Lewis, Sr. Preston graduated from Crowley High School in Louisiana. He studied at the Louisiana State University with an A.B. degree in 1911. He was captain of his military company. He taught first at Houma, La., but the Waynesboro High School made him the Assistant Principal. While at the Waynesboro High School, he organized the first regular football team in the school's history.

He was a member of Co.E., First Georgia Infantry of the National Guard and went to the Mexican border to patrol the U.S.A. border. When in 1917 the U.S. sent over the 151 Machine Gun Battalion with a first contingent of the 42nd Rainbow Division and served in Europe. He served until he was returned to the States as a machine instructor and stationed at Camp Hancock. During W.W.-II he was a Captain and County Commander of the Georgia State Guards.

After W.W.-I, he entered into the practice of law. He had already read law in Mr. Fullbright's office. He was the City Attorney and he built up a fine reputation.

Mr. Lewis was an active member of the Waynesboro Methodist Church all his adult life and served it in many official posts, including Sunday School Superintendent for 25 years, teaching of the Brinson Bible Class, Chairman of the Official Board and both trustee and steward.

He was a ranking Mason. He was a past Master of the Waynesboro Masonic Lodge, receiving his 50-year membership pin in 1965. He was a charter member of the Waynesboro American Legion Post and was past president of the Waynesboro Rotary Club. He was also a member of the Waynesboro Country Club and of the Oranto Barracks, Veterans of World War I.

He was first married to Clifford Gray McElmurray, who died in 1946, and in 1948 he married Janie Coleman Edmond who survives him. She was the daughter of Nannie McMillan of Atlanta and her father, F. Woodrow Coleman. Her father was originally from Alabama.

Other survivors included two daughters: Miss Clifford Gray Lewis, Atlanta, Ga.; Mrs. Jesse C. Palmer, Jr., Waynesboro; a son, Preston Brooks Lewis, Jr., Waynesboro; a step-son, Robert Edmond, Waynesboro; a sister, Mrs. William H. Powell, Waynesboro; a brother, Julian F. Lewis, and Ralph Lewis, a brother, and nine grandchildren, all of Waynesboro at the time of his death. He died on Aug. 19, 1965, and was interred in the beautiful Waynesboro Magnolia Cemetery.

ROBERT CALDWELL NEELY, SR. was b. in Savannah on May 17, 1856, the son of Philo Whitehead and Capt. Thomas W. Neely. His father served in the Southern Confederacy throughout its history and his son inherited from him a strong sense of duty and personal responsibility. Completing his education in Savannah and the preparatory school of Richard Malcolm Johnston in Baltimore, he then studied law in New York, but returned to Georgia in 1876 and became manager of Major Wilkins' business in Waynesboro. Later he formed the firm of Mackenzie and Neely, general merchants; his subsequent business interest being with the firm of Wilkins, Neely and Jones, and then the R. C. Neely Company. In 1899 he organized and became President of the Citizens Bank of Waynesboro, and a member of the State Highway Commission. For 25 years he was President of the Burke County Board of Education. In his religion he was an active member of the Methodist Episcopal Church.

He married first Willie Leora Addison, daughter of Sarah Lawson and Thomas Addison, and niece of the Lawsons. They had a son, Robert C. who died at age three. His mother died Jan. 25, 1885. His second wife was Lillian Wilkins, the daughter of Moselle Carswell and Maj. W.A. Wilkins. She was b. in Louisville, Ga. She served as State President of the Missionary Society of the Methodist Church. She was also a charter member of the Colonial Dames, a member of the Daughters of the Revolution and United Daughters of the Confederacy, and organized and was the President of the local American Legion Auxiliary. She was also President of the Woman's Club in Waynesboro. She maintained homes in Waynesboro, Augusta, and Asheville, N.C. She lived seven years after his death. They had three children: Mozelle Neely (Mrs. John R. Palmer), Alvin W. Neely, and Robert C. Neely, Jr.

Mr. Neely was a member of the State of Georgia Society of Colonial Wars. Thomas Gamble was Historian and Secretary of the Savannah Office.

The editorial of The True Citizen (T.C. Nov. 3, 1923) rightly saw Mr. Neely as the great man that he was. The history of any nation or subdivision thereof is most largely made up from a study of the lives of its great men. They are the factors that shape and mold the ideals for the advancement of that community, and a community is known more and regarded for the men it produces.

In the death of Mr. R. C. Neely, the city, the county, and the State has suffered a loss that cannot be estimated. Mr. Neely was active and aggressive, fearless and courageous, and had faith in his ability, in his fellow man and in his country. He built up a business--that of farming, and a supply house that was second to none of like character in the State.

In all his dealings at home and abroad, Mr. Neely was esteemed and honored for the integrity of his character and his fair dealings. Mr. Neely was highly regarded for his unusual business ability, his careful judgment and his splendid character. He enjoyed the highest standing in the commercial and credit centers of the South and East. He was a member of the Bankers Club of New York and enjoyed the esteem of the wide circle of friends with some of whom he had continuous business dealings for a long number of years. With the banks of Georgia and New York he had established himself as one of the soundest businessmen of the State and with them his word was his bond. Mr. Neely was known and loved for his many charities, was liberal and helped thousands of colored people during his long business career.

Personally, Mr. Neely was a most attractive man; handsome in his bearing and carriage and most pleasing and engaging in his manner. He was a thorough gentleman and could easily be recognized in any group of men as a leader by reason of his superior talents and attainments.

Mr. Neely loved his own town and county and all during his successful career he never thought of it as too small to hold him. He labored faithfully and earnestly at all times for its upbuilding and it was at home that he was loved best because he was known best.

The universal sorrow expressed upon Mr. Neely's death by his own people was the tribute that would have pleased him most. Sorrow was general wherever he was known and hundreds of telegraphs to the family joined in their bereavement.

May the labors and examples, his bfty and splendid characters, be an inspiration to the youth and young manhood of this community.

ROBERT CALDWELL NEELY, JR. was b. June 27, 1888, the son of Lillian Wilkins and Robert Caldwell Neely, Sr. He studied in the Waynesboro and Augusta schools and at the University of Georgia.

In 1910 he had reached manhood and was help with his father. He worked in the cotton business in Augusta where his father had a co-partner. On Nov. 14, 1912, he married Louise Calhoun Phinizy, the daughter of Marion Coles Phinizy and Stewart Phinizy. She was b. in Augusta and could be proud of distinguished masters, such as Gen. Andrew Pickens and John C. Calhoun, Statesman of South Carolina.

Robert Neely, Jr. became a farmer and civic leader; served as Mayor of Waynesboro and also a member of the Burke County Commissioners. He was a driving force in obtaining paved highways, the sale of the City's power electric light, and the Waynesboro golf course. His father died in Nov., 1923. He had already worked in the Neely Bonded Warehouse, the R. C. Neely, Sr. Gin and was learning farming. This was the time when the farmer had to work harder to save their cotton crop. On Jan. 12, 1924, he was made the A & S Director of the Augusta and Savannah Railroad in his father's place.

In March 21, 1925, he bought out all the interests of Mr. C. H. Herrington and the firm of Herrington and Braswell, lumber dealers and building supplies. This gave him a broad base to become the agent for the new automatic cotton pickers (which covered six ounties); carload of nitrate of soda; calcium arsenate; molasses; three-row dusting machines, as well as lumber, building supplies, and other materials.

He served as President of the Georgia Cotton Warehouse and Compress Association for several years, was director and charter member of the National Cotton Compress and Cotton Warehouse Associations, and was one of the organizers and charter member of the National Council of America.

His wife, Louise P. Neely, was very active in her garden club activities, being charter member and President of the Waynesboro Garden Club; many of the Sand Hills Garden Clubs in Augusta, and life member and President of the Garden

was developed and the State Headquarters House of the Garden Club of Georgia on the University campus in Athens was completed. Beautification of highways, parks, St. Michael's Episcopal Church in Waynesboro and "Shadows", her antebellum home and garden, can be in her accomplishments.

Robert C. Neely, Jr. died May 30, 1964, and his wife followed the next year, Jan. 5, 1965. Both are interred in the Waynesboro Magnolia Cemetery.

MARION NEELY WALKER, b. Oct. 6, 1913, the daughter of Louise Calhoun Phinizy and Robert Caldwell Neely, Jr. Her paternal grandparents were Robert Caldwell Neely, Sr. and Lillian Wilkins Neely. Mr. R. C. Neely, Sr. was a prominent farmer and businessman in Waynesboro and Burke County for many years. His wife was the daughter of Maj. William Wilkins, also prominent in business and farming in Burke County.

Maternal grandparents were Mr. Stewart Phinizy and Mrs. Marion Coles Phinizy both of Augusta, Ga. Mr. Phinizy was prominent in the textile business in Augusta and one of its' leading citizens.

Marion Walker was educated in both the Augusta schools and Waynesboro schools as her father's original business made it necessary to spend part time in each city. After graduating from high school in Waynesboro she attended Ward Belmont College in Nashville, Tenn., and Gulf Park College, Long Beach, Miss.

In 1935, shortly after completing her education, she married John W. Walker, Jr. of Augusta, where she resided for several years and gave birth to her first child, John W. Walker, III. In 1942 she and her husband moved to Waynesboro where her husband accepted a position with her father at the Neely Bonded Cotton Warehouse. In 1942 her other child, Louise P. Walker was born.

Subsequently, Marion actively entered her many civic undertakings, among which were cleaning of the tombstones and restoration of the Confederate Cemetery in Waynesboro; preserving the landscaping and beauty of the Magnolia Cemetery; actively supporting as Chairman of the Burke County Bicentennial Committee; giving full-time attention to the continuing activity of the Burke County Historical Museum and the Burke County Historical Society; all of this, plus dedicated interest in the work of the Waynesboro Garden Club. In 1978 the Waynesboro Chamber of Commerce awarded her "Citizen of the Year , for her outstanding contributions to her community".

At the present time she has one sister, Mrs. Ralph B. Willis, and one brother, Robert C. Neely, III, both of whom reside in Waynesboro.

SAMUEL GAINES STORY, II was b. Oct. 29, 1870, the son of Burmah Steed and Samuel Gaines Story. He was a native of Richmond County, but lived in Burke County the greater part of his life.

He married Ida Gresham, born May 21, 1876, the daughter of Annie Lassiter and Job Anderson Gresham, C.S.A. They had five children. Their first home was at the "Story's Mill" but later they moved to Waynesboro and had a nice home on Jones Ave.

He had a large farm and was a successful farmer. In addition, he served for several terms as Sheriff of the County and at all times he was one of the best.

Mr. Story was a Deacon in the Waynesboro Baptist Church. A jovial man, he seemed to laugh inside and out, and very few ever had more fun out of life. Befitti his type he was completely bald; his dome seemed more for crystal gazing than thinking, but it served for him the normal purposes.

One Sunday morning as he sat in his pew close to the front, listening intently to the sermon; those in the back of the church, which is excellent for observation but not always for concentration, saw a tiny white feather slowly waft downward from somewhere above. Eventually it came to rest on Mr. Sam's baldness, but only after some tense moments for a few who had seen in advance this hoped-for possibility. Yet so soft and fluffy was it, that the aforesaid Deacon noticed it not. Many back of him, however, had witnessed the blessed event; and no doubt, the smiles going the rounds, the minister interpreted for listeners' pleasure in the series of illustrative stories which he was relating.

When the service was over, Mr. Sam was informed of his new acquisition and what a "do-do" he made over it, smiling and handshaking with friends and acquaintances as he left the church. Why, he had praised that the Lord would cover the nakedness of his head; the Lord had provided. Like manna, He had sent it from Heaven; He was the great Restorer, etc. Our doubts whether any other one little bird, ever intentionally or unintentionally, gave so much pleasure to so many, with so little.

Mr. Story died at Valona, Ga. on July 25, 1923, where he was spending the summer. He had been in feeble health for some time and had never fully retained himself since being paralyzed several months before. He seemed to be improving until recently he was stricken again, finally succumbing to the attack.

He was survived by his wife, Mrs. Ida Story and five children: Misses Anita and Ida, Margaret and Emily; one son, Gaines Story, III and one grandson. The interrment was in the Magnolia Cemetery.

ELIZABETH JONES WADE was b. July 2, 1865, the daughter of Seaborn Augusta Jones of Millhaven. She married Capt. Jesse Turpin Wade, b. Aug. 24, 1851, and d. Aug. 20, 1918. He was a graduate of the V.M.I. Capt. Wade's sister, Mrs. Martin, lived in Fredericksburg, Va.

They both were communicants in the Brick Methodist Church in Screven County. Both Capt. Wade and his wife are interred in that cemetery. She lived until March 6, 1952.

Elizabeth's father was known as "Devil Seaborn" and was a first cousin of Col. J. J. Jones in Waynesboro. The Colonel remembered that Seaborn (a young man) had arrived at the big house and insisted that the two or three young ladies, who had gone to bed, should dress again, so he could see what they looked like.

Capt. Wade late in life sold (or leased) the Millhaven Plantation for $60,000 to R.C. Neely. Later the plantation went to the Comers of Alabama (or Macon).

YOUNG JOHN ALLEN, missionary, was b. in Burke Co., Ga., Jan. 3, 1836, s/o Andrew Young John and Jane (Wooten) Allen. His parents d. when he was an infant and he was brought up by an uncle and aunt, Wiley and Nancy (Wooten) Hutchins, in Meriwether Co., Ga. He received his preparatory education in Ga. at the Brownwood Institute, LaGrange, and at Morgan Looney's schools at Palmetto and Starrsville. He attended Emory and Henry College, Emory, Va., during 1853-54, and was graduated A.B. at Emory College, Oxford, Ga., in 1858. He was admitted to the Ga. Conf. of the Methodist Episcopal Church, South, in the latter year and appointed a member of the board of missions for China. He then disposed of considerable property which his father had left him, and after raising collections in behalf of missions and being ordained a deacon and elder, sailed for China in Dec., 1859. He arrived in Shanghai in July, 1860, and immediately began to study the Mandarin dialect. Later he began to preach in and around Shanghai. At the outbreak of the Civil War in the U. S., Dr. Allen was placed in charge of the China mission field and held the post until 1865. He opened up new work at Nau-tsiang and Kading in 1863, and at Soochow in 1864. As a means of support and to keep the mission property intact, Dr. Allen entered the Chinese gov't service in 1864 as an English teacher in the Kiangnan Arsenal School, remaining active as an educator until 1881. In addition he established the first Chinese newspaper in China, the "Wan Kwoh Kung Pao" or "Review of the Times" in 1868, and also engaged in translating scientific books and other works for the gov't. He was appointed superintendent of the China mission in 1881 and in addition took charge of the woman's foreign mission board. In 1882 he established at Shanghai both the Anglo-Chinese College and the McTyeire Home and School for Girls. The work of the China mission organization was so extended by Dr. Allen that it was formally erected into a regular conference in 1886. He was elected president of the Anglo-Chinese College in 1887, and continued in that post until 1895 when the Shanghai conf. released him to devote his entire time to literary work. He helped found Soochow Univ. in 1901 and the Anglo-Chinese College was merged with it in 1911. "Dr. Allen was a sincere, brilliant and powerful preacher and a sympathetic teacher. He conducted his work upon the principle that the foreign missionary should serve the nation and not the individual, and that the native missionary should reach the individual as pastor of the churches. His name in Chinese, Lin-lo Chih, is still known in China, and during the last 15 years of his life he was more widely known than any foreigner who had ever worked in the Chinese mission field." He was one of the most voluminous writers for the Chinese that the missionary body had produced and through his writings reached not only to three empires, China, Japan and Korea, but wherever there are Chinese. His collected works include some 90 volumes of translations for the Chinese gov't; "The War Between China and Japan" (16 vols.); "China and Her Neighbors" (1876); and "Women in All Lands; or, China's Place Among the Nations" (21 vols.). He was an organizer of the Christian Literature Society of China and edited, at various times, in addition to the "Review of the Times", the tri-weekly "Chinese Gazette" for the government and the "Christian Advocate." In 1877 he was elected a delegate by the North Ga. conf. to the gen. conf. of his church and he was a delegate to the centennial conf. in Shanghai in 1907 to celebrate the 100th anniversary of the beginning of Protestant missions in China by Robert Morrison. Emory College conferred upon him the degree of Litt.D. in 1876 and the degree of D.D. in 1878. The Young Allen Memorial Church was established at Shanghai, China, in his honor. He was married in 1858, to Mary, d/o Samuel Houston, of Coweta Co., Ga., and had in all ten children. Dr. Allen d. in Shanghai, China, May 30, 1907.[1]

---

[1] Nat-Cyc of American Biography, Vol. 11, 1983.

Allen, Elisha Anderson 2
    Young John 206
Applewhite, Joseph P. 3
Attaway, Douglas 4
Barnes, Goodwin M. 5
Bell, Simeon 6
Belt, Lloyd Jones 7
Berol, Henry 8
Berrien, Major John 9
    Laura Maria 9
    Thomas Moore 10
Blount, Edward H. 10
    Hugh M. 12
    Stephen W. 13
Borom, Marcus P. 14
Bostic, Zillah Lee 1
Botsford, Rev. Edward 15
Braswell Family 17
Brinson, Judge Edward L. 17
    William Leslie 18
Bryan, William H. 19
    William H. (Jr.) 19
Burton, Thomas 20
Bussey, Adele J. 21
Buxton, Needham A. 22
    Samuel 22
Byne, Rev. Edward 23
    James Miller (Sr.) 24
    James Miller (Jr.) 24
Callaway. Enoch H. 25
Carswell, Arabella 27
    John Devine 28
    John Wright 29
    John W. (Sr.) 26
    Porter W. 30
Carr, Patrick 32
Carter, John C. 33

Cates, Francis M. (Sr.) 34
    Fancis M. (Jr.) 35
Cates Family 36
Carter, Alexander 39
    Isaiah 40
Chalker, Roy F. 192
Chanler, William 40
Cherry, G. Frank 41
Childers, Kennedy C. 41
Coalson, Paul 42
Cooley, Joseph E. 43
Corker, Frank G. 44
    Stephen A. 44
Cox, George F. 45
    P. Duncan 46
    Sidney C. 46
Craven, William H. 192
D'Antignac, William 48
Daniel, Henry C. (Sr.) 48
    Henry C. (Jr.) 48
    J.H. 50
Davies, Myrick 51
Davis, Marion T. 51
    William H. 51
Dent, John M. 54
Dickinson, William H. 54
Dixon, Eve Walker A. 55
Dolinssky, Arnold J. 56
Drew, Troy 56
Emanuel, David 56
Evans, Arthur Forte 58
Felder, Thomas B. 59
Ford, Lewis R. 60
Franklin, Alonzo L. 60
Fryhofer, George W. 62
Fulcher, Edwin (Sr.) 63
    Edwin (Jr.) 64

Edwin Dent 64	**Hodges Family** 37
William M. (Sr.) 65	**Holland**, Josiah....................86
William M. (Jr.) 66	**Holmes**, William R. 90
Fullbright, Henry J. 194	**Hubert**, Allison T. 92
Galhin, George 67	**Hurst**, C.W. 92
Garlick, Blount G. 69	**Irwin**, Jared 93
Garner, Cicero.......................69	**Iverson**, Alfred 93
Gay, Evelyn W. 70	**Jackson**, Abraham 94
Givens, Howard W. 70	George L. 95
Gnan, J. Holland 70	**Johnson**, C. Preston 95
Goulding, Francis R. 71	Herchel W. 95
Gray, Simeon A......................72	L.D. 96
Green, Charles C. (Sr.) 195	**Johnston**, Phillip P. 97
Charles C. (Jr.) 195	**Jones**, Allen W. 98
John 74	Batt 98
William 75	Elizabeth 205
Greenwood, Henry D. 76	Henry A. 104
Gresham, Edmund B. 196	Inez F W. 103
Emmett B. 198	John James 99
John Jones.....................198	John J. 99
Lena Shewmake 200	Margaret A. 100
Oscar Milledge 199	Philip 102
Harden, Ross U. 76	Seaborn H. 105
Hargrove, Roy S. 77	Warren W. 105
Harlow, John A......................78	William E. 106
Southworth 78	William Wilkins 106
Hatcher, Herbert C. 79	**Kelsey**, Andrew Z. 106
Hayne, Linwood C. 80	**Kilpatrick**, James Hall 107
Heath, Evans Virgil 201	James Hines 108
Herrington, Lovick (Sr.) 81	Washington L. 109
Lovick (Jr.) 82	**Lance**, Thomas J. 109
Mary Louise 87	**Law**, Joseph 110
W.J. 87	**Lawson**, Alexander J. 111
Hillhouse, Albert M. 84	Edward F. 112
William C. 84	Hugh 113
Hillis, Wm. Wycliffe 86	**Lee**, Isam S. 114
Hines, James K. 88	**Lester**, Rufus E. 114

Lewis, Clifford 115
    Jonathan 117
    Josiah 117
    Preston Brooks 201
Lisle, George........................119
Lively, Alexander 119
Lord, William 120
Lyons, Judson 121
Macaulay, Hugh A..............122
Mackenzie, Annie Reid 122
McCathern, Sidney 123
    Walker 123
    William W. 124
McCloud Family 124
McElmurray, Evans H. 125
    John F. 126
    Judson S. 126
    Mary Louise 127
    2nd & 3rd Generation 128
    Thomas J. 130
    William L. 130
McMaster, Hugh B. 131
Milledge, Richard 198
Miller, Baldwin B. 132
    Julia Carter 133
    Joseph B. 134
    Robert Lee 135
Mills, Ellis W........................135
Milner, Charles T................136
Milton, John 136
Morris, William S. 137
Murphree, Robert M. 137
Murphy, Robert A..............138
Neely, Alvin W. 139
    Lillian W. 140
    Marion 204
    Robert C. (Sr.) 202
    Robert C. (Jr.) 203
Odom, Horace P. 141
    Joyce P. 141
Oglethorpe, James 141
Oliver, James H...................142
Pagenhart, C.L....................142
Palmer, Howard E.W. 143
    James P. 144
    Jesse C. (Sr.) 145
    Jesse C. (Jr.) 146
    John Turner (Sr.) 147
    John Turner (Jr.) 147
Pemberton, Atton 148
Perkins, Edward A. 148
    John H. 149
Perry, Heman H. 150
Pettigrew, Roderic 150
Pintchuck, Louis 151
Polhill, Thomas 152
    Joseph 153
Powell, John 154
    William H. 154
Poythress, John Carter 155
Pugh, James L. 155
Rainwater, Ella Mary 155
Rauers, Kate Thomas 156
Reynolds, Joseph Jones 157
Riordan, Margaret Storey ..160
Rowland, Grattan W. 161
Sanderford, John W. 162
Sapp, George W. 163
Sapp Family 163
Scales, Floyd L.....................166
Schley, Henry J. 166
Scott, Robert Lee 167
Sherwood, Adiel 168
Shewmake, Burke 169

John Troup 169
SKINNER, Charles W. 170
    Franklin Moore 170
STEMBRIDGE, Henry H. 172
STORY, Samuel Gaines 204
STURGES, John R. 172
    Samuel 173
TANHAM, Thomas F. 174
TARBUTTON, Ben James 175
TARVER, Charles 175
THOMAS, Ethelred 176
    George C. 176
    Jethro 177
    J. Pinkney 178
THOMPSON, Peyton W. 179
    Wall Tatnall 180
TUCKER, Memory King 180
Twiggs, John 181
Wakelee, Kate C. 182
WALKER FAMILY 182
WALKER, John W. 184
WALL, Thomas W. 184
WALTON, W.T. 185
WARNOCK, George O. 185
WARREN, Eli...........................186
    Lott 186
WHITEHEAD, Amos W. ..187-188
    Florence B. 189
    James Harper 189
    John Philpot 190
    William D. 191
WILLIAMS, Ezekiel 191

www.ingramcontent.com/pod-product-compliance
Lightning Source LLC
Chambersburg PA
CBHW060600080526
44585CB00013B/633